THE SUNDAY TIMES
WEEKEND
BREAKS

THE SUNDAY TIMES
WEEKEND
BREAKS

Edited by

WILL ELLSWORTH-JONES
CHRISTINE WALKER

Hodder & Stoughton
LONDON SYDNEY AUCKLAND TORONTO

Illustrations by Gavin Rowe

British Library Cataloguing in Publication Data
Ellsworth — Jones, Will
   The Sunday Times weekend breaks.
   1. Great Britain. Visitors' guides
   I. Title II. Walker, Christine   III. Rowe, Gavin
   914. 1'04858

   ISBN 0–340–50894–9

Published by Hodder and Stoughton,
a division of Hodder and Stoughton Ltd,
Mill Road, Dunton Green, Sevenoaks, Kent TN13 2YE
Editorial Office: 47 Bedford Square, London WC1B 3DP

Photoset by Litho Link Limited, Welshpool, Powys, UK

Printed in Great Britain by St Edmundsbury Press Ltd,
Bury St Edmunds, Suffolk

CONTENTS

INTRODUCTION

When *The Sunday Times* launched a separate Travel Section in January 1988 one of the essential ingredients that we knew had to be included was a guide to weekends away. At first we wondered if there would be enough places to keep the Weekend Away page going all through the year, but we soon discovered that the weekend break had become a veritable industry. We found companies offering such diverse breaks as a weekend in Iceland or Istanbul, clay pigeon shooting in Devon, or cottages to rent in Shropshire, and when we found readers clutching our guide to Bradford as they tried out the City's Indian restaurants, we knew it was a service that readers wanted.

Our only problem since then has been what might be called the "good intention syndrome", when readers make a determined note to clip out a weekend break in Suffolk and then forget to do so. We next hear from them when we are trying to meet our deadline, when they come on the phone to us: "I know you did a piece on Suffolk some time last year. Can you find it for me?" It is a good test of politeness under pressure.

So here for all those readers who mean to clip those articles and never do, and for those readers who might never have read the Travel Section of *The Sunday Times* but simply want new ideas of where to go or what to do over the long weekends, we have chosen the best of our Weekends Away for you to enjoy. Whether your taste runs to St Tropez in winter (where our photographer inevitably bumped into BB) or to the more austere delights of the Romney Marshes, we hope that everyone will find something that attracts them in this collection.

There is however one word of warning. The prices and all other details were checked in July 1989 before this book went to press and prices and schedules do change rapidly. Please only take details as a guideline and check all facilities before you travel.

We hope that with the help of this book your two day weekend will seem like two weeks and that you will return home on Sunday ready and willing to face the week.

Will Ellsworth-Jones
and Christine Walker

ENGLAND

Tintern Abbey

Central and Southern England

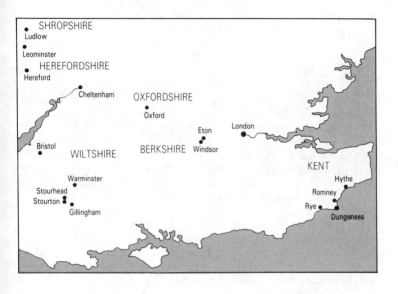

SHROPSHIRE
Ludlow

Leominster

HEREFORDSHIRE
Hereford

Cheltenham

OXFORDSHIRE

Oxford

Eton

London

Bristol

WILTSHIRE

BERKSHIRE

Windsor

KENT

Warminster

Hythe

Stourhead
Stourton

Romney

Gillingham

Rye

Dungeness

Cheltenham

Justine Picardie

. . . .

"**M**OST people seem to remember Cheltenham for no other reason than visits to see their aged aunts," said the man from the tourist office sadly. And indeed, there is a pervasive air of gentility associated with this Regency spa town.

But there is more to Cheltenham than aged aunts and retired colonels. After all, it is the home town of the eccentric ski jumper Eddie "the Eagle" Edwards. (As the tourist office pointed out, "Eddie Edwards and GCHQ have done more to put Cheltenham on the map than we could have in years.") Cheltenham also offers a fine music festival in July — an annual event since 1945.

Two hundred years ago George III, on the advice of his physicians, arrived to take the waters in what was then a small Gloucestershire town, after he had suffered "a pretty smart bilious attack". True, Cheltenham's saline springs had been discovered fifty years earlier, but with the King's patronage, the town quickly became a fashionable spa resort.

I spent a very pleasant weekend at the Queen's Hotel. Overlooking the Imperial Gardens in the centre of Cheltenham, the hotel resembles a splendid wedding cake with its façade of white colonnades. Inside, it looks like Glasgow's Kelvingrove Art Gallery, with art nouveau wallpaper in the halls and corridors, and dark Victorian oil paintings.

The weekend started, as is to be expected in an English summer, with rain. But there are all manner of things to do on a rainy Saturday in Cheltenham, such as shopping in the elegant terraces of Montpellier, around the corner from the hotel where the Georgian buildings are adorned with graceful caryatids. Less classical — but offering more shelter from the bad weather — is the Montpellier Courtyard, a small modern development with stylish craft and clothes shops, delicatessens and brasseries; and sitting in splendour in the middle of it all, Henry, a large white cockatoo who likes having his head stroked and squawks in the rain.

Tearing ourselves away from the beseeching eyes of Henry, my companion and I adjourned to Gardner's Coffee Shop, where one can sit and gaze out of the window at the rain-drenched Montpellier Gardens. Inside, there are fragrant toasted tea cakes to eat, and elegant ladies of a certain age to observe. (We shared a table with a venerable old gentleman, who had an impressively large white moustache and a dashing yellow waistcoat.)

The rain cleared in time for a short drive to the Cleeveway House Restaurant and Hotel, in Bishop's Cleeve, on the outskirts of Cheltenham. (To get to Bishop's Cleeve, go north on the A435 Evesham Road). After admiring the house — an early eighteenth-century manor built of golden Cotswold stone — we had the most delicious lunch imaginable: locally grown asparagus, followed by perfectly cooked Dover sole with fresh vegetables from the garden, and then the best summer pudding I have ever eaten. Afterwards, we sat in enveloping armchairs in the sitting room, drinking coffee in front of the open fire (very comforting on a dreary day). There was even home-made fudge for the particularly greedy (like me).

I would have happily slumbered there all afternoon, but I was tempted back to the town centre by the prospect of Morris dancing in the Imperial Gardens. This is a popular spectator sport in Cheltenham — though there were more teenage hippies there than retired colonels and aged aunts — but sadly, on the stroke of four when the jollity was about to commence, it started raining again.

So we went shopping instead, along the tree-lined Regency Promenade where county ladies browse at Jaeger, while their daughters nip into Next. Then we found the new Regent Arcade ("Gloucestershire's shopping experience"), which is like any other 1980s shopping mall — beige walls, marble floors, and the usual chain stores — but is redeemed by its centrepiece, a marvellous clock designed by Kit Williams. Looking like an intricate Heath Robinson construction, it has a duck at the top laying eggs, a wooden fish at the bottom that blows bubbles on the hour, and a mouse that pops out from different places every minute.

I was so taken by the clock that we got to the Cheltenham Art Gallery just as it was closing, but there was time to browse through a dusty second-hand bookshop next door. (And if I hadn't been so full from lunch, I would have eaten a slice of the lemon Bakewell tart at Choir's, an attractive teashop around the corner in Well Walk.) Exhausted by all this activity, I then retired for a quiet nap at the hotel, in preparation for Saturday Night Out in Cheltenham.

Lured back by Henry the cockatoo, the evening began at the Montpellier Courtyard. As Henry was by now asleep in his cage and locked away in a baked potato shop, we had to content ourselves with a drink at the Shambles, across the courtyard. Actually, it was a very pleasant drink, even without Henry, and we sat outside as the rain had stopped. An elegant French party sat at the next table, and it was rather Parisian for a while. (And certainly much less noisy than the crowded Montpellier Wine Bar up the road, where young Cheltenham ladies and gentlemen in striped shirts and Barbours quaffed their drinks and guffawed loudly.)

Our Night Out continued at Pizza Piazza in Montpellier Street. The service was friendly, the pizza was good, and the surroundings (Georgian, as ever), were congenial. Then we ambled back to the hotel, for a drink at the Napier Bar, where the stern face of Sir Charles Napier gazes down at the good burghers of Cheltenham as they enjoy a final nightcap. There were plenty of retired colonels in evidence, drawn perhaps by the stuffed tiger's head on the wall, with guns, sabres, and mounted tusks and whiskers from boars shot in Delhi and other outposts of the empire at the turn of the century.

On Sunday the rain had stopped, so we went to Cheltenham Race Course. There were no races, and no horses, but there was a flea market selling a variety of interesting bargains: anything from a pink crocodile candlestick to a macabre collection of real plaited hair. ("It's 1920s hair," said the stallholder, though how she could date it, I do not know.) I spent 50p on a large blue glass bowl and a small silver teapot (big enough for one cup), and then we had tea and an iced bun.

As the sun grew hotter, and the racecourse became more and more crowded, we escaped down the road to the Pittville Pump Room, which was empty. Designed by Joseph Pitt to resemble a Grecian temple, the building was opened in 1830 as a fashionable spa (and its history is chronicled in a museum on the upper floors, with displays of costume and jewellery from the 1760s to the present day). The spa water is still available, free of charge, from the marble pump: I drank a cup, which tasted rather like Andrew's Liver Salts without the fizz.

Suitably revived by our medicinal doses, we wandered around Pittville Park, to look at the peacocks, and budgerigars in various small aviaries, and the lake, where a pair of swans was building a nest, helped by an elderly lady who brought them leafy branches from a nearby bush. And, of course, there was a teahouse in the park, serving neat cheese and pickle sandwiches to those with an appetite after their Sunday afternoon strolls. (The taking of tea is a serious business in Cheltenham.)

Yet more peacocks demanded to be admired at Sudeley Castle, seven miles to the north of Cheltenham, just outside the town of Winchcombe. A site of castles since the time of King Ethelred the Unready, the present house dates from 1450, and was the last home of the sixth wife of Henry VIII, Queen Catherine Parr (her tomb dominates the chapel at Sudeley Castle, where she was mourned by her companion, Lady Jane Grey).

After stalking the peacocks around the garden — an exceedingly beautiful formal affair, with manicured topiary and sweet-smelling herbs — we settled down to watch a medieval pageant performed by the local amateur dramatic society. Having been denied the pleasure of Morris dancing in the Imperial Gardens the day before, I was determined to become fully involved in the celebratory spirit of things on my last afternoon, but in the end the pageant's plot became too elaborate for me to follow, so I skulked around the corner to sample the tea in the castle's old kitchen.

There was no tea to be had at Cleeve Hill, but a very fine view of Cheltenham from one of the highest points in the Cotswolds; we climbed up to the top for a final look at the city, and beyond towards Wales and the Black Mountains, and Tewkesbury and the Malvern Hills. All around were birds and daisies and buttercups, and — as one might expect in a Cheltenham beauty-spot — a well-founded golf course. For Cheltenham will always be the most English of towns, quietly restrained, but with a very civilised appeal.

GETTING THERE
By road, 96 miles from London to Cheltenham on A40/M40. M5 from Bristol or Birmingham. British Rail information (tel: Gloucester 29501).

HOTELS
Queen's: The Promenade, Cheltenham (tel: 0242-514724); double room from £85; weekend break, from £48 per person per night, inclusive of dinner and breakfast.
Cleeveway House: Bishop's Cleeve, Cheltenham (tel: 0242-672585); bed and breakfast: single room, £28.50; double room, £45.
Prestbury House Hotel: The Burgage, Prestbury (tel: 0242-529533); bed and breakfast: single room, from £30; double room from £40.

MUSIC
The Cheltenham International Festival of Music: July. (Information can be obtained on: 0242-523690).

MUSEUMS
Cheltenham Art Gallery: Clarence Street (tel: 0242-237431): Arts and Craft collection, 17th-century Dutch paintings, 17th to 20th century British paintings; open Monday-Saturday 10am-5.30pm; admission free.
Gustav Holst Birthplace Museum: 4 Clarence Road (tel: 0242-524846): open Tuesday-Friday noon-5.30pm; Saturday 11am-5.30pm, admission free.
Pittville Pump Room and Gallery of Fashion: Pittville Park (tel: 0242-512740): open Tuesday-Sunday 10.30am-5pm (open Sundays, April 1-October 31 only).
Sudeley Castle: open daily, April 1 to October 31, noon until 5 pm (tel: 0242-602308). Admission: adults £3.40, children £1.85.

PLACES TO EAT
Cleeveway House Restaurant (see under hotels).
Pizza Piazza: 6 Montpellier Street (tel: 0242-221845).
The Shambles: Montpellier Courtyard (tel: 0242-577458).
Choir's: Well Walk (tel: 0242-510996).
Gardners Coffee Shop: 16 Montpellier Walk (tel: 0242-583947).

Oxford

*Brian
Jackman*

. . . .

LET the smell of hot loaves lead you by the nose. Once inside, other aromas take you past ripe cheeses, salami, roasting coffee; between banks of fresh fruit and vegetables: fat bulbs of fennel, golden pears, sweet muscat grapes bursting from their boxes. Elsewhere there are mussels, carp and silver sprats; and a game dealer's shop half-buried in fur and feather: wild duck, pheasant, brown hares and fallow bucks.

Oxford's splendid covered market is just one of the unexpected pleasures to be found beneath the dreaming spires; and like so much of the city it is wedded to the pursuit of excellence — not a bad theme for a winter weekend in Europe's third-oldest seat of learning.

It may take a morning to find your bearings, and a guided walk to unravel the mysteries of the medieval college system. In the heart of the city, in the square mile which is still more Gown than Town, there are more than 900 buildings of architectural and historical interest. In age and style they range from the Saxon tower of St Michael at the North Gate to the classic set-piece complex surrounding the Bodleian Library and the great dome of the Radcliffe Camera.

Save the thirty-five university colleges for a rainy day. Opening times vary, but most offer a glimpse of inner sanctums: quadrangles, chapels and dining halls hung with portraits of distinguished former students and benefactors. Choosing is invidious, but your weekend would be incomplete without a visit to Christ Church. It has the largest quadrangle (Tom Quad), the biggest pre-Victorian hall, its own art gallery and one of England's smallest cathedrals.

Other rainy-day delights include the Ashmolean Museum (all kinds of treasures from the Alfred Jewel to Picasso's *Blue Roofs*), the excellent Museum of Oxford, and Blackwell's Bookshop with its green shutters and 200,000 titles to browse through.

So much for undercover Oxford. Out of doors the city lends itself to winter. Lucky the visitor who sees it under snow; but at any time there is a chameleon charm about its pale stone buildings and pinnacled skylines that are every bit as magical in a wash of winter sunlight as when, more frequently, they are sulking in the subfusc gloom of a Thames valley fog.

Everyone, student or casual visitor, will carry away a favourite image. Perhaps of the High, an elegant curve of college façades; or the Broad (Broad Street), whose medieval paunch frames a magnificent prospect of the Sheldonian Theatre.

Or maybe the Thames from Folly Bridge; or my own favourite, from the banks of the Cherwell looking across the peaceful expanse of Christ Church meadow with its grazing cattle and winter trees to see Christ Church,

Merton College and all the city spires beyond: a textbook vision of *rus in urbe* without equal in Europe.

And should your weekend spill over into Monday, a glance at your map will give you endless ideas for a day in the country. Oxford, embedded in the soft underbelly of Middle England, is perfectly placed for short forays into the Cotswolds or upper Thames valley; to Blenheim Park, Burford, and the willow-bordered landscapes of the William Morris country around Kelmscott.

HOW TO GET THERE

From London the best way is by British Rail. Buy a Network Saver at Paddington station for £12.00, valid for one month, for any time after 10am. Fastest train is at 6.25pm — arriving 7.10pm.

GETTING AROUND

Oxford railway station lies outside the city centre, to the west. You will need a taxi; or take a bus to Carfax, in the city's historic core.

HOTELS

Randolph: Beaumont Street, 110 rooms. Best in town. Victorian gothic meets Trusthouse Forte. Good central location opposite Ashmolean Museum. Tel: 0865 247481.

Eastgate: off the High, 37 rooms. Another Trusthouse Forte hotel. Newly refurbished. Not quite in same league as the Randolph, but in even better position near Magdalen College. Moderately expensive. Tel: 0865 248244.

LUNCH

Head of the River: St Aldate's. Stylish 3-storey riverside pub at Folly Bridge. Excellent and imaginative traditional English menu with each dish priced at about £5. Tel: 0865 721600 or 726158.

Pastificio: George Street. Fresh pasta in bright modern surroundings. Special set lunch often available. Tel: 0865 791032.

AFTERNOON TEA

Randolph Hotel for a traditional tea in the grand manner. Finger sandwiches, home-made scones and pianist. £6.25.

Rosie Lee, halfway down the High. Afternoon teas served between 3pm and 5.30pm. Toasted tea cakes, Earl Grey or Rosie Lee's own blend from 75p per pot.

PUBS

Eagle and Child: St Giles. Interior divided into snug firelit parlours. C. S. Lewis and J. R. R. Tolkien used to meet here. Ideal for a pub lunch.

Turf Tavern: St Helen's Passage, off New College Lane. 13th-century building with low ceilings, head-splitting beams, hot cider punch in winter.

DINNER

La Sorbonne: off the High. Half-timbered 17th-century building hidden in narrow lane. Eat in the Casse-Croûte Room — somewhat cheaper than the (expensive) restaurant but still offering the same excellent French cuisine. Tel: 0865 241320.

Michel's Bistro: Little Clarendon Street. Good, typical bistro dining and decor in upwardly mobile street of boutiques and eateries. Moderately expensive. Tel: 0865 52142.

Brown's: Woodstock Road. Where students take their parents. Crowded, rambling restaurant, all mirrors and hanging plants. Cooking is more steak and mushroom pie than haute cuisine. Inexpensive. Tel: 0865 511995.

SHOPS

Blackwell's Bookshop: Broad Street. Established opposite the Sheldonian Theatre in 1879 and now one of the world's biggest.

Frank Coopers: High Street. Makers of marmalade since 1874.

Stamp of Oxford: Broad Street. College scarves, hand-painted bow ties.

The Paperback Shop: Broad Street. Everything fit to print in soft covers.

KEY SITES

Radcliffe Camera: splendid domed building designed by James Gibbs and completed in 1749. Now a reading room for the Bodleian Library.

Bodleian Library: named after St Thomas Bodley, its 16th-century benefactor. Now one of the world's greatest, with some 5 million books. Some parts open to visitors, Mon-Fri 9am-7pm, Sat 9am-1pm.

Divinity School: has been called the most beautiful room in Europe — a perfect example of 15th-century Perpendicular Gothic now containing an exhibition of Bodleian treasures. Opening times same as for Bodleian Library.

Sheldonian Theatre: built by the young Christopher Wren between 1663-69, in the style of a D-shaped Roman theatre. Nowadays its restored interior is the setting for matriculation and degree ceremonies; also concerts presented by Music at Oxford. Open Mon-Fri 9am-4.45pm, Sat 9am-12.30pm.

COLLEGES

Tiptoeing around college quadrangles, halls and cloisters is one of the great tourist pleasures of Oxford. Opening times vary; some are open to visitors only in the afternoon. Among the most interesting are:

Christ Church: St Aldate's. Founded in 1525 by Cardinal Wolsey and refounded in 1546 by Henry VIII. Architectural glories include Tom Tower (designed by Wren), Tom Quad and the medieval dining hall. Its chapel is also Oxford Cathedral (stewards will give you a guided tour).

Magdalen College: High Street. Founded 1458. Has famous 15th-century bell tower, cloister, lawns, three quadrangles, own river walk and deer park.

New College: New College Lane. Founded 1379 by William of Wykeham. Magnificent quadrangle, chapel and beautiful gardens bounded by ancient city wall.

Merton College: Merton Street. Founded 1249. The quadrangle (Mob Quad) is the university's oldest. The 14th-century library is reputedly the oldest in England (it contains Chaucer's astrolabe and the first printed Bible in Welsh).

Other colleges worth making an effort to see include All Souls, Balliol, Brasenose, Oriel, Corpus Christi, Pembroke, University and Exeter.

MUSEUMS AND GALLERIES

Ashmolean Museum: Beaumont Street. Britain's oldest public museum. Founded in 1683 but now housed in classical 1840s building. Contains antiquities, paintings, ceramics, musical instruments. Special attractions include everything from Michelangelo drawings to Guy Fawkes's lantern. Admission free. Open Tue-Sat 10am-4pm; Sun 2-4pm.

Museum of Oxford: St Aldate's. The story of Oxford from mammoths to motor cars. Should be regarded as essential viewing before you visit the colleges. Admission free. Open Tue-Sat 10am-5pm.

Pitt Rivers Museum: Parks Road. One of the world's greatest museums of ethnology, archaeology, weapons, musical instruments. Admission free. Open Mon-Sat 1-4.30pm.

PARKS AND GARDENS

Botanical Garden: High Street. The oldest in Britain (1621). Bounded by the Cherwell. Serene and sheltered behind its high walls, magnificent even in winter. Best in afternoon when the glasshouses open. Admission free. Open Mon-Sat 9am-4.30pm; Sun 10am-12 noon and 2-4.30pm. Glasshouses daily 2-4pm.

Christ Church Meadow: off St Aldate's. For a country walk without leaving the city, stroll along the Broad Walk to the River Cherwell, or go the longer way round via the New Walk and the Thames towpath. Open 8am until dusk.

BIRD'S EYE VIEWS

Two to choose from: up the wooden staircase to the cupola at the top of the Sheldonian Theatre; and the gallery near the top of the spire of St Mary's Church in the High.

BEDSIDE READING

Oxford, by Jan Morris (Oxford University Press paperback, £4.95). A celebration by a distinguished author who knows and loves the city.

Further information: City of Oxford Information Centre, St Aldate's (opposite the Town Hall). Talk to the staff, plunder their maps and leaflets. Or tel: 0865 726871.

EXPLORING OXFORD'S COUNTRYSIDE

Blenheim Palace: Woodstock (8 miles), is closed in winter; but Capability Brown's great park alone is worth a visit to see its bare beeches, lake and Vanbrugh's bridge, and the palace itself on the skyline. Afterwards, in Woodstock, the Blenheim Tea Room serves excellent afternoon teas by the fire (toasted tea cakes, hot muffins, scones and cream, home-made hot apple cake).

Burford (17 miles): a perfect stone-built Cotswold town. Its steep main street climbing from the lovely River Windrush is full of antique shops. The Bay Tree Hotel in Sheep Street offers fragrant log fires and wonderful 3-course lunches featuring fresh game, meat and fish at £10.50 a head. Also in Sheep Street: the editorial offices of the *Countryman* magazine. Its entrance leads to a beautiful secret Cotswold garden — admission free.

Wantage (14 miles): has a statue of King Alfred, who was born here in 849. Better still, it is a springboard for winter walks along the prehistoric Ridgway which runs across the roof of the chalk downs to the south, past the Uffington White Horse and Wayland Smith's Cave.

Further information: Thames and Chilterns Tourist Board, 8 the Market Place, Abingdon, Oxfordshire OX14 3UD. Tel: 0235 22711.

Romney Marshes

*Elizabeth
Grice*

. . . .

OCTOBER 1988. The winding, leafless way through Kent to the Romney Marshes is strewn with upended trees and houses wrapped up like parcels, waiting for the loss adjuster to call and peer under the protective packaging of polythene and batons. In the path of the Great Storm, the Kentish oast houses have been whipped to the bone and stand uncowled or flayed of tiles. The great weatherboarded barns, that marched so solidly across the marshes a few months ago, lurch uncertainly out of the loamy plain.

The marshes, being low and featureless, were better able to withstand the hurricane than most parts of southern Britain, but even the everlasting images of churches and sheep, glimmering eerily out of a winter fog, have a weather-beaten air, resigned and patient.

There may be easier times to tramp this moody landscape inside the triangle of Rye, Dungeness and Hythe, but the season of short days and sharp nights is perfectly suited to its atmosphere, and to appreciating the crackle of a log fire at the end of a day's damp excursion.

No part of England, except perhaps East Anglia, is so generously designed for church-crawlers. As John Piper found: 'Wherever you go in the Romney Marsh, you are seldom out of sight of a church." And what churches. Box-pewed. Decorated with biblical texts. Most of them grazed to the porch, and sometimes beyond, by the burly, fat-faced Kent sheep, which William Cobbett, riding from Appledore to Hythe in 1823, called "white as a piece of writing paper". They are far from white just now, but in their speckling thousands they are as synonymous with the marshes as the brave churches.

At Ruckinge, a rough plank marks the burial place of the infamous brandy smugglers, the Ransley brothers, who were hanged in 1800. At East Guldeford we almost mistook the massive, double-roofed church for a tithe barn. Was the medieval population of these isolated villages really so large as to fill a church such as St Clements, Old Romney, or were they just immense thanks-offerings for the fat of the land?

But of all the beautiful

churches that rise out of the marshland mists, the little cap-towered building at Fairfield is most worth a meandering detour. It sits alone and beckoning in the bare windswept fields like a stranded ark out of which has poured nothing but sheep.

Until quite recently, the marshland was flooded so often that worshippers arrived by boat. The huge key hangs outside Becket's Barn farmhouse, almost the only other visible edifice.

Of the various defences that were supposed to frustrate an invasion of England through Romney Marsh — Martello towers, pillboxes and "dragons' teeth" obstacles to German tanks — the finest is the grandly named ditch, the Royal Military Canal, to the north. This broad waterway, though wildly optimistic as a deterrent to Napoleon, has a good towpath for much of its twenty-odd miles and makes a fine walk,

especially for birdwatchers. The three-mile stretch between Appledore and Warehorne is owned by the National Trust.

Part of the ancient coastal path from Gravesend to Rye, the Saxon Shore Way traverses the marsh, following the canal from Warehorne to Appledore (apple tree to the Saxons), a little town that once stood open to invading Danes and French on the bank of the then tidal Rother. A late-afternoon dyke-walk is magical when the fog lifts and everything is dyed red — water, window-panes, boat-tops and even the motionless wading birds.

Along the River Rother you can walk or drive into battle-scarred Rye through the ancient Land-gate, one of three that once guarded the town. The smell of seaweed and salt creeps up from the harbour and lingers in the cobblestoned streets.

Slither down the glistening

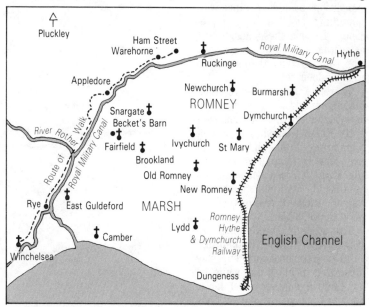

cobbles of West Street, past Henry James's old home, Lamb House, to the Mermaid Inn for a toasting in the snug bar. With its comfortable old hostelries and fascinating corners, Rye would have made a practical camp for meandering in the marshes. But it is a natural journey's end rather than beginning and we chose Pluckley, some miles north, near Ashford, as our base instead.

Here, isolated in a misty bowl and brimming with local stories of hauntings, we found Elvey Farm Country Hotel, a place where we could kick off muddy boots in a stone-flagged porch and collapse in front of a hissing log fire. The beautifully converted barn, stables and oast house are in the middle of a working farm which looks out to the hills and woods of the Weald of Kent.

While our young son set out after breakfast with the farm children to collect eggs, the day's expeditions could be planned with something less than military precision. The marshes, though best navigated by Ordnance Survey map, do not lend themselves to rigid manoeuvres.

There are two pieces of essential reading for anyone contemplating, enjoying or reviving old memories of the Romney Marshes — both of them always in plentiful supply in Rye. One is *Romney Marsh and the Royal Military Canal* written by that devoted marshman and walker, Richard Ingrams (Wildwood House, £5.50).

The other is *The Saxon Shore Way* by Alan Sillitoe (Hutchinson, £10.95). Both books are superbly illustrated in black and white by Fay Godwin, another marsh lover. They are not guides and yet they are full of information. The historical, the literary and the personal come together in a way that above all makes you want to *be there*, just as John Piper's dramatic paintings of marsh churches give you a pilgrim's zeal to find them.

When Ingrams started work on his book, he went to see Piper, whose own King Penguin book, *Romney Marsh*, came out in 1950. After the interview, Piper apologised: "I feel I didn't tell you anything about Romney Marsh, but I don't think I *know* much about it. What I really like about it is that it is all — 97 per cent — atmosphere." That feeling is what drew us back for the second time in twelve months and will do so again.

WHAT TO SEE

You cannot miss the 14th-century *Landgate* and you should not miss *Ypres Tower*, built about 1250, housing Rye Museum. *The Mermaid Inn* is Rye's largest medieval building, hugging a small central courtyard. It is lopsided, timber-framed, latticed, full of smuggling connections and incredibly cosy, despite its size.

Lamb House: West Street, was lived in and loved by Henry James. He used it as a setting for his books. Now owned by the National Trust, but only 2 oak-panelled rooms on the ground floor, and his beloved garden, are open to the public. Joseph Conrad and Ford Madox Ford used to walk over to visit him from Winchelsea.

Winchelsea: more village than town, lies two miles south of Rye and is full of superb old houses. Most fascinating of all, its curious church which looks like a ruin but is in fact just the nave of a grandiose ground plan that was never completed.

Romney Hythe and Dymchurch Railway: this miniature line with its 15-inch gauge, running between Hythe and Dungeness, seems to attract just as many adults as children. It was built in 1927 by an eccentric millionaire, Capt J. Howey, and still provides a regular hourly service in the summer.

A few miles west of the marshes take a steam train on the *Kent and East Sussex Railway* (sometimes called the Tenterden Railway, from its starting point).

Bodiam Castle: near Robertsbridge, is a truly romantic ruin, rising majestically out of a duck-strewn moat. It was built in 1385 against a French invasion that never came. It has been uninhabited since the 17th century but remains remarkably intact. The floors have been replaced in some towers, rewarding those brave enough to mount steep spiral staircases with stupendous views. Admission: £1.30 adults, 70p children. National Trust shop. Open Mon-Sat, April to end October 10am-6pm, Nov to end March, 10am to sunset. Five miles from Robertsbridge station. One mile east of A229. Three miles south of Hawkhurst.

WHERE TO STAY

Elvey Farm Country Hotel: down a lonely track out of the village of Pluckley. From Charing, go straight through the village down a steep hill. Turn right by the Blacksmith's Arms, first right, first right again. This 15th-century Kentish yeoman farmhouse, in 75 acres, has 10 rooms in all, some of them in the allegedly haunted oast house. Comfort and cooking are both excellent. Children welcome. No special weekend break rates, but a double room costs from £45.50 per night. Single: £23.50. Set dinner: £12.50. Children under 10: £6.25. Tel: Pluckley (023384) 442. *The Old Vicarage Guest House:* 66 Church Sq, Rye, is a most civilised bed-and-breakfast house in the prettiest corner of the town, looking right out on to the church. Single from £22, double £32, suite £40. Tel: Rye (0797) 222119.

23

Shropshire

Julian Critchley

. . . .

ENGLAND between the Severn and the Wye, or between Shrewsbury and Hereford, is as unspoilt as it is beautiful. Textbooks call it the Middle Marches: A. E. Housman, his "land of lost content" and the British Tourist Board the "Heart of England". Telly commercials puffing Telford New Town sing of "its beautiful British countryside". British? The copywriter must be as unlearned as he is untravelled.

Shropshire and Hereford are English counties looking towards Wales, with their backs turned firmly against Brummagem and its Black Country. It is a castellated land, blue, green and gold, a country of long vistas in which the horizons are indented with the sharp profiles of distant hills. To those who have read Housman's poetry it is the home of places with magical names like Wenlock, Clun and Knighton, names plucked from the gazetteer by the poet. Its "capital" is Ludlow, the town towards which his doomed lads were for ever striding on some long-forgotten first of May.

Go to Ludlow and make it your base. Within a twenty-five mile radius is some of the prettiest scenery in England. Villages such as Eardisland, Weobley and Pembridge, where even the lavatories are in black and white and the churches have detached towers for protection from the marauding Welsh. Towns like Tenbury Wells, Leintwardine and Leominster, where Georgian houses can still be bought for half the price of property in Surrey. And Ludlow itself, the prettiest small town in England, where Broad Street with its mansions runs down from Buttercross to the town's last remaining gate.

The A49 trunk road is the north/south axis. Juggernauts thunder along it bound for Liverpool from Bristol and the south. Everything along the Welsh border runs north to south; the trick is to find roads that go east to west. Drive north out of Ludlow to Craven Arms, turn towards Wales and follow the road that climbs to Newtown in Powys by way of Clunton, Clunbury, Clungunford and Clun. You are likely to be on your own.

Or turn east from Craven Arms and drive up the Corve Dale towards Much Wenlock. The earth of the dale is red and the farming the richest in Shropshire. The valley lies between the Wenlock Edge and the two Clees, Brown and Titterstone, which, rising to nearly 1,800 feet, stand between Shropshire and the world beyond.

Diddlebury has a Saxon church, and high up the slopes of the Brown Clee, near the aptly named village of Cold Weston, is the chapel at Heath, a Norman construction untouched since the twelfth century, standing alone in a deserted field. It is unlocked.

Holdgate has a church built like a castle and completely unrestored. So remote are the villages of the dale that not even the Gilbert Scotts, those indefatigable Victorian restorers, managed to lay their hands on it.

The joys of the Welsh border country lie at the end of lanes that wind interminably beneath high hedges from one stately farmhouse to another; a switchback progress offering spectacular views from the tops of high hills and lonely valleys, where the silence is broken only by the wind and the distant hum of a tractor. One lane can end in the muddy yard of Cold Comfort farm, another at the foot of a ruined keep, undisturbed since the Civil War.

South Shropshire is a land of hills. North Herefordshire, of vales. To the north is The Wrekin, a hill under which lies Uriconium, once Britain's fourth-largest Roman city and still largely unexcavated. The Stretton Hills lie anchored to the east of Church

Stretton, like a line of great ships. The Long Mynd is to the west of the town, a dark whaleback where the last great bustard in Shropshire was sighted in 1826.

Further west are the Stiperstones, a range of hills crowned by tors of quartzite, the most prominent of which is the Devil's Chair. Cordon, a sinister volcanic peak, lies immediately to the north of the Clun Forest, a tableland bisected by the most obvious stretch of Offa's Dyke, the Saxon frontier between Mercia and Wales.

Travelling west across south Shropshire the country changes perceptibly from English to Welsh. The Clees and Corve Dale are like Devon. The Wenlock Edge stands above Ape Dale like the escarpment of the Cotswolds. The Long Mynd and the Stiperstones have a wilder, Welsh quality, a line of hills above 1,600 feet, brown in winter, green in summer and blue in the early autumn.

North Hereford is a pastoral country where trees cling to the steep sides of hills, the soil is brick-red and the houses black and white. The boxes of matches proclaim "England's Glory". The most attractive part lies to the west of Ludlow, the plain of Wigmore, the site of an Ice Age lake imprisoned by a circle of hills. Here are to be found villages like Burrington, where the time is counted by the Post Office's twice-daily van and exquisite eighteenth-century houses like Elton Hall lie hidden behind a screen of trees. Through this Arcadia flow the rivers Teme, Onny and Lugg.

Shropshire men are not the sort to blow their own trumpet. Shrewsbury, the county town, is not even a city, and in cricketing terms Shropshire rates only as a minor county. The area is sparsely populated. There are no dukes, and the great houses are not the sort with zoos. Shropshire is famous for its Tories, its scenery and its sheep. Go while the going is good, and keep the secret to yourself.

WHERE TO STAY

Ludlow's most spectacular hotel is the Feathers, a carefully renovated black and white building constructed in 1603. It has 37 rooms; doubles from £78, singles from £54. The Feathers is situated at the top of the town, and, thanks to the bypass, has reverted to its medieval silence. Tel: 0584-5262.

I sometimes stay at Church Bank, Burrington, a tiny village 6 miles west of Ludlow. The cost is only £11 per person. This is a bed and breakfast of the very best sort, run by the Lauries. Alan was a housemaster at Shrewsbury School and his wife, Rosemary, cooks 4-course dinners (£7 a head, believe it or not) of a standard that would have persuaded me to stay on at Shrewsbury as an assistant master. Tel: 0568-86426.

WHERE TO EAT

There are 3 serious restaurants locally. The Old Post office at Clun, The Country Friends at Dorrington, and The Poppies in the Roebuck pub at Brimfield.

The Old Post Office, overlooking the Clun Valley, has 8 tables, a bar and comfortable bedrooms for those who seek the peace and plenty of the Marches. I have lunched and dined there, and have rarely been disappointed. Dinner is £18 a head, the meat and fish is local and the cheeses excellent. It is quiet and comfortable. Just the place to eat in the back of beyond. Tel: 0588-4687.

The Country Friends at Dorrington, 6 miles south of Shrewsbury on the A49, is a more ambitious place. The 1988 edition of *The Good Food Guide* awarded it 14/20 and listed it among its Restaurants of the Year. It is large, black and white, and comfortable with an à la carte that ranges between £13.50 and £18. I have lunched there well. *The Good Food Guide* remarks "snack lunches and dinners on quiet nights (only during the week) are cheaper, and bargains." Tel: 0743-73707.

The Poppies at Brimfield, 3 miles south of Ludlow, is the most exciting of the 3. It is a pub (the Roebuck) with a restaurant room and 3 bedrooms above, where the food is very good indeed. Carole Evans is more adventurous than her rivals and I cannot think of a better "comfort station" when touring the Shropshire Hills. Tel: 0584-72230.

For lovers of pork pies of the old-fashioned kind, the Blist Hill open-air industrial museum at Ironbridge has a replica shop, Charles Jesse, which sells the real thing. A large pie and a bottle of decent burgundy from Tanner's of Shrewsbury and I can guarantee you can drive through Telford without even noticing it.

Stourhead

Christopher
Somerville

. . . .

THERE'S nothing like a stiff climb, allied to a good appetite, to put an edge on a long-anticipated view. Our first gaze west from the top of White Sheet Hill, at 8am on a half-freezing winter's morning, was wonderful. The meeting point of three counties — Wiltshire, Dorset and Somerset — spread twenty miles of thickly wooded, deeply rural countryside at our feet.

A carpet of pearl-grey and pink mist was broken by vein-like bunches of bare treetops, swells of hillside and the four little spires on the corners of St Michael's church tower down in still-sleeping Mere village. Slap in the centre of the view, drawing our eyes irresistibly, exactly as they were designed to do, the pillars and portico of Stourhead House stood out in striking domination of everything else in sight.

For a winter walking weekend, this little-visited corner of the West Country is hard to beat. In summer there are visitors enough to please the tourist board and local traders. Longleat and the lions are only just over the hill, and at Stourhead there are

musical parties, picnics, fireworks and all kinds of jamboree in the park and gardens — not to mention the superb Palladian house itself, full of Chippendale and eccentric family history. From early November until Easter the house closes to the public, but the gardens stay open all day for all-comers. We took a whole morning to get round the lakeside walk under the trees, and met only two other couples.

Hoares erected Stourhead on banking money in the eighteenth century, and Hoares still live there today. There were so many Henrys in the family that they were known by nicknames. Henry the Good built the house in the 1720s, and his son Henry the Magnificent dammed old fishponds and the springs of Dorset's River Stour to create a spectacular and harmonious water garden known as the Pleasure Grounds. Strolling along the path round the lake, we passed high-flown temples to Flora and Apollo, as well as simpler rustic nooks. In an icy-cold grotto, Ariadne slept in statue form over the river's springs, while beyond her a river god shook his weedy tresses and an admonishing finger. Every few yards a new view opened, unobscured by leaves at this season, over a blend of water, masonry, hillside and woodland as subtle as master craftsmen could plan. Everything was reflected without a ripple in the thick, smoky water of the lake, slipping from one shade of grey to another.

Water splashed in the distance, but everything else in Stourhead gardens was utterly quiet — one of those still, sharp winter mornings when blackbird alarms and duck chatter ring like iron in the air. Against a washy blue sky the spindly branches of oak, birch and beech made a backdrop for the Stourhead conifers. The gardens are rich in these stately trees — cedar, cypress, juniper, spruce, pine — as well as many more exotic species planted by successive Hoare baronets. Some, well over 100 feet tall, have been growing on these Wiltshire slopes for two centuries and more. The summer and autumn colours of the deciduous trees at Stourhead make poor, drab relations of the conifers, but in winter they come into their own — great dark rockets of trees, whose resinous fragrance still ghosts across the path.

Tree list in hand, we followed the number tags on the trunks past temples and grottoes, until the watery sun gave up the unequal struggle and bequeathed us a softly spitting afternoon. We cut dead the last handful of trees, and made for the log fires and welcome elbow-room of the Spread Eagle Inn at Stourton, just outside the garden gates.

Built shortly after Stourhead House to cope with overflows of Hoare guests, the Spread Eagle carries on its hospitable trade under the ownership of the National Trust and its managers, Robin and Christine Wills. There's nothing particularly smart about the inn. The public bar, where estate workers gather among other regulars, is smoked orange from floor to ceiling. One of the bar window panes holds the diamond-cut signatures of, among many others, David and Primula Niven from 1941.

The atmosphere is more like a club than a pub. "In summer at weekends," said Robin Wills, "I often wonder how we'll fit everyone in. Three hundred people can descend at one time. But as things are now ..." — he waved a hand at the family with gurgling baby at the next table, the only other occupants of the room — "it's all very quiet ... very pleasant."

The home-made steak and kidney casserole and the good bitter of the Spread Eagle revived us: the scent of the fire made us drowsy. Only one thing for it — a well-anoraked trot by way of Search Farm and Zeals Knoll into Mere, on the far side of the A303. This road, one of the West Country's great pre-motorway through-routes, skirts Mere closely as a dual carriageway; but the village

29

goes on about its business regardless, accepting trade off the road without actively seeking it.

The grey stone streets of Mere are full of old-fashioned shops with wood-framed, plate-glass Victorian frontages. The Old Ship Hotel and The Talbot face each other in the village centre, two dark, poky, heavily beamed and creakingly comfortable old coaching inns. Narrow side alleys ramify from these main streets. Waterside, cutting back from Upper Water Street, winds beside a stream spanned by bridges, which lead to more little roadways a couple of feet wide between the neat gardens of tiny grey cottages. From this intimate maze of paths we looked up to find the dun-coloured backs of the downs swelling into the gathering dusk, seemingly close enough to reach out and touch.

Next day we set out to tackle those downs. We stretched out from Stourton through the woods to Alfred Tower, then east and up from limestone valleys on to the chalk ridge of White Sheet Hill. Alfred Tower is a model for all those Rapunzel towers. It rears up on a prominent site 900 feet above sea level in three-sided, red brick phallic magnificence, taller than the tallest Stourhead tree. Its little arched windows in rows, soaring overhead, were just made for tumbling plaits of golden hair. Henry Hoare the Magnificent put up the tower in 1772 to glorify both King Alfred and himself, in the days when a landed gentleman could do what he damned well pleased on his own land.

The oldest road in England runs right past Alfred Tower, and we followed its straight course for three miles up to the downs. The Harroway (Hoary or Ancient Way) was a tin-distribution route in Bronze Age times, but its origins lie thousands of years further back than that. Under various guises it runs right across southern England from Devon to Kent by way of Stonehenge. Our little section turned quickly from a minor road into a boggy lane, then to a stony chalk track that curved up to the Iron Age fort, Bronze Age barrows and Stone Age enclosure on the summit of White Sheet Hill. Sir Richard Colt Hoare, second baronet and a keen amateur archaeologist, came up from Stourhead two centuries ago to slice his way into these barrows, and found several "interesting antiquities" inside.

The previous morning's early view from White Sheet Hill had been filled with mist, but today's clear light gave us a living topography lesson — limestone lanes, woods and farmlands of Somerset, long curves of the River Stour into lush Dorset; and, running east along the ridge, the rolling flanks of the Wiltshire downs.

Along the ridge we walked, passing crumbling old milestones beside the path — "XX miles from Sarum, XCVIII from London, 1750" — relics of the days when this waterlogged, rough old track was the main coaching route between London and Exeter. Our boots clogged with coffee-coloured chalk clay, our faces nipped with cold until hard walking warmed them, our eyes were on those waves of smoothly rounded plough- and grass-land where barrows, mounds and strip lynchets showed thousands of years of human occupation. We must have covered seven miles by the time we felt like turning round.

Part of the pleasure of walking weekends in winter is making oneself cold, damp and tired in the cause of both inner and outer glow. The other part, of course, is undoing all that good healthy work with knife, fork and glass by a proper fire. Friends had recommended just the place to do maximum agreeable damage of this sort, at Trudoxhill near Frome. We went to find Rob and Julie Viney at the White Hart there, and were glad we did — not just for the restorative excellence of their food. There's no better way to cap a winter walk than a couple of pints of home-brewed Ash Vine bitter by the Vineys' open fire. Once settled there, however, don't expect to stir another step.

GETTING THERE
By road from London — M25, M3, A303 to Mere. From Midlands and north — M5, M4 to junction 18, A46 to Bath, A36 and A361 to Frome, B3092 to Stourhead. Nearest railway stations to Mere — Gillingham (5 miles); Bruton (10 miles).

WHERE TO STAY
Spread Eagle Inn: Stourton, Wilts; tel: 0747-840587 (Robin and Christine Wills). Bed and breakfast, twin or double with bath £42, single £37. Winter breaks (2 nights including à la carte dinner): £48.50 per person. Family suite: £68 for family of 4 (room and breakfast). Dinner: £12.50 plus wine.
Stag Cottage: Zeals, Wilts; tel: 0747-840458 (Marie Boxall). Bed and breakfast, double £20, single £10.50. Packed lunch on request. No evening meal, but high teas on request, and *White Lion* at Bourton is 5 minutes up the A303 — good vegetarian and other menu, about £10; Sunday lunch £5.50; all fresh vegetables. Also try *Old Ship Hotel:* Mere; tel: 0747-860258. *Cornerways Cottage:* Zeals (Irene Snook); tel: 0747-840477. *Red Lion:* Kilmington (on the Harroway); tel: 09853-263. Tourist Information Centre, Mere, displays local accommodation list in window.

WHERE TO WALK
Stourhead gardens and parkland (open 8am to dusk); *Mere* village; *White Sheet Hill* nature reserve and the Harroway (OS ref 745351 to 853338).
End up at *White Hart:* Trudoxhill (Rob and Julie Viney) — OS ref 748438. Good food, big fire, 20 fruit wines, Ash Vine bitter; new brewery open; tel: 0373-84 324 to view.

WHAT TO BRING
O.S. 1:50,000 Sheet 183 Yeovil and Frome; stout boots and thick socks; winter woollies; tree and bird book.

BEDTIME READING:
The Old Road by Hilaire Belloc.

Windsor

Patricia Mowbray

. . . .

WHEREVER you are in Windsor, the castle rises lordly overhead, a monument of memories dominating the skyline. It doesn't matter that the grand, sandcastle towers and turrets were added to make it more picturesque, nor that charabancs of tourists endlessly unload beside Queen Victoria's impassive statue to crawl over the royal homestead, en route from Big Ben to Anne Hathaway's cottage. Windsor has always been tarted up and played ambivalent host to the invader.

Well, ever since William, guarding his title of conqueror, surrounded his capital with fortresses and chose the chalk hill above the Thames, between water meadow and wild open country, as the site of the motte to complete the ring. For more than 900 years a stronghold has remained there, the present majestic monument being the largest occupied castle in the world.

You don't have to invent ghosts in Windsor when, beneath banners of the Knights of the Garter in St George's Chapel, you can stand on the royal vault, which holds the earthly remains of Kings George III and IV, William IV, Henry VIII and Charles I, whose body was brought back here after his execution. As his coffin was carried across the castle courtyard, falling snow turned the black pall white, before the casket was lowered into an unmarked spot, while the Bishop of London, denied prayers, wept.

It was in his fortress-palace that Charles awaited his fate, reading Shakespeare and walking the long terrace. Here monarchs have been born and have died, have fallen in love and womanised, been held captive and mourned, have announced abdication to a nation waiting by wireless sets.

It has been the scene of ostentatious feasts and revelries, acted as a royal retreat from plague and been abandoned to squatters and local ragamuffins. There is a continuity even in the gusting garbage. The council dustcart now sallies forth several times daily. In 1519, with nobles swarming to Henry VIII's Garter Feasts, horsemen were limited to sixty for a duke, fifty for a marquess, because of the squalor. Horse muck or McDonald's cartons, life has never been easy for a cleansing operative in the royal borough.

During the bleak Civil War years, with the castle reduced to a garrison-prison, Dean Christopher Wren bravely hid chapel treasures, refusing to give up his keys to the Puritan governor. His son, who grew up in the castle grounds, was to become one of our greatest architects.

Sir Christopher it was who completed the Windsor Guildhall. At loggerheads with a pedantic council which demanded columns to support the open ground floor, Wren capitulated but had the last laugh. His columns do not actually touch the ceiling.

It was at his family home beside Windsor Bridge that we stayed: Sir Christopher Wren's House Hotel has been rescued from no-star state to three stars (none being on offer for sympathetic restoration). Under the resident director, Michael North, the attractive Orangerie restaurant has earned a reputation for good food, and the "theatre weekend" has been introduced.

While Noël Coward's light comedy, *Present Laughter*, at the Theatre Royal on Friday evening wouldn't normally have tempted me, it presented an ideal opportunity to witness a Windsor night out. There was an abundance of crêpe de chine and cultured pearls and even the under-twenties sported best frock or collar and tie. Picking up their pre-ordered gins in the interval, the theatregoers seemed to have wandered off-stage into the bar.

Later a group of denimed youngsters danced amid refuse sacks in front of Pizza Hut, delivering a beery, bonhomous "God Save the Queen" up at the castle

ramparts. But the Union Jack, not the Royal Standard, was flying — the Queen was not at home.

Saturday morning we met the hotel's motherly breakfast ladies, renowned for urging black pudding on dieting businessmen. They produced an enormous bag of bread for the tinies to take to the river bank. Copious supplies are essential. Drop one crumb into the Thames hereabouts and swans surge up like a snowdrift, with vicious fighting down the pecking order.

We took a canary-yellow motor-boat to Bovney Lock, keeping time with the butting coots but easily outpaced by a sandy-haired, thirteen-year-old Etonian oarsman. There were almost as many Etonians as swans on the sunlit river.

Life looked far more idyllic for the boys than for their predecessors, all seventy of whom were taught for twelve hours a day by one master in the classroom, built circa 1500, which still stands in School Yard.

We "did" the castle and the old town with a group of Americans who assembled wherever their guide raised her umbrella as a rallying signal. And gratefully we climbed into John Seear's open landau to be tucked in under tartan rugs by his liveried groom.

"Look out, here comes the opposition," grinned John from under his topper, urging the pair of gleaming horses out in front of the approaching open-topped sight-seeing bus, which followed our more gentrified conveyance until we left the High Street to trot off up the Long Walk.

Half an hour's drive in the landau takes you the three miles to Snow Hill, at the southern end of the Long Walk, and to the Copper Horse equestrian statue, erected in memory of poor "Farmer George", his last melancholy decade lived out at Windsor Castle while his son ruled as regent.

Looking as though it might at any moment clatter down from its lofty pedestal and gallop home, the statue can also be reached by a short stroll through the park from Bishops Gate, past the entrance to the Queen Mother's residence at the Royal Lodge. At the Fox & Hounds, outside the park gates, there's a chance to sample "the best steak and kidney pie in the Thames valley".

The 4,800-acre Great Park, tamed from "forest" where once wild oxen, boar and wolves roamed, offers the beautiful Virginia Water lake, dug by the Duke of Cumberland's troops after the Battle of Culloden, and the internationally famous woodland of Savill Garden and Valley Gardens.

Up on Smith's Lawn, where Prince Charles played a dashing No 2 for Windsor Park on Sunday afternoon, little seemed to have changed since the Black Prince jousted in victory tournaments against the team of his warrior father, Edward III. The press pack, corralled behind a bank of paparazzi lenses at one end of the ground, was still looking for fallen garters.

We had come to the Guards Polo Ground via Windsor's popular Safari Park, where the baboons can be relied upon to pee on your windscreen while swiping the wipers. Here we saw such unlikely feats as dolphins hurling their trainer twenty feet into the air and a parrot called Rocky riding a bike on a high wire. That's Windsor: you can watch your future King play polo in the green and pleasant land of Barbour jackets and Range Rovers, or parrots riding bicycles, while peacocks strut majestically among the chicken nuggets.

In search of serenity before heading homewards, we drove to Dorney Court, where there is honey still for tea and Palmers managing to keep the roof on after twelve generations.

Behind fat walls of yew, the pink brick of the Palmers' Tudor manor house glowed in the late afternoon sun, which danced across the panelled Great Hall, burnishing the gallery of family portraits which stretch back four and a half centuries. Lady Barbara Palmer, mother of six of Charles II's illegitimate children, smiled seductively on.

The thunderstorms struck just before we left, causing much stoical Canute-like activity. Once home we feasted on delicious asparagus from the Dorney Court gardens.

WHERE TO STAY

Sir Christopher Wren's House Hotel: Thames Street Windsor (tel: 0753-861354). Theatre weekend (dinner and theatre Friday, breakfast and dinner Saturday, breakfast Sunday), £95 pp per night.

Oakley Court: Windsor Road, Water Oakley, Windsor (tel: 0628-74141). Victorian gothic mansion with modern extensions, on the Thames 3 miles from Windsor. Weekends: single rooms from £99; doubles from £119.

Moor Farm: Ascot Road, Holyport SL6 2HY (tel: 0628-33761). Working farm and 700-year-old listed farmhouse 4 miles out of Windsor; bed and breakfast in room with private facilities £30-£34.

Tourist information centre: at Windsor Central station (tel: 0753-852010) supplies accommodation guide, availability and makes bookings (from about £12 bed and breakfast); 9.30am-6.30pm, Sundays 10am-6.30pm.

WHERE TO EAT

The Watermans Arms: Brocas Street, Eton. Landlord Jeff Collibee cooks a 30-item menu from cod and chips, £2, to chicken Kiev, £3.

Eton Wine Bar: 82 High Street, Eton (tel: 0753-854921). Three courses about £12 and main course about £5 — minted lamb and lemon pie particularly good.

Fox & Hounds: Bishopsgate Road, Englefield Green, Egham (tel: 0784-433098). Three courses about £10-£15, main course from £7; marvellous haddock and egg crumble and steak and kidney pie.

Hinds Head: High Street, Bray (tel: 0628-26151). Three-course dinner about £25, lunch £19, Sunday lunch £21.50.

THINGS TO DO

Windsor Castle: precincts free 10.30am to about 7pm summertime, changing of the guard 11am. State apartments (except when in use) 10.30am-4.30pm, Sundays 1.30-4.30pm (adults £2, children £1).

Queen Mary's dolls' house: times as for state apartments (adults £1, children 50p).

Royal mews exhibition of Queen's carriages and gifts 10.30am-4.30pm, Sundays 10am-2.30pm (adults £1, children 50p). Castle information, tel: 0753-868286.

St George's Chapel: in castle grounds. Occasionally closed for ceremonies, otherwise 10.45am-4pm, Sundays 2-4pm in summer (adults £1.50, children 60p). Services open to the public. Information, tel: 0753-865538.

Guided tours: of old town, 1 hour, from tourist information centre at 10.45am and 1.45pm, Sundays 1.30pm (adults £2.50, children £1.50).

Madame Tussaud's Royalty and Empire exhibition: in Central station's royal waiting room and under glass canopy; 9.30am-5.30pm (adults £3.55, children £2.55).

Eton College: open 10.30am-4.30pm (Sept 5-Oct 2, 2-4.30pm). Guided tours: adults £2.40, children £1.80.

Carriages: Orchard Poyle Carriage Hire, South Gates, Wick Lane, Englefield Green, Surrey (tel: 0784-435983). Edwardian and Victorian carriages touring countryside, visiting polo or horse shows; £10-£40 per seat. On fine days, half-hour landau trips up the Long Walk, £15 per party.

River trips: leaving Promenade, Windsor Bridge. Gamble and Logie rowing boats £6 an hour, motorboats £9 half an hour (tel: 0753-863160). Salters Steamers (tel: 0753-865832) runs a variety of daily trips.

Windsor Safari Park: Winkfield Road, Windsor, daily from 10am, adults £6.95, children £5.50.

Savill Garden: Wick Lane, Englefield Green, Surrey, 35 acres of woodland gardens, 10am-6pm, weekends 7pm or sunset if earlier, adults £1.80, children (each escorted by adult) free.

Polo: Smith's Lawn, Windsor Park, entry from Blacknest Gate. Usually 2 matches Saturday and Sunday, the first at 3.15pm. Parking on Smith's Lawn £8 per car, spectators on foot free.

Dorney Court: Dorney, Windsor. House and garden Sundays 2-5.30pm, adults £2.30, children over 10, £1.

The Wye Valley

Mark Wallington

. . . .

ONE of the most spectacular bends in Britain is on the Chepstow to Monmouth road as it follows the River Wye upstream. Having hugged the rim of a gorge for a number of miles, the road suddenly emerges from woodland and there below is the cold, grey shell of Tintern Abbey, a superb stone skeleton crouched by the riverside. The sight makes you lunge for the brake pedal.

This is the road on which most people approach the Wye valley and it's advisable to make the trip in daylight. It's also a good idea to be there out of season: in the autumn, when the cider apples are picked and there's a sweet smell of fermentation in the air; or in the winter, when the trees are bare, the views extended and the browns and pale greens run into the grey of the river. Also, you have the place to yourself.

We were staying just south of Ross-on-Wye at Flanesford Priory, a fourteenth-century Augustine retreat recently converted into self-catering units, which incorporate much of the original detail with a style and elegance that is

striking. The conversions are of varying sizes but each has a special feature. Ours, for example, had a five-ton cider mill in the middle of the kitchen.

The Priory is in the heart of the valley and makes a fine touring centre. On the hill above are the splendid remains of Goodrich Castle, while below, the river sweeps in a curve under Kerne Bridge and heads off towards Symonds Yat at the start of its dramatic route.

Also within easy distance is the river's less spectacular — although arguably more interesting — course to the north, where it reflects a softer landscape, running across water-meadows and along some of the splendid timbered and thatched villages that Herefordshire has such a wealth of — places like Hampton Bishop where the church has a black and white timbered belfry.

A network of lanes crisscrosses the river here, and over the brow of every hill there's some curiosity, normally a church or a pub: in Hoarwithy, for instance, we came across St Catherine's, a delightful Italianate church built by a vicar with a passion for Tuscany and a dislike of the brick design he was presented with when he arrived at the parish. At Kings Caple we stumbled across the British Lion pub, with two farmers at the bar and a landlady who said: "It's not normally this busy." She does bed and breakfast for £7.50 — it would probably be a memorable night.

Of the larger centres on the river, Hereford is the more interesting but Ross is the one in which you're more likely to spend time, mainly because of its situation, high above a horseshoe curve in the river. By day, Ross is a market town, with business centred around its seventeenth-century market house. By night, it's more of a ghost town, the spire of St Mary the Virgin casting a long reflection in the river, and the illuminated gothic-style town walls contributing to the eerie effect.

The walls, as you might expect, aren't authentic. They were built in 1830 in an attempt to decorate the town as it began to realise its potential as a resort. Tourism isn't new to the Wye valley. As long ago as the eighteenth century the area attracted visitors on what had become known as the "Wye Valley Tour", and it quickly received the kind of endorsement about which every tourist board dreams: a painting by Turner and a poem by Wordsworth.

In those days Tintern was the cultural highlight of a visit, and the rocks above Symonds Yat the natural. These attractions are still the most popular and one suspects that the area has been protected better than most. Even the motor car has been comparatively ineffectual in Herefordshire; there truly seems to be less traffic here than one is used to and driving can be a pleasure.

Walkers are also well catered for thanks to the Offa's Dyke path which begins in Chepstow on its long journey north; and the Wye valley walk, which runs for fifty miles from Hereford to Chepstow mostly along the river.

Both are waymarked paths but, if you want to be more creative with an Ordnance Survey, there's enormous scope. We found a good and varied circular walk that took us an afternoon starting from the Priory and following the Wye valley path for a distance downstream, then walking round and back along the top of Coppet Hill with fine views of Yat Rock.

But to have the real Wye valley experience, you must tackle the river itself. In the heyday of the Wye Valley Tour visitors would hire boats in Ross with awnings and oarsmen and a well-stocked

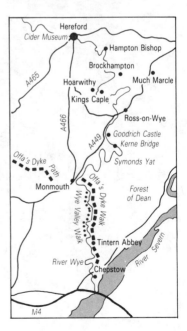

dining table and set off down to Monmouth and beyond. We had a canoe and a couple of pork pies but the thought was there and I can recommend the trip to anyone. The people — or rather person — at Monmouth Canoe Hire is very accommodating and will drive you to a suitable launching point from where you paddle back to wherever you left your car.

We started by Kerne Bridge,

and the first thing that struck me was: while it's nice to have a river next to you when you're on the road, it's damned annoying the other way round. Fortunately, the river soon veers away and slips into the gorge and the scenery is stunning, passing Yat Rock and then the Yat itself where we stopped at the Saracens Head on the riverside before tackling the rapids.

We'd heard a lot about these, mostly from locals who sat in dark corners and shook their heads and drew their fingers across their throats when we told them we were going to canoe to Monmouth. But it was all talk: any able-bodied person or child could manage the trip — all you've got to do is sit in the thing and the current will take you down to Monmouth in a few hours — and it really is the best way to see the river.

WHERE TO STAY

Flanesford Priory: a converted ancient monument and Grade One listed building with an assortment of accommodation. Weekend breaks are available only in winter between end-October and end-February (excluding Christmas). Prices are from £73 to £165. Tel: 01-948 8500 (brochures); 01-940 1398 (reservations).

Broome Farm: a working farm 2 miles from Ross. B&B, £12.50; en suite, £14.50. Evening meal available. Also a very pleasant place to stop for cream teas. Hilary Johnson, The Broome, Peterstow, Ross-on-Wye, Herefordshire. Tel: 0989-62824.

Chase Hotel: Four Crown Hotel in Ross-on-Wye, in its own grounds. £38.50 per person for 1 night's accommodation with bathroom, breakfast and £15 towards evening meal. Weekend breaks, minimum 2 nights, £47.50 per person, per night. Gloucester Road, Ross-on-Wye. Tel: 0989-763161.

THINGS TO DO

Westons Cider: an interesting and charming old, family-run cider business. Tel: 053184-233 to arrange a visit.

Hereford Cider Museum: story of cider making through the ages. Whitecross Road, Hereford. Open Mon-Sat 10am-5.30pm until the end of October. For November to March, check times on tel: 0432-354207. Price: adults £1.50; children £1.

Goodrich Castle: a Norman ruin, with moat, drawbridge and barbican beautifully sited over the river. Open Mon-Sat, 9.30am-6.30pm. Sun, 2pm-6.30pm. Adults 75p; children 35p.

Tintern Abbey: highly recommended. Open all year. Site of a Cistercian monastery since 1131.

PUBS

The Rose and Crown in Ross-on-Wye has a "devil amongst the tailors" table. *The Cross Keys* in Goodrich has a skittle alley.

CHURCHES

St Catherine's, Hoarwithy: an Italianate church in the middle of Herefordshire.

All Saints, Brockhampton: a thatched church with an original design. Inside is a celebration of arts and crafts — impressive misericords and tapestries from the William Morris workshop.

BOOKS

The Wye Valley by Richard Sale (Wildwood House), with photographs by Rosie Waite; *Paths and Pubs of the Wye Valley* by Heather and John Hurley (Thornhill Press); and The Ordnance Survey Wye Valley Guide.

Eastern England

North Norfolk

Cal McCrystal

. . . .

THE east coast of Britain is an unlikely spot from which to observe the western sun setting on the sea. But Hunstanton's striped cliffs of carr stone and red and white chalk are happily placed for the spectacle, since they face west over The Wash. Tired eyes may be bathed here at the end of a gritty working week.

And this is where we pause on our first west Norfolk evening, seeking balance in the soul of the world, a force that insists on equilibrium.

Having struggled, groaned and clocked ourselves through another urban stint, we have fled to the edge of the flattened land, to watch the tide rise up from the far-off Lynn Deeps, and run towards us, a fresh vitality, incarnadined, pouring in to right the tilted scales and raise the jaded mind.

Hunstanton is but a short drive from Grimston village, where we have made our weekend base in an eighteenth-century former manor house. The hotel, Congham Hall, is surrounded with orchards, country gardens, woodlands, ditches, hedgerows, and music from the blackbird's flute. A trumpet-call away lies Sandringham, where the monarch goes from time to time to preserve *her* equilibrium. This increasingly rare state can be attained in places all around: in Walsingham's streets where pilgrims meet, in nature trails through conifer woods, in stately homes and in good hotels and inns, and even within the ancient walls of nearby King's Lynn.

With the sun now beneath The Wash, we dine with good appetite amid the tranquillity of Congham Hall. There is an à la carte menu. What decisions are required of one over the apéritif! "Warm pastry of wood mushrooms and truffle; chicken mousseline with pine kernels in a rosemary-scented cream sauce; wafers of monkfish marinaded in sesame oil and lime ..." Our eyes devour fillet of lamb, medallions of veal, roast quail, a lime mousse with ginger cream, a blackcurrant parfait and a chocolate marquise before we make our minds up.

We turn to the second menu entitled "Hobson's Choice". It is for gourmets, among whom I do not include myself. We opt for it anyway, and it goes down as inspiringly as the Hunstanton sun: fresh asparagus with lemon butter; rich beef consommé with port; escalope of salmon steamed with ginger and served with crab and a shellfish sauce; kiwi fruit sorbet; grilled breast of duck with herbs and raspberry vinegar; a plate of cheeses; hot apple pastry with calvados sorbet, and, later in the quiet lounge, coffee and petits fours.

The à la carte dinner costs £25 per person, including VAT but not wine. Hobson's Choice is more ex-pensive — £32 — but is in the all-inclusive price of the weekend, which is £130 per person if, like us, one pays an extra £15 a head for the half-tester Grimson Room.

The palate and the stomach pleased, our thoughts are slight, and far from worldly care. Taking heed not to overstretch our wits, we sip coffee and listen to the owner's tale of abandoning his job in aircraft building in Hertford-shire and coming to Congham Hall seventeen years ago. Here, the people are prosperous, clean,

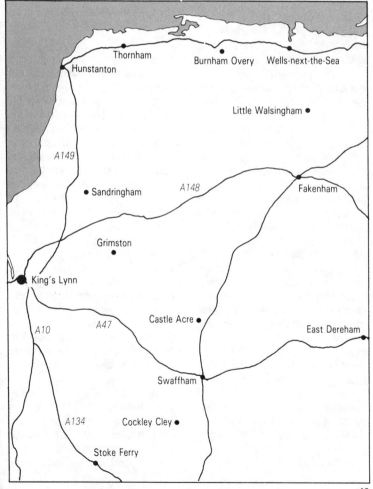

polite, hospitable. Good Dutchmen and their wives cross the sea to occupy his beds and exclaim over his victuals. In changing careers, he could not have chosen a more agreeable place (his name, incidentally, is Forecast).

At 10.30, his wife appears, kindly and pink-faced, and says: "I'm going on, or I'll keel over." We too retire early, for there will be a lot to see tomorrow.

If the half-tester was built for short sleepers (those less than five feet eight inches tall), it gives me long slumber. The electronic shower is disappointing, producing a weak spray and inadequately hot water. This, Mr Forecast forecasts later, will be fixed, for as it happens there are electricians working in the house at that very moment. But it isn't, so we make do with good old-fashioned baths.

We return to Hunstanton, planning to have lunch there. This time, the journey is unrewarding. The Golden Lion Hotel beckons us with its windows overlooking the promenade. We leave the sounds of surf sizzling on sand and seabird cries and enter a muzak zone. Through the clouds of cigarette smoke, we discern only a half-dozen customers in a vast lounge. We take a seat and a barman glances over. We wait. A waitress glances over. Nothing happens. After ten minutes we shed our peevishness and leave.

A short distance along the coast is Thornham and the King's Head Hotel, which has rose bushes on either side of the entrance and an old, low bar inside where excellent leek and potato soup and jolly patrons restore good humour.

It had been our hope to see

Sandringham, a site surrounded by rhododendrons that appears as "Sant Dersingham" in the Domesday Book. Here the Queen farms 3,310 acres, while as much again is devoted to forestry and stud farms. Alas, we learn that the place is closed to the public, the monarch currently being in residence where, as a seventeenth-century poet would have it,

> Th' uneasie Pageantry of State,
> And all the plagues to Thought and Sense
> Are far remov'd.

In this corner of East Anglia with its rolling fields and heaths and flinty villages, drainage schemes have taken away much water but little history. The heavy wheels of trade to and from King's Lynn's busy port barely disturb the landscape. Only 100 miles or so of M11 and A11 separate it from London, but within a day of arrival, such is the ensuing adjustment, one might as well be 1,000 miles away.

Hayblown lanes by day and salt-scented waterways at night help us to reassess our sympathies and antipathies with things, and relearn the grammar of a mystic communion we are forced to shun in the shouting capital. We relearn it not only from contemplating Hunstanton's pink surge, but from frequent flashbacks to antiquity, passing before our eyes like barges on the Ouse.

An Iceni village at Cockley Cley, between Stoke Ferry and Swaffham, reveals the way of the early Britons and their fight for survival in moated compounds. A Roman road to facilitate troop

movements after the defeat of the Iceni and Trinovantes tribes led by Boadicea, is traceable for fifty miles. The largest surviving medieval guildhall in England graces King's Lynn. The town's ceremonial silver testifies to its pro-Restoration bias (alone among East Anglian boroughs), an independence of mind that prevails to this day. In yonder fields of the Burnhams, Lord Nelson scampered as a boy.

Georgian façades and interiors disorient and confuse (behind the fifteenth-century Trinity Guildhall with its stone and flint chequer flushwork front are the town's assembly rooms, built in 1766). The Victorian corn exchange is among the grand survivors of nineteenth-century houses, factories and workshops; demolition took most of the rest in the name of progress and modernity.

In Little Walsingham, there is a shrine to the Virgin Mary where, in the 500 years before Henry VIII, many kings and nobles paid homage. Some believe that angels helped to build it, and there is an angel there to this day. Her name is Sharon, and she makes us laugh.

We have afternoon tea at Sharon's Pantry, a cramped place full of seductive odours. Seeing us hesitate before an array of cakes, Sharon cries: "Oh go on, have one of those big creamy meringues! Spoil yourselves!" Later, unbidden, she sits at our table to wrap up for us in her Norfolk vowels a secret recipe for Norfolk punch. Sharon assures us it was "never meant to be an aphrodisiac". We are still laughing as we leave the village along a street named Holy Mile.

The weekend assumes a gradual, unwanted urgency. There is just time for a stroll on the broad beach of Wells (there is mud; Wells demands wellies), to skirt Titchwell's nature reserve and pause briefly at a black windmill where the road squeezes over a narrow bridge on the way to Burnham-Overy Staithe. We force ourselves not to rush hither and thither.

The light begins to fade as we approach Castle Rising, once a rotten borough, now a place of pleasant mystery. Five miles north of King's Lynn, and inland, it recalls an ancient jingle.

Rising was a sea-port town, when
     Lynn was but a marsh,
Now Lynn it is a sea-port town,
     and Rising fares the worse.

While it is true that King's Lynn emerged largely from drained marshland, Rising's origins remain a puzzle. Although there is a 1738 painting of Castle Rising Castle, showing tall ships in the background, records going back to the late eleventh century make no reference to a port.

The Norman castle is a windswept ruin. But if you stand, out of the wind, in the arched eastern gateway, and look upwards at the massive keep, silhouetted against this, your last weekend sky, you will see the sun descend slowly on the tower, etching it in red, before falling towards Hunstanton. It is as good a picture as any to be going home with.

WHERE TO STAY

Congham Hall Hotel (11 bedrooms, open all year; AA 3 red stars and rosette, RAC 3 star and blue ribbon award): 6 miles from King's Lynn, 5 from Sandringham, and 40 from Norwich. A short distance to the north are uncrowded beaches and tiny fishing villages; to the east are the Norfolk Broads, 100 miles of lock-free navigable waters. The hotel has its own swimming pool, tennis court and cricket pitch. Horse riding can be arranged nearby.

Weekend tariff, £115 per person (2 sharing), including English breakfast and dinner. All rooms with private bathroom, colour TV and direct dial phone. No facilities for children under 12 years. Restaurant open to non-residents (tel: 0485-600250). The hotel is a member of the Pride of Britain group of independent hotels and town houses. For a copy of the Group's brochure tel: 0242-862352.

WHERE TO GO

Antiques and books: Old Curiosity Shop, King's Lynn; Saddle Rooms Antique Centre, Heacham; Teecees, Hunstanton and King's Lynn; Torc Books, Snettisham.

Arts and heritage: annual festival of music and the arts: King's Lynn, last week in July. Museum of Social History: King's Lynn, open Tues-Sat, 10am-5pm. Guildhall regalia rooms: King's Lynn (town treasures and charters), Nov-Apr, Fri and Sat, 10am-4pm; May-Oct, Mon-Sat, 10am-4pm. Bygones at Holkham: Holkham Park, Wells-next-the-Sea (4,000 items, incl old cars, farm equipment, smithy, craft demonstrations), June-Sept, Sun-Thurs, 1.30-5pm. Castle Rising Castle: open all year, daylight hours. Closed Mon-Tues in winter. Bircham Windmill: May 20-Sept 30, 10am-6pm. Cockley Cley Iceni Village and Museums: daily 1.30-5.30pm from Easter to Oct. Houghton Hall: Fakenham (Shires and Shetlands and militaria), 12.30-5.30pm Easter-Sept 24. Sandringham House and country park: Mar 26-Sept 28 (except July 17-Aug 5) Sun-Thurs, 10.30am-5pm. Tel: 0553-772675.

Garden Centres and Wildlife Parks: African Violet Centre: Terrington St Clement, open daily 10.30am-4.30pm. Park Farm: Snettisham, daily 10.30am-5pm (except Sat). Pensthorpe Waterfowl Park: Fakenham. Sea Life Centre: Hunstanton.

West Norfolk is rich in pubs which, with few exceptions, serve wholesome snacks, from around £2.50, and full-course lunches, from about £9. The King's Head in Thornham and the Black Horse Inn at Castle Rising were sampled and are recommended.

For more information telephone the West Norfolk Tourist Information Centre, King's Lynn, 0553-763044.

Rutland

Elizabeth
Grice

. . . .

EVEN if it was only his second memorised historical fact next to the date of the Battle of Hastings, every schoolboy used to be able to name the smallest county in England: Rutland. Ever since Leicestershire gobbled it up in the boundary changes in 1974, Rutland has been fighting to keep its identity and though it may no longer qualify for a general knowledge question, it still has the character of a little kingdom, a perfect English shire in miniature.

If ever a place lived up to its armorial motto, *multum in parvo* (loosely, small is beautiful) this is it. Imagine the lush pastures of Warwickshire, the red earth of Herefordshire, the crocketed steeples and four-eared towers of Lincolnshire churches, imagine the Cotswolds without the trippers, Lake Windermere without the encircling traffic jams and you have something approaching the robust delights of Rutland.

Add to this a fine tradition of cheese-making, stout sausages and good beer (it is the headquarters of Ruddles and it becomes immediately obvious why Rutland bristles with independence.

The most transfiguring thing to happen to Rutland since it lost the great oak forest that clothed it at the time of Domesday was the creation of a freshwater lake the size of Windermere. It is fifteen years since two hamlets and 3,100 acres were drowned to make it, yet Rutland Water is still a surprise, a sudden oasis off the grey stretches of the A1.

You cannot be secretive about a beautiful plane of water that ranks as the largest man-made lake in Europe, but you can be clever. Rutland's cleverness lies in not having oversold or overdeveloped its immense reservoir. People, rather like the thousands of waterbirds which have gradually colonised its westerly nature reserve, have had to find it for themselves. "The district council will direct them once they're here, but they won't tell them how to find it," we were told, with a touch of local pride in perversity.

We arrived at dusk on the edge of Rutland Water's southern shore, guided by its great landmark, Normanton Church. Looking at night like a ship at anchor, this church was once part of the Normanton estate and when the valley was flooded it was saved on a rampart of stone, jutting out into the water. We stayed in converted stables (all that is left of Normanton Hall) as close to the water's edge as one could prudently be.

Our window looked across the cobbles to the floodlit church. We went to bed and woke again to the tinny chimes of the stable-block clock; and when we opened the curtains on a blustery Sunday morning, more than 100 coloured sails were already doing a mad minuet on the choppy lake.

The Oundle division of Anglian Water, which manages the reservoir, has an understandable obsession with fluids and has created a water museum inside Normanton Church. Enter this cool edifice, descend a few stone steps into the vault and you are plunged into the gloriously titled Story of Sewage, a full and frank exhibition which makes you grateful to be living in the last quarter of the twentieth century.

Intending one afternoon to sniff out a Stilton-making factory (the best Stiltons come from this area) we found ourselves on the edge of the Vale of Belvoir, irresistibly diverted to its pompous castle, sitting high up on a hill like a bristling and rather ill-constructed crow's nest. Belvoir Castle, seat of the Dukes of Rutland, is not for purists but offers a superb vantage point for the vale.

It underwent restless rebuilding for centuries but just as the fifth Duke and his architect, James Wyatt, were about to call it a day in 1816, the whole northeast and north-west fronts were destroyed by fire and the reconstruction began all over again. It shows.

Belvoir Castle, outwardly a youngster in its class, has a slight air of dilapidation inside which is part of its charm. Ancient hangings are rotting away on their poles and some of the upholstered antique furniture looks as though it has suffered from the attentions of the Belvoir Hunt's pack. Stuffing spills out like bursting bulrushes.

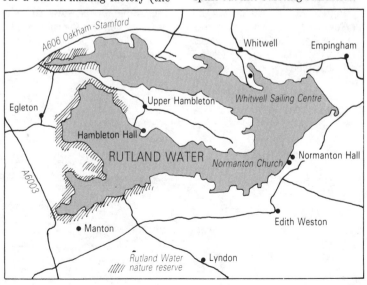

Our route back to Rutland Water took us through the warm stone villages of Knipton, Saltby, Wymondham, Teigh (pronounced tee) and Ashwell.

Teigh is tiny and its church unlike anything else to be found in Rutland. Except for the thirteenth-century tower, it was entirely rebuilt in 1782. Its pews are arranged in tiers, conversationally facing the centre, as in a college choir; and high up at the west end is a little wooden pulpit flanked by two reading desks.

We called in at Oakham, Rutland's capital, for tea and a glimpse of the castle. Tea there was, but the signs to Oakham Castle led us through wrought-iron gates to a humpy grass compound, the great earth bank of the eleventh century castle bailey. As we left, we peered through the windows of the Great Hall, all that remains of the once massive castle complex.

There are so many lambs being born in this part of the country in spring that the sound can be deafening. Making our way across country back to Rutland Water after a day's pottering, we felt we had stumbled on some invisibly sign-posted lamb route. They and their dozy mothers had to be scooped off the road as we meandered through the Deene Park estate, near Corby, to Kirby Hall.

Kirby Hall is one of those rare finds: a country house the guide-books have utterly failed to capture and therefore to package.

Half-ruin, half-house, this magical Elizabethan mansion lies in a gentle hollow, its church and village long since swept away. Its pinnacles, bull's-eye windows, enormous chimneys and great stone gables rise slowly from the dip as you approach, then the massive twin-bow windows appear, catching the sun.

The place has been despoiled of its fittings, furniture, hangings, carpets, pictures and all the other appurtenances that detract from the appreciation of a great building. It has not been lived in for one and a half centuries. English heritage is slowly reclaiming the geometric gardens with their great table-topped yews, and the "privy garden and the wilderness". I hope they are never tempted to do more to the house than keep it safe.

WHERE TO STAY

Normanton Park Hotel: on the south shore of Rutland Water. A 16-bedroom hotel in the coach house and stable block of the old Normanton Hall, demolished in 1925. Rooms comfortable, food excellent and every window in the restaurant overlooks the water. Single rooms with bathroom from £38; double rooms from £52; family rooms from £68. For special weekend break rates, tel: 0780-720315.

Boultons Hotel and Restaurant: Oakham, effectively the capital of Rutland, offers birdwatching weekends, £57.50 per person for a 2-night stay (dinner, bed and breakfast included). Bird-watching with a guide costs £67.50 per person for 2 nights. The Boultons is a 16th-century former hunting lodge only 2 miles from Rutland Water. Tel: Oakham (0572) 722844.

Hambleton Hall: one of the best small hotels and restaurants in the country, sitting on top of the Hambleton peninsula overlooking Rutland Water. Noël Coward wrote *Hay Fever* here. Fifteen luxurious rooms. Double from £85. Tel: 0572 756991.

WHERE TO GO

Rutland Water: lies off the A606 Oakham-to-Stamford road and is open all year. It has 27 miles of shoreline which you can walk, cycle, fish from or sail around. There is canoeing, sailing, windsurfing and, for the less energetic, a pleasure cruiser called the *Rutland Belle* which operates from Easter to September from Whitwell car park. Adventure playgrounds for children.

Normanton Church Water Museum: open Easter to October, 11am to 5pm daily. Admission 40p, children 20p.

Whitwell Sailing Centre: the Whitwell peninsula is open all year round for dinghies and sailboards.

Rutland Water nature reserve: a narrow strip of land stretching for about 9 miles around the western end of the lake and covering 350 acres. There are 3 bird-watching hides at Lyndon Hill reserve and 10 at Egleton. With a winter wildfowl count of about 20,000, it has become one of the country's most important sanctuaries.

For information about permits, contact The Warden, Fishponds Cottage, Stamford Road, Oakham, Rutland, Leicestershire (tel: 0572-724101).

Cycling: cycles can be hired from Whitwell or Normanton. Most are fitted with baskets for picnics and some have children's seats.

Wing Maze: this little oddity is so close to Rutland Water that it would be a shame not to walk it. Wing village lies 3 miles south of Uppingham on a hill above the Chater valley. The old turf maze, about 40 feet in diameter, may date from medieval times.

Kirby Hall: 2 miles off A43 Corby to Stamford road. Magnificent half-ruined mansion open all the year. For times, tel: 0902-765105, or English Heritage.

Belvoir Castle (and military museum): 7 miles south-west of Grantham off the A607 and seat of the Dukes of Rutland since Henry VIII. Open from March to the end of September. Tel: 0476-870262.

Burghley House: William Cecil's famous house set in parkland laid out by Capability Brown. Best known for its beautiful china, silver, tapestries and paintings. Open from Easter until October, 11am to 5pm.

Shotley Peninsula

Christopher Somerville

. . . .

"COULDN'T free the bloody tiller," growled the stout party in muddy gumboots to his son. "Come and give us a hand."

The younger man drained his pint and they tramped out of the Butt and Oyster. From our window seat over the river we watched them weaving between the black wooden hulls of retired Thames sailing barges, splashing vigorously in a tiny rowing boat out to their mooring in the River Orwell.

Salt, water, wind and mud all flavour the shoreline of the Shotley peninsula, a tongue of low-lying land pinched between the estuaries of Orwell and Stour on the Essex/Suffolk border. The Butt and Oyster — famed locally for its hospitality, relaxed atmosphere, good food and ancient decorations stained orange by countless years of tobacco smoke — stands with its outer wall lapped by the broad waters of the Orwell. In the dark bar, lit by reflections from the river, tweed coats and leather jackets mingle with canvas shoes and mud-streaked jerseys in a boatish smell of varnish and salt.

People come down the narrow lane to Pin Mill to sail — mostly owners of small boats, or families with one dinghy on time-share among six children. As non-sailing outsiders, content just to watch the boats go by, we did not feel excluded. Sailing from the hard here is for outdoor fun and exercise, not the gin-and-burgee stuff of south coast marinas. Arthur Ransome often sailed from Pin Mill, and that no-nonsense spirit of hardy adventuring that still clings to the place is celebrated at Pin Mill Sailing Club's regatta in September, a mixture of serious racing and out-and-out fun: mud football, greasy poles, tug of war on the green, Punch and Judy. And then there is the wonderful sight, each June or July on the day of the annual barge race, of twenty or more old barges setting off from Pin Mill under red sails like a flock of lumbering exotic birds.

To those who don't (or can't) sail, Pin Mill offers other delights — National Trust woodland along the shore; superb river scenery; a ramshackle collection of outdated coasting vessels, some inhabited, others slowly sinking, moored in a quietly creaking township at the water's edge. It is a distillation of the serene pleasures of the Shotley peninsula: breathing space, elbow room, wide horizon, remoteness. Water and sky — the keynotes constantly in view.

To spend the weekend here between the two rivers is to let last week and next go hang, eat hugely and well in the many excellent pubs, ramble around the salt marshes of the shore trying to hold wind-blown binoculars steady on oystercatchers, shelduck, terns and dunlin.

You leave the A12 just ninety minutes from London — no more hour-long crawls in first gear through Chelmsford, now the bypass is open — and slip straight away into relaxation. There is one B road — the B1456 — winding its way under the giant legs of the new Orwell Bridge and on down to Shotley at the peninsula's tip. Away from this, you can put the clock and calendar aside.

Tattingstone village perches on the edge of Alton Water reservoir. This is the place to siphon away the strains of the week by sailing, diving or sailboarding, fishing or strolling around the inlets and creeks.

The Waterloo House in Tattingstone must be one of the smallest pubs in existence: "An old Suffolk alehouse, never been changed," says the landlord/postmaster. Victorian farm labourers drank their beer here and ate breakfast in this tiny box of a room attached to the village Post Office.

At the far end of the reservoir a slender clock tower rises over the military-classical pomp of the Royal Hospital School for sailors' sons, a splendidly formal collection of buildings through which the road runs to reach the white-boarded mill and black-spotted, cinder-built Mill House at Holbrook.

Here bed-and-breakfasters go fishing for carp in the milpond; and here a tangle of lanes winds towards Shotley. The roadside banks are low enough to allow enticing glimpses over field slopes and copses towards the widening River Stour as it leaves the lush meadows of "Constable country" for the windier and more exhilarating world of the estuary. Flatford Mill, Willy Lott's Cottage, Dedham Vale and all John

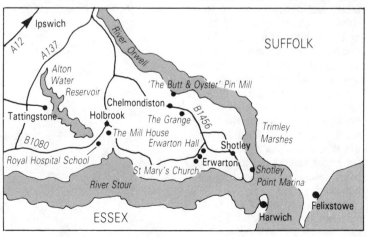

Constable's best-known scenes are only fifteen minutes' drive to the west.

This southern side of the peninsula is quiet and remote, with sweeping views of solitary flint church towers and pink-faced medieval halls so highlighted by that astonishing East Anglian clarity of light that they stand up out of the trees as if printed on the sky.

A network of footpaths leads down to the marshes and bird-haunted saltings by the Stour. As we walked off our Butt and Oyster fisherman's pie, we wandered over the spine of farmland to fetch up at the ivy-hung St Mary's Church at Erwarton. Mossy stones, lichened bricks and flints from five centuries of building and repairing make up a beautiful patchwork body to the church; its interior is flooded with soft light from clerestory windows. A heart-shaped casket discovered in the chancel wall in the 1830s contained a pinch of dust, supposedly the remains of Anne Boleyn's heart. A somewhat far-fetched local legend has it that Henry VIII used to be rowed in a barge by discreet serving men round from Hampton Court, some 100 miles away, to dally with Anne at her uncle's house, Erwarton Hall, half a mile up the lane from the church and unfortunately not open to the public. The present hall, alas, is not the one where the lovers met. It was built about fifty years after Anne lost her head — but it is everything a Tudor country house should be: mellow red brick, latticed windows, high and handsome gables.

At the sharp end of the peninsula the sea exerts its influence. The wind is keener, and smells ever more tangily of salt. Here, generations of boy seamen gritted their teeth to ascend the great rigged mast that still soars above the barrack-like buildings of HMS *Ganges*, a famed and feared Royal Navy training establishment until a decade ago. There is a spanking new marina just below, and pillar-box red lightships moored in mid-river.

At Shotley Point on the very tip of the peninsula we sat looking south to the yellow cranes of Harwich and east to the red ones of Felixstowe. Stour and Orwell converged before us in a bustle of enormous ships as we lingered on the shore, watching the real world at work.

Later we lazed back the four miles to Pin Mill along the Orwell shore, stunned by good beer, fresh air, salty breeze and exercise. The mud flats of Trimley Marshes across the river — under constant threat these days from expansion by neighbouring Felixstowe docks — hold enough invertebrates per square yard to enslave a huge population of birds; and we must have seen most of them that afternoon, though we did not meet another person.

GETTING THERE

Travelling by car from London — M25, A12 and A45 (Felixstowe direction) to turn-off before Orwell Bridge (A137/B1456). Driving from the north — A1, A604, A45 and as above. By train — nearest stations are Ipswich and Manningtree.

WHERE TO STAY

The peninsula is not geared to tourism and accommodation is rather sparse, but try the following:

The Grange: Chelmondiston (at the head of the lane to Pin Mill). Tel: 0473-84744. Jacqueline Holmes will ring you the day before you arrive with details of the weekend's menu, so you can bring your own suitable wine. Excellent home-cooked food. Guests have their own sitting room complete with crammed bookshelves and an open fire. Little delicious treats like bara brith come included in the price — bed and breakfast £30 double, £16 single. Dinner about £10 a head. Children are welcome. Cot available.

The Mill House: Holbrook, tel: 0473-328249. This is a 17th-century mill house with a bed and breakfast business run by Jean England. Views over ponds and trees from bedroom windows. Bed and breakfast costs £28 double and £18 single. Bed and breakfast only; but at

The Compasses in Holbrook, just a few hundred yards up the road, you can eat well in the restaurant (3 courses and wine: about £25 for two) or in the bar for half the price. If fully booked, Holmes and England can recommend a few other places on the peninsula. If these fail, Ipswich is north, Dedham west, Colchester south — all only a few minutes' drive away.

THINGS TO DO

You will probably just want to wander and enjoy the wonderful bird life of the two estuaries, the friendly pubs and profusion of footpaths (O.S. 1:50,000 Sheet 169, Ipswich and The Naze). But you can also visit:

Alton Water Reservoir: Open 7 days a week. Boats, sailboards, wetsuits etc for hire. Special provision for handicapped. Fishing permits obtainable from local tackle shops.

Marinas: At Shotley and Woolverstone.

Pin Mill Sailing Club regatta: for details, tel: 0473 84271.

Barge Race: end of June or early July.

HOLIDAY READING

Ordinary Families by E. Arnot Robertson (Virago, 1982). On sale behind bar of Butt and Oyster.

Suffolk Coast

Lailan Young

. . . .

THE wind-lashed coast of Suffolk, as atmospheric as Benjamin Britten's sea interludes that it inspired, feels like one of the remotest parts of the island kingdom. Roads are few, trains fewer. In the pierless stretch of coast between Aldeburgh and Southwold there is not much to tempt the visitor in search of bright lights and the noisy pleasures of the seaside.

It is a coast of salt marshes bright in spring with kingcups, tinged in summer with sea lavender, and of wetlands busy with the courtship dances and aerial acrobatics of terns and waders, eccentric grebes and the opportunist heron. Migrant geese graze the green pastures in winter under open skies. Spring is the time for swallows and swifts to wing in from deepest Africa.

The coast has mysterious areas where whole towns have disappeared into the North Sea. Ruined chapels and aged walls nestle under trees and gorse, and some that teeter now on sandy cliff-tops are also doomed to a watery end. Small towns and villages of clapboard houses with steep roofs blend into a landscape that makes the walker, cyclist or birdwatcher feel less obtrusive than the callous motorist.

No road runs along the coastline, so there is an expectation of something new and different at the end of each narrow road that leads off the A12 to the sea; it is as if one arrives at journey's end ten times a day.

Aldeburgh is the place most readily associated with Britten, for it is in this small seaside town that he wrote *Billy Budd* and *The Turn of the Screw*.

Inland, beside the River Alde, the white funnels of Snape Maltings stand out like those of an ocean liner beached among the glistening mud flats and shimmering waters of the estuary. The cluster of nineteenth-century granaries and malthouses, all mellow brick and painted clapboard, are now a place of exultation and exaltation for music-lovers and music-makers.

The wonder of Snape is not only the perfect acoustics of the unembellished brick concert hall, but that a short walk out along the river one can be alone and hear the sounds of pianos and sopranos from the rehearsal rooms mingling with the intimate chatter of swallows and the piping of redshank. This is the main venue for the magical Aldeburgh Festival every June.

Browse the shops in Aldeburgh High Street and you would never suspect that you were at the seaside: "No ice-creams or lollipops etc" plead the shopkeepers' signs. At number 110, a Salton turbo fan is switched on at night in the window display of cakes and cookies of the Cragg Sisters' tea-room. Is it keeping today's goodies cool for tomorrow's customers?

E. M. Forster liked Aldeburgh, where he lodged with fisherman Billy Burrell. As the telephone directory states, Billy is still to be found at the "Fisherman's shed opposite Wentworth Hotel". His clients come from counties around, from London and even America, for his lobsters, fish and dressed crabs.

Near the fishermen's huts the lifeboat sits high above the pebbled shore, all sparkling navy, orange and white, a list of its historic moments displayed on the outside walls of its shed: "Saved boat and three" and "Landed a body".

The moot hall, built in the time of Henry VIII, squats quaintly and timorously in the shelter of the shingle bank. Through the town and past the fish and chip shop, one can stroll along the sea wall to the Martello tower, northernmost defence against a Napoleonic invasion.

Northward lies Dunwich, most of it under the sea. Once the capital of East Anglia, it had a population of 4,000 cited in the Domesday Book. A small museum tells the story of the once-city, and its disintegration. Today's 160 inhabitants live quietly in cottages in narrow leafy lanes. The famous fish and chip café by the beach burnt down on re-opening at Easter 1988 but, in a village unaccustomed to bustle, the proprietor brought in a concrete mixer within days to churn its ingredients for the floor of a new café that had to be open and ready for a wedding party within a month.

Peaceful and not to be missed are Minsmere, where the Scrape is the place to see the elegant avocet and rare birds on migration, and Walberswick, a village of old walls and leaning chimneys, two greens, and a view over heath and marshes to Southwold, the jewel in the Suffolk coastal crown.

Southwold is the most relaxing and complacent of seaside towns. The church is magnificent, the best houses have a touch of grandeur and style, the white lighthouse is set prudently inland in a side street, and from the open greens spangled through the town like emeralds there are wide views of sea and water-meadows.

The shops are various and friendly. Denny & Son, who used to describe themselves as "tailors of Southwold and Savile Row" (in that order) have introduced a line of men's underpants covered in red hearts for the season. At Avril, across the road, they are collecting donations for a wooden seat in memory of Ben, a golden labrador whose fan club stretched the length of the High Street.

Down by the beach, brightly painted huts in band-box colours have names such as Ma's Bar, Dodge City and Here's Hoping. On the crumbling cliff above, the Sailors' Reading Room keeps a more cautious watch over the troublesome sea. Faded photographs and cuttings books tell of floods, wreckage and disaster.

Look down the coast and there is one sore thumb on the southerly horizon: Sizewell, box-like, brooding, and ominously bleak. But scan the great sweeps of land and sea, past a church tower in the distance and the boats drawn up on the shore, and there is reassurance that Suffolk is, and will remain, beautiful.

WHERE TO STAY

Wentworth Hotel: Aldeburgh (tel: 0728-452312). Pleasant with some rooms facing the sea. Bed and breakfast from £32.75.

Theberton Grange: Theberton, Nr Leiston, Suffolk, IP16 4RR (tel: 0728-830625). Spacious, comfortable, friendly, family-run country house and restaurant. Six rooms. Bed and breakfast from £18.50 single, £27.50 per person, double. Three-course dinner £11.50.

The Crown: Southwold. Bed and breakfast from £25.50 (see below).

The Aldeburgh Tourist Office also has details of cottages to rent.

WHERE TO EAT

Aldeburgh Fish & Shop Shop: 226 High Street. Tue to Sat, 11.45am-1.45pm and 5pm-9pm. Cod and chips £1.65.

Festival Club Wine Bar: Aldeburgh (behind Aldeburgh Festival offices). May to August, noon-7pm. About £4 main dish.

Regatta: 171 High Street, Aldeburgh (tel: 0728-452011). Pleasant meals about £9. 12 noon-2pm and 7pm to late. Telephone to book.

At Snape Maltings there is a good selection of places to eat.

Plough and Sail: Pub (cottage pie and vegs £2.95); *River Bar* for steaks, scampi in summer months, 12 noon-2pm and 7-11pm.

Granary Tea Shop: 10am-6pm, open all week; *Concert Hall:* self-service food counter is open 2 hours before concerts and for 30 minutes after. Good salads from about £4.

Flora Tearooms (the fish and chip café): by Dunwich beach. Open until early December. Cod and chips £2.55. Bring your own bottle (no corkage charge).

The Ship: Dunwich. Pleasant pub food.

The Crown: Southwold (tel: 0502-722275). Adnams' flagship hotel with superior bar food and stylish restaurant. Lunch: 2 courses £10.50, 3 courses £12.50. Dinner: £13 and £15. Excellent wine list. Open 7 days a week. Visit the *Cellar & Kitchen Store* at the back of the hotel for good wines, "super plonk", accessories. Mon to Sat, 10am-6.30pm.

ARTS AND LEISURE

At Snape Maltings the *Aldeburgh Festival* is every June; *Maltings Proms* in August; *Showcase Concerts* in September; *Britten/Mozart Festival,* September; *Master classes* open to the public April-August; *Winter concerts* at Christmas and New Year. To join the Mailing List (excellent detailed and advanced information) send £5 for 2 years' subscription to Aldeburgh Foundation, Aldeburgh, Suffolk, IP15 5AX. Box office tel: 0728-453543.

Suffolk Craft Society, all August at the Peter Pears Gallery.

Alde River: trip from Snape Quay at the Maltings by motor launch, past marshes and birds and Iken Church. Adults £2.20, children £1.50.

Minsmere RSPB Reserve: take the B1122 out of Leiston to the reserve entrance near East Bridge. Nature trails: bird-watching hides accessible from Dunwich Cliffs National Trust car park. Open 9am to sunset; closed Tuesday; Sunday and Bank Holiday weekends for RSPB members only. Admission £2.

St Edmund's Church: Southwold; superbly proportioned columns soar above a light-filled nave; screens with painted figures.

Blythburgh Church: on the A12, where carved angels in the roof witnessed Cromwell's cavalry smash the floor below.

FURTHER INFORMATION

Details of bed and breakfast, inns and guest houses from Aldeburgh Tourist Office, The Cinema, High Street, Aldeburgh (tel: 0728-453637).

Northern England

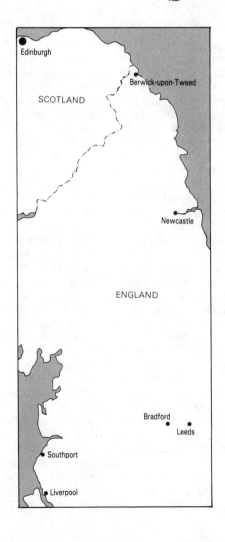

Edinburgh

SCOTLAND

Berwick-upon-Tweed

Newcastle

ENGLAND

Bradford

Leeds

Southport

Liverpool

Berwick-upon-Tweed

*Anne
Wilson*

. . . .

THE cry of seagulls and the slow beat of the mute swans' wings as they rise from the River Tweed symbolise the haunting, isolated beauty of Berwick-upon-Tweed. The river dictates the lie of the town. It comes in a wide sweep to meet the sea, enfolding the town in a near complete embrace of water. The coastline to the north and to the south is bare and windswept, with long stretches of white sand, mud flats and rocky outcrops frequented by rare sea birds.

Berwick is, officially, the northernmost town in England, though its townsfolk still consider it a matter of opinion as to whether they are Scottish or English. The controversy is less bloody nowadays, but the fine Elizabethan walls encircling the town and the many castles scattered across the Cheviot Hills to the west are testament to its embattled past. The Berwick accent also reflects its border position, being an extraordinary mix of Scottish and Geordie.

A walk round the Berwick walls is a good way to get the measure of the place. (The distance is just over a mile and a leaflet describing the walk is available from the Tourist Information Centre.) From King's Mount to Brass Bastion, you get the best sense of contrast between the gentility of the buildings within the walls and the raw beauty of the coastline without. Looking on to the town, the granaries and stately grey merchants' houses with their red pantile roofs are the epitome of neat Georgian architecture; looking outwards, a sharp breeze from the sea about half a mile away chills your cheeks and the eye is drawn to the long, white ribbon of deserted sand which stretches away to the south.

The view from Meg's Mount adds another dimension to Berwick's character — the River Tweed, gently curving, with traditional Northumberland cobles (shallow fishing boats) bobbing peacefully in the water.

Take a town tour with one of the local history buffs if you like bloody tales of heroic deeds and cannon fire (tours can be arranged through the Tourist Information Centre during the summer). Otherwise, visit the museums which, as well as offering a welcome refuge from the often unpredictable elements, have some fascinating exhibits, housed in interesting buildings.

The beautifully restored Barracks — the first barracks built in Britain — contain three separate museums. The Regimental Museum of the King's Own Scottish Borderers has uniforms, equipment, arms, pictures and models relating to the regiment's history. The most evocative exhibit is two reconstructed rooms: one the sleeping quarters for soldiers and their wives in the 1750s which shows their lack of privacy; and the second, a Victorian soldiers' schoolroom. The English Heritage Exhibition puts the regimental history in a wider context by colourfully depicting a soldier's life from Cromwell to Victoria.

The third museum, the Art Gallery, consists largely of Berwick's share of the Burrell Collection — some French Impressionist paintings, pottery, glassware and brass. But there is another section of greater local interest showing modes of transport in local agriculture.

There are two other museums in Berwick, one of which has a compelling, if gruesome, appeal. At the far end of Marygate is the Town Hall. Its rear entrance takes you up to the Cell Block Museum where the guide delights in showing the tiny cells with their branding irons, whipping hooks and manacles. The unspeakable conditions are neatly summed up by Elizabeth Fry, the prison reformer, who began her 1819 report with: "Nothing can be much more defective than this small prison." The Wine and Spirit Museum, by comparison, is slightly disappointing. There are some nice old bottles and a display of wine-making equipment, but the museum is essentially a tasting and buying point for Lindisfarne Mead, a sweet wine made to a receipe devised by the Lindisfarne monks.

If you tire of the museums, stroll around the town. Berwick is a place of narrow streets dotted with little shops — not the smart antique shop variety, more the sort of shops which reflect Berwick's age, position and interests. Game Fair and Jobson's in Marygate sell hunting, shooting and fishing gear; The Black Sheep on Bridge Street offers "sheep design" hand-frame knitted sweaters at a fraction of their price in Covent Garden. Cowe's, the grocer's shop on Bridge Street, gives a reminder of our pre-supermarket past. The shop still has dark wooden counters with drawers and shelves behind; ask for what you want and relish the rare attention of personal service. You might like to buy a tin of "Berwick cockles", mint-flavoured sweets shaped like cockles, unique to Cowe's.

A pilgrimage to Holy Island, known before the eleventh century as Lindisfarne, about ten miles south of Berwick and joined to the Northumbrian coast by a mile-long causeway, is an essential part of the Berwick experience. If you have come without a car, take the 477 bus — there are two bus services a day, depending on the tides, though after September they run only on Saturdays.

I have rarely encountered so spiritual a place. Perhaps it is the stark loneliness of the small island, cut off from the mainland at high tide, its romantic sixteenth-century castle perched on an outcrop. Perhaps it is the sound of the sea crashing against the rocks and the stories of ascetic monks living in the freezing, austere conditions of primitive huts to evangelise Northumbria. In autumn, the flat golden light enhances the sense of standing on sacred ground. Transported back to the dawn of British Christianity, one imagines St Cuthbert, that extraordinary hermit monk, taking to his small coble to seek further isolation on Inner Farne where, for nine years, he lived a life of prayer and contemplation.

The Priory, now an atmospheric ruin, dates back to the eleventh century. It was here that the Lindisfarne Gospels were written and illuminated. The Priory Museum depicts the life and times of St Cuthbert, St Aidan and the monks in a fascinating exhibition on the arrival of Christianity to the area. The museum bookshop has a good collection of books on the history of Holy Isle. The castle, which was built partly with stones from the ruined priory, owes its existence to an order issued by Edward VI that all havens be fortified against the Scots. The rooms are filled with English and Flemish furniture, mostly oak, from the early seventeenth century.

Ghosts abound in the town of Berwick and on this lonely stretch of coastline, but, in the end, the place is about its people. The Holy Islanders are proud and slightly reserved; Berwick is large enough to have people moving in and out, but small enough for everyone to know about it. Expect a warm, friendly welcome, and, if you can imagine so odd a mix, Edinburgh refinement tinged with Geordie charm. Wrap up warm, by all means, but prepare to be inspired.

HOW TO GET THERE

By train: a 4-hour journey from King's Cross leaving 6 times a day between 9am and 6pm. Standard return: £96, first class £140; from Glasgow: 6.25am direct, otherwise 9 trains a day changing in Edinburgh. Standard return: £23, first class £34. From Leeds: 7.10am and 4.55pm direct, otherwise every 2 hours changing at York. Standard return: £42, first class £63.

WHERE TO STAY

King's Arms Hotel (tel: 0289-307454): a restored coaching inn in the centre of the town. Doubles from £59.50 a night including full breakfast.

There are a number of guesthouses in the town. I found *Albury House* (tel: 0289-304433) good value and comfortable. (Ask for a room with a view of the Tweed.) For Georgian splendour, try *The Walls* guest house (tel: 0289-308320), from £20 per person bed and breakfast. Also contact the Tourist Information Centre (tel: 0289-330733) for further suggestions on accommodation.

WHERE TO EAT

Funnywayt'mekalivin' (tel: 0289-308827): preparing good, fresh food with care and artistry may be a funny way to make a living, but Lizzie Middlemiss manages it. Dinner (about £13.75 a head) is more elaborate: a 4-course set menu with dishes such as cauliflower and fennel soup, salmon soufflé and Northumberland roast beef. Dinner Friday and Saturday, pre-booking essential. Warn if you require vegetarian.

The *King's Arms:* offers 3 pleasant settings. King's Room, the oak-panelled dining room, has an à la carte dinner for about £13.50; the Bistro restaurant for lunch or dinner, dishes such as Farmhouse grill (£7.25); or the Garden Bar and Restaurant for large "submarine" sandwiches (90p) and light lunches.

Another good snack place in an historic setting is *The Townhouse* (tel: 0289-307517) in the town hall (where the butter market used to be). Open 9am-5pm. *The Shuttle* (tel: 0289-330281) is a newly opened restaurant, a short bus ride from the town centre on Main Street, Spittal. Lunches 12.30pm-2pm, dinner from 7pm. À la carte prices vary, but a dish such as fresh salmon in fresh cream and sherry sauces or scallops mornay costs £8.75. Prebooking for Saturday evenings is essential.

Pubs tend to be more like Scottish bars; a notable exception is *Meadow House* (tel: 0289-304173), which has an extensive bar menu and vegetarian food, but is only open noon-2pm daily; 7.00pm-9.30pm last orders; Sunday lunch orders to 2pm.

Bradford

*Gill
Charlton*

. . . .

FORGET those images of dark, satanic mills and the depressed north. Bradford is a monumental Victorian city that is proud of its heritage — the wool capital of the world. There is optimism in the air here.

The best-preserved northern industrial city, it lines a deep basin on the edge of the starkly beauti-ful Yorkshire Moors. The black grime and the appalling urban squalor of Victorian Bradford has been cleaned away, but you can still look down over the snaking streets of terraced houses and back-to-backs, the massive bulks of the mills and the grand civic buildings, all built of locally quarried millstone grit. Bradford's textile barons modelled their mills and warehouses on the palaces of

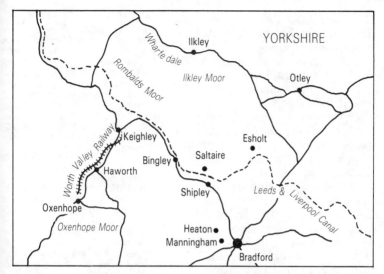

Renaissance Florence. Mill chimneys resemble Italian campaniles, Lister's spinning works has more than a little in common with the Uffizi Gallery, and City Hall's 200-foot tower is a copy of the Palazzo Vecchio's. Bradford has style.

Mill owners built for their workers too. Saltaire is a pretty model village beside the Liverpool and Leeds canal, built in the 1850s by Sir Titus Salt. Some terraced cottages are plain two-up-two-downs, others have porches and ornate arched windows; the house you were given depended on your rank at the mill. There is a hospital, a Nonconformist church (Sir Titus's mausoleum stands behind it), schools and alms houses for the elderly. Workers were paid in tokens to be spent in purpose-built shops or exchanged at Sir Titus's bank. The only thing the village lacks is a pub; he did not approve of alcohol.

Salt's Mill has been bought by a local entrepreneur, Jonathan Silver, who is turning it into a massive arts and leisure centre —

already one of the vast, iron-pillared spinning rooms houses a permanent collection of paintings by David Hockney, a native son.

Although many mills became unprofitable this century, Bradford still spins and weaves some of the finest woollen cloth in the world (imagine a mix of cashmere, mohair, mink and wool) and nearly half the city's working population is employed in the textile industry. If an order destined for America or Japan fails to meet its export deadline, or if the dye is one shade off, the material and often the made-up clothes end up in one of Bradford's many mill shops selling at cost with the designer labels cut out. I could not resist a navy-blue cashmere coat (unsold end of a run) for £75.

Bradford is now the home of a large, thriving Indian community centred around Manningham where J. B. Priestley grew up. Some of the best Indian restaurants in Britain are found here, most notably the Aagraha, which is listed in the Michelin guide.

There are Indian superstores selling freshly packed spices, lentils, cashews and pistachios, and sari centres where Indian silks and Kashmiri wool shawls are sold at prices which it would be hard to beat in India itself.

Despite all the southern prejudices about the uncivilised north, there is much more to Bradford than mills. The Alhambra Theatre is the northern home of the Festival Ballet and a touring venue for the National Theatre and the RSC. Everything from opera and rock concerts to wrestling matches can be seen at St George's Hall, and it takes half a day to tour the National Museum of Photography, Film and Television, part of the Science Museum.

And, if you feel the need to get out of Bradford, the Yorkshire Moors and dales are a short drive away. You can take a local bus to Haworth, home of the Brontës, and follow their footsteps along marked walks to places like Ponden Hall (the Thrushcross Grange of *Wuthering Heights*) or try to remember the words of "Ilkley Moor Baht 'at" as you cross that famous moor to the Victorian spa town of Ilkley. Nearer still is Esholt, a dying village (no one wanted to live next to the sewage works) until it became the celebrated setting for *Emmerdale Farm*.

When I stepped on to the train at King's Cross in London, I did not know what to expect from Bradford. Now I'm determined to return for more browsing round the mill shops, another session at the addictive IMAX cinema, perhaps some horse riding on the moors and definitely for some good Indian food.

HOW TO GET THERE
Bradford lies on the M62 linking Manches and Leeds, which in turn connects with M1. Gold Star Holidays (tel: 0904-6389 has excellent weekend break offers travell by rail. Return rail ticket and 1 night's acc modation in Bradford's best city centre ho costs from £53 from London and the sou east; from £48 from East Anglia and Welsh Borders and from £53 from cen Scotland. Extra nights cost £21 a pers Book through travel agents.

GETTING AROUND
Buses from Bradford Interchange cover city and nearby towns and villages. Lc trains from Forster Square station run to S aire, Ilkley and Keighley, where you can ju on a steam train to Haworth along the Wc Valley Railway.
The Wayfarer Waterbus cruises along Leeds and Liverpool Canal from Shipley Bingley past wharves, mills, canalside c tages and over an aqueduct. Tel: 02 595914.

HOTELS
Bankfield Hotel: Bradford Road, Bingley miles from town centre): a neo-Tudor cou house overlooking the River Aire, built 1848 by William Murgatroyd, Major Bradford. Fine panelled reception rooms spacious bedrooms. Special weekend t from £34 per person per night in double rc including dinner. Minimum stay 2 nights Sun. Tel: 0274-567123.
Victoria Hotel: Bridge Street, Bradford; Gr Victorian hotel with attractive stuccoed pu rooms opposite railway station; many b rooms recently refurbished. Weekend t from £32 a night half board. Minimum sta nights Fri-Sun. Tel: 0274-728706.

LUNCH
Moorland pubs are the best bet. *Roch Heifer Inn* (Rock Lane, Thornton) serves o cious roast beef and Yorkshire pudding, a should be made: a huge puff with a hole in middle for pouring in the delicious t gravy.
Dog and Gun: Oxenhope; overlooks a bea ful moorland valley. Serves Yorkshire p ding, cottage pies and chilli. Wash down a delicious Taylor's bitter, brewed Keighley.
National Museum of Photography, Film Television's bar and restaurant serves ho made pies and salads and affords great vi over city centre.

AFTERNOON TEA

Village Bakery: in Saltaire, a Victorian coffee shop frequented by retired mill workers, serving Yorkshire curd tart, toasted teacakes and cream cakes made on the premises.

Betty's: The Grove, Ilkley; run by descendants of Frederick Belmont, a Swiss confectioner who moved to Yorkshire in 1919. Home-made cream scones, tarts and tea breads including the Yorkshire Fat Rascal, a crumbly buttery fruit bun. Exotic selection of teas and coffees specially imported from all over the world.

DINNER

Indian: not the usual greasy, how-hot-can-you-take-it curries, but delicately spiced tandooris, kormas and biryanis from the Punjab, Kashmir and Bengal. Recommended are the *Sabraaj Dining Club* (20 Little Horton Lane, opposite Alhambra Theatre): good food in a port-a-cabin; *The Bombay Brasserie* (Simes Street, Westgate): in the extraordinary setting of a converted Methodist chapel; *The Aagraha* (27 Westgate, Shipley): about £12 for two.

European: *Restaurant Nineteen* (19 North Park Road, Heaton, tel: 0274-492559): a candlelit restaurant in a Victorian house, serving "imaginative English food" which made it a finalist in Egon Ronay's Restaurant of the Year for 1988. About £48 for 2.

The Box Tree (Church Street, Ilkley, tel: 0943-608484): with one Michelin star is an opulent but cosy restaurant said to be the best in the area. Imaginative French menu includes coquilles St Jacques with pasta in a mustard sauce; perfectly cooked local lamb and game, and, unmissable but fattening, puddings or rosewater sorbet. Set menu is £17.50 a head; but à la carte is a stiff £80 for two, excluding wine. Now open for Sunday lunch at £13.95. Closed on Monday.

SHOPS

The Golden Shuttle (Albion Mills, Greengates, Bradford): men's and women's clothes (up to size 26) including fashionable designer labels such as Jaeger, Alexon and Hugo Boss for half-price or less. No seconds. Open Tues-Sat, 9.30am-4.30pm.

British Mohair Spinners (Midland Mills, Cape St, off Canal Road): for hand-knitting yarns in pure mohair; 58p per 25 grams; 50 colours. Open Mon-Fri, 10am-4pm.

Suit Length Centre (918 Wakefield Road, Dudley Hill): for finest quality Huddersfield and Scottish worsted suitings. A 3.2-metre length costs between £29 and £52. Also cashmere mixes for coats and suits at around £16 a metre; including fabulous exotic mix of mohair, cashmere, mink and wool. Open Mon-Sat, 8.30am-5pm.

Skopos Mill Shop (Otley Road, Shipley): for curtain and upholstery fabrics. Will make up lined curtains for about £40 a pair, average length. Open Mon-Sat, 9am-5.30pm.

Bombay Stores (Shearbridge Road, Bradford): for Indian silks, chiffons and satins (ranging from £1.50 to £8 a metre). Open 10am-8pm every day.

MUSEUMS AND GALLERIES

National Museum of Photography, Film and Television: Princes View, Bradford: illustrates the history, technology and uses of every type of film; lots of audience participation. You can try your hand at reading the news on television, operating a television camera or editing a drama programme. Not to be missed is the IMAX cinema: its 45x62-foot curved screen makes you feel part of the action. Open Tues-Sun, 11am-6pm.

The Industrial Museum: Moorside Road, Bradford: the history of steam power and the technology of the Victorian woollen textile industry are displayed in this former spinning mill. Adjacent mill owner's house shows domestic life at turn of century. Open Tues-Sun, 10am-5pm.

Colour Museum: 82 Grattan Road, Bradford: tells the story of dyes, dyeing and textile printing as well as exploring the nature of colour with working models and views of how the world looks to a dog, a fish and a bee. Open Tues-Fri, 2-5pm, Sat 10am-4pm.

Cartwright Hall: Lister Park. A beautiful baroque mansion displaying 19th- and 20th-century art and sculpture and Old Masters including Sir Joshua Reynolds's *Brown Boy*. Open Tues-Sun; 10am-5pm.

BEDSIDE READING: *Victorian Bradford, the Living Past* by Ian Beesley and David James (Ryburn Publishing, £5.95). J. B. Priestley's *Bright Day*, about his youth in Bradford, and *Lost Empires*, about the early music halls.

Further information: Bradford Tourist Information Office (City Hall, Bradford BD1 1HY, tel: 0274-753678) has excellent guides and maps and can book tours of area and visits to mills.

Southport

Paul Gogarty

. . . .

IT WAS raining as I made my nostalgic return to Southport, boarding the Northern Line from Liverpool Central Station and shunting through the city's post-industrial landscape.

Litherland, my old home town, had vanished and some new place had inherited its name. As we left the suburbs, kids in wellies splashed through puddles beside the gloriously overrun embankment. Dunes started to rise, stubbled with marram grass. These were the dunes where I had seen my first condom as a schoolboy; dunes that seemed to scream for secret sex and were the setting for the whole school's fantasies.

In those early days of Beatles, Bessie Braddock, Screaming Lord Sutch and Everton's Golden Vision, we would hop on this same line to Southport's open-air, sea-water pool. Our mission was to pester the sunbathing girls who littered the paving slabs like pink confetti.

My Auntie Rose had made similar pilgrimages thirty years earlier when men and women were corralled at opposite ends of the pool. In those days any man sliding a strap down on his bathers to bronze a shoulder would get a flick from the ever-watchful attendant employed to uphold decorum.

The best pool in the world is still there, its vast irregular shape now embellished with the intricate liquorice knots of two huge water slides. In one of four projects in the pipeline for Southport, the pool will soon be gaining a retractable roof, nightclub, sports facilities and 140-room accommodation to accompany the stately restaurant overlooking it.

Tourism is bubbling in the resort and confidence so buoyant that the town is even selling sand to Saudi Arabia. An £82-million winter garden complex is planned for 1991 with a conservatory three times as long as its predecessor, but the biggest project is the £300-million Southport Marina. If this comes about, the development will have its own village, but more important, Southport will once more be reachable by sea-going vessels.

Beyond the pool are the never-ending Southport sands and the miniature railway which, Sisyphus-like, shuttles visitors backwards and forwards along the three-quarters-of-a-mile-long pier.

Southport is the great British seaside with saharas of sand but no sea. We all know it is there somewhere and we could no doubt swim in it if we walked halfway to Ireland, but to all intents and purposes it might just as well not exist. The best most of us can hope for is that we, like the pier, will get our toes wet at high tide. It comes as no real surprise to learn that Verdi Godwin, the local lifeguard who has been patrolling the sands from Ainsdale to Southport for forty years, has yet to record his first fatality.

Perhaps, anyway, the great British seaside resort is a generic misnomer, for isn't it eccentric individuality that is the hallmark, not some commonly shared experience? Southport is a one-off: its character strong enough to withstand capricious fashions and incorporate only those modern elements that enhance rather than endanger it.

Blackpool, as always, takes the bulk of the two-week summer holiday bucket-and-spade brigade but in Southport you won't see brown paper going up in guest house windows in October, its season lasts all year round. Six and a half million people live within an hour's drive and just as many arrive for weekend shopping expeditions as come for the more traditional seaside amusements.

Southport is what Brighton pretends to be: a genuinely elegant seaside town. Its sense of space contrasts keenly with most other resorts whose guest houses stop abruptly where their beaches begin. Here the promenade overlooks a half-mile-deep maze of hedgerows, manicured lawns, bowling and putting greens, lakes and bridges before Marine Drive separates the funfair from the beach.

Despite its claim to a mild, sunny climate, my arrival coincided with one of those melancholic rain-swept seaside days. Grim faces, glimpsed through drenched window panes in guest houses, sipped endless cups of tea.

I walked along the promenade past the Floral Hall where in a former incarnation as a mod in 1966 I side-shuffled across the vast floor with an ocean of immaculate mohair-suited Scousers and Mancunians to the sounds of American soul records. Now it was Ken Dodd and Engelbert Humperdinck and the only concession to youth was a regular heavy-metal slot.

A little further along the promenade I popped into the Lakeside Inn: "The smallest pub in Britain". While questioning the rigour of the research, I can certainly vouch for the snugness: it's a bit like having a drink in a shoebox.

In my grand four-poster bed that night, at a loss without my duvet, I feared I might be strangled by the intricate lace bedspread. The next morning I was still there and, drawing back the curtains, a glorious day awaited me.

My room in the Scarisbrick Hotel overlooked Lord Street, the finest shopping street in the north-west. The strangely harmonious potpourri of Victorian and Edwardian architectural styles was already bathed in sunshine. People sat at the Parisian café terrace, strolled through the boulevard's gardens or under the wrought-iron canopy that runs along the more stylish of its shops.

Its Wayfarer's arcade perhaps best symbolises the sense of space and graciousness that epitomises Southport. The wrought-iron rib cage holds up a glass sky that radiates light over the fountains, palms, café tables and bandstand. Baskets overflowing with trailing lobelia, petunia and geraniums hang from the belvedere and balconies. Pride of place goes to a bronze statue of Southport's favourite son, Red Rum, whose advancing years have forced him to forego his morning canter along the sands with his stablemates.

At lunch I met my parents on the bowling green. One of the main reasons they settled just outside Preston was its proximity to Southport. It's a place many retire to. It is clean: even in the arcade streets you will not find upturned ice-creams or mushy peas decorating the pedestrian walkways. It is green: there are the Botanic Gardens, Victoria Gardens, Princes Park, Hesketh Park, endless golf links, bowling and putting. It's compact: everything worth seeing, outside Churchtown, is located within easy walking.

These factors are also the key to its wider appeal today and the blue-rinse brigade is not as overwhelmingly in evidence as in the past. Forty-one per cent of Southport's visitors are now under thirty-five and windsurfs and jet skis are just as visible as bingo halls.

Satiated on five saucerfuls of Southport shrimps, we drove to nearby Churchtown whose antiquity is preserved in Lilliputian thatched homes and shops. The main street houses the oldest saddler in Lancashire as well as a lacemaking cottage industry.

In St Cuthbert's Parish Church we found a memorial stone with skull and crossbones dedicated to John Sutton, an eighteenth-century pirate, and another to a member of the hanging Pierrepoint family. Opposite the church are the 1,000-acre grounds of

Meols Hall, the Fleetwood-Hesketh family home. We then adjourned to the Hesketh Arms, Southport's most famous pub.

Behind it, in the Botanic Gardens, a miniature train laden with maroon-uniformed eight-year-olds chug-chugged through the pansies. The gardens boast a museum, aviary, fernery and a wonderfully tacky café, a kind of Fifties equivalent to the Seventies strippedpine movement in its veneration of plastic.

Later we met for dinner at the stately Prince of Wales Hotel, where the manager John Barrington-Fortune entertained us with stories of their various theme weekends. When he first took over, they staged a murder weekend. Anxious for things to run smoothly and to play his part, he turned an ambulance with siren screaming away from the forecourt, convinced it was two hours early. Later, he discovered one of the guests groaning in his room. He had fallen ill and called the ambulance himself. Fortunately it was nothing serious.

Another leading hotel, the Scarisbrick, has also been stepping up its weekend break themes: clay-pigeon shoots and golfing are just a few.

The prize this year must go to the Clifton, which organised a "gnomes' convention". Owners of garden gnomes sent their loved ones ahead for a few days' holiday and then joined them for the weekend convention and banquet. I've been to the garden centre and Bashful and I can hardly wait for the reunion.

GETTING THERE

By train: Euston-Liverpool Lime Street, about 2 hrs 50 mins; Central Station (linked by underground or a 5-minute walk) to Southport 40 minutes (trains run every 15 mins). Return prices: Blue Saver (off peak Mon-Thurs or Sat and Sun anytime) £28; White Saver (leaving Friday) £38, Standard £66, First Class £93.

By car: from the south exit M6 at junction 26, take M58 to Ormskirk and then Southport road. From the north exit M6 at junction 30, then take the A59 from Preston.

ACCOMMODATION

Guest houses, bed and breakfast from £9.50 per person. A full list is available from the tourist office. Guests staying at the 2-star Finer 5 Hotels (*The Dukes Folly*, tel: 0704-33355, is one in the group of 5 hotels), can eat at each other's restaurants and share their facilities. Costs from £40 for bed and breakfast doubles. Three-star *Scarisbrick Hotel* (0704-43000), Lord Street, bed and breakfast from £38. Two-night bed and breakfast weekend breaks from £62 per person. Four-star *Prince of Wales* (0704-36688), Lord Street; doubles from £74. Two-night weekend breaks from £76 per person.

RESTAURANTS

Cheap and cheerful restaurants in the alleys offer good 3-course meals for as little as £3.25. Popular Italian restaurants are *Pizzeria Mama Mia*, £8 per head, and *Casa Italia*, £16 per head (both in Lord Street); and the *Café Bar* in Wright Street.

Prince of Wales: table d'hôte £9.95 (highly recommended); à la carte about £25 per head with wine. *Scarisbrick:* table d'hôte £10.50 (excellent value).

THINGS TO DO

Open-top bus tour; pleasure flights from Southport Sands from £7.50. There are also the zoo, aquarium, the botanic gardens, the Steamport Transport Museum and stellarium that are well worth visiting.

INFORMATION

Staff at the Southport tourist office are extremely helpful. For advice on the area's facilities, contact them on tel: 0704-40404/33133.

The
West Country

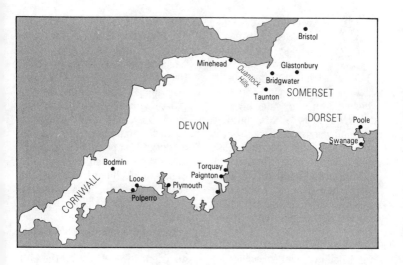

South Devon Coast

Paul Gogarty

. . . .

A peculiar noise — like a cross between a donkey and a jackal — woke me. Two hundred feet below my window, gulls wheeled over the water-lily pads and reed beds of Slapton Ley. Ornithologists were already out in force staring through binoculars across the patchwork fields, seemingly into space. A few other early risers, newspapers under their arms, wandered around the gaggle of shops at the ley's southernmost point.

My trek had begun the day before. I had taken an early morning train from London to Totnes, a boat to Dartmouth and then eased in my muscles with a brisk seven-mile walk to Torcross.

Between the ley and the two-mile stretch of shingle beach, a Sherman tank stood guard, a memorial to 800 US marines who died offshore during the Second World War. At the far end of the old coastal toll road was the Strete Gate picnic area where, the day before, I'd watched gulls re-inventing the barbecue spit as a giant nutcracker for opening snail shells.

Howard Garner, the owner of the Greyhomes Hotel, escorted me on the first stage of the day's walk. Before long we were negotiating orthostat walls (primitive boundary slates), hopping over hedges and wading through waist-high undergrowth. One moment he would be warning me against trampling a rare blue orchid; the next pointing to an abandoned mine he had camped in as a boy. Just 100 yards from the coastal footpath, this forgotten world had provided Howard as a child with the perfect jungle playground. Exhausted after their labyrinthine adventures he and his friends would rest on the cliff edge, imitating the adders sunning themselves on the rocks below.

As Jacob's Ladder — the old route to Beesands — was inaccessible, we approached via the old lime kilns of Beesands Cellars. At the Cricket Inn I chatted with Frank Crocker, one of the village elders, who had fished these waters all his working life and who talked of the twenty boats working here just after the war. The local fishermen had withstood storms and a plague of octopus but had no means of competing with Dartmouth's larger mechanised ships. Frank had watched the young people move to the city and his colleagues pass away one by one.

The next village along, Hallsands, disappeared more dramatically. Undermined by reckless silt dredging, thirty-seven homes were lost to the sea on the night of January 26, 1917. It is an eerie place, and the few remaining walls stand perilously on the wave-cut platform and continue to crumble a little more each year.

The most glorious section of the walk started at Hallsands and continued through to East Portlemouth. Along the narrowest of paths — which undergrowth constantly threatened to engulf — pink and blue thrift, mournful foxgloves and the hideously

named bloody cranesbill chanced their frailty to the harsh environment.

I ate my lunch overlooking the lighthouse at Start Point. It was here that Henri Muge was hung in chains in 1581 as a warning to passing ships of the dangers of piracy. Seven years later, when they lit the Armada beacon, bits of him were still hanging there. Below, the jagged edge of a rusting shipwreck cut the water's surface and on the fibrous lichen-covered rocks, cormorants stretched out their wings to dry like prehistoric pterodactyls.

Occasionally the remnants of a smugglers' cave or abandoned mine were spotted among such porcine-named promontories as Gammon Head, Pig's Nose and

Ham Stone. As the day wore on, the translucent waters of the succession of mostly uninhabited sandy bays became increasingly tempting. At Rickham Sands I succumbed and the day's heavenly labour came to an end.

The next morning, leaving the Gara Rock Hotel on the third and final day of my walk, there was a bounce in my step. As I rounded the huer's hut, which for a short period in the 1970s was a pub catering for three customers at a time, I saw the raised lines of Celtic burial grounds behind me and the surf breaking up the beach 200 feet below. The early sun had already sent nature into rapturous song. Three miles later I took the ferry across to Salcombe and started the ascent to Bolt Head. The walk across the cliff to Bolt Tail had spectacular views.

A heady pagan delirium lasted until mid-afternoon, when my deprived and abused feet started to scream for deliverance. By then I had reached Hope Cove, where the storm of tourism had laid the village to waste. Noisy people sat outside pubs that stayed open all afternoon and there seemed something frenetic and snatched about their pleasure.

It was not until I had left the golf links at Thurlestone, a few miles on, that the marvellously rugged, inhospitable coast reasserted itself and shook off its imposed domesticity. At Bantham Bay, the meeting point of the open sea and the River Avon, my walk ended. A fleet of windsurfers bobbed on the smooth waters while children wrote messages in the sands. In the car park, a sign shattered the bay's beguiling tranquility: "Thirteen lives were saved by the lifeguard at the beach in 1987. Keep to the right side of the beach to avoid the strong rip currents." Later that evening, strolling through Thurlestone churchyard, I found the message underlined in a graveyard epitaph dating from the 1850s: "Drowned bathing at Bantham".

The sea was not the only danger in past centuries. Bantham Bay and Thurlestone Sands were the setting for some of the most infamous acts of butchery during the wrecking years. One renowned case concerned the *Chantiloupe* as it returned from the West Indies in 1772. On learning that the ship was about to run aground, Mrs Burke (a relation of the parliamentarian Edmund Burke), bent

on saving what she could of her precious jewellery, bedecked herself in whatever she could. Her relief at being saved from the seas by helping hands soon turned to cold terror as her frenzied rescuers hacked at her sea-swollen fingers to get at her rings. Her body was buried in the sands like so many before her. Even today, locals claim bones from unmarked graves are exposed during storms.

The contrast in landscape along the Heritage Coast is stunning. But from the austere slate-like teeth which the wind howls through at Bolt Head to the secluded bays shielded by giant sycamores at East Portlemouth; and from the homogeny of medieval and Tudor buildings in Dartmouth to the bluebell-clad hillside at Start Point, the soothing mantra of the sea never left me.

On the train home my throbbing feet heated the carriage but already I was planning more punishment as I wondered how long it would take to walk the South-West Peninsula Coast from Minehead in Somerset right round to Poole Harbour in Dorset . . .

GETTING THERE
Paddington to Totnes British Rail Blue Saver £33; White Saver (Fri and Sat) £45; standard return £61, 1st class £92. The journey takes just under 3 hours. Taxis: Totnes to Torcross about £13; Bantham to Totnes about £10.

HOTELS
Greyhomes Hotel: at Torcross (tel: 0548-580220), bed and breakfast from £22 per person per night. Evening meal £8.65.
Maelcombe House: at East Prawle (tel: 0548-51300). Three-quarters of the way to Prawle Point from Start Point, overlooking Lannacombe Bay, offers bed and breakfast from £11.50 per person. It doesn't serve alcohol but you can bring your own.
Gara Rock Hotel: at East Portlemouth (tel: 0548-842342). From £29 per person bed and breakfast (half-board £40). Outdoor heated pool, good for afternoon cream teas, super views.
Thurlstone Hotel: Thurlstone (tel: 0548-560382), from £57 per night per person bed and breakfast. indoor and outdoor swimming pools, sauna, Jacuzzi, golf, plus superb views.
Sloop Inn: at Bantham (tel: 0548-560489), 5 double rooms. About £18 bed and breakfast per person per night. Very good food.

FOOD
Most of the bed and breakfasts will provide you with packed lunch on request from £2.50 to £4.

Start Bay Inn: (tel: 0548-580553) Torcross, has the best fish, caught by its owner, Paul Stubbs. I had jumbo plaice for about £5.
Gara Rock Hotel: table d'hôte starts at £11.50 (the sole I had was as large as the sharks that bask offshore).
The Sloop: had the best and most reasonably priced food: avocado prawns, trout with new potatoes and fresh vegetables, and pavlova cost about £10.

THE WALKS
Plenty of scope with an uninterrupted coastal path. The route from Dartmouth to Torcross is approximately 7 miles; Torcross to Gara Rock is about 11 miles; Gara Rock to Bantham about 13 miles.

ORNITHOLOGISTS
Ringing hut overlooks the bridge between north and south leys at Torcross. You will find the bird logbook in a tin under left side of hut. Slapton Ley Field Centre, Slapton, Devon. Tel: 0548-580466.

FURTHER INFORMATION
Walk leaflets and other literature from Su Powell, South Hams Tourism or Ian Kemp, South Devon Heritage Coast officer. Both can be contacted at Follaton House, Plymouth Road, Totnes, Devon TQ9 5NE (tel: 0803-864499).
Salcombe Publicity Association: tel: 054884-2736 for full list of accommodation in Salcombe.

Polperro

Elizabeth Grice

. . . .

"THESE little back-street shopkeepers must be awfully pleased to see *us* this week," intoned a plummy youth in the bread queue outside Polperro's bakery. Well, they were and they weren't. The baker's wife was in the act of rubbing down her display cases with a damp cloth when the young man raised his unfortunate voice, and it was as much as she could do to restrain herself from rubbing the silly grin off his face at the same time.

"Little backstreet shopkeepers!" she exploded, mimicking the departing customer for the amusement of her regulars. "Most of these little backstreet shopkeepers could buy him up twice over."

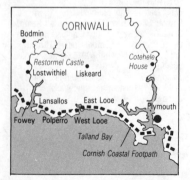

Underneath its honeypot exterior, Polperro is a proud, self-respecting fishing village which in high summer is positively menaced by its tide of visitors, most of them funnelling in on foot down one narrow street. Its attitude to them is rather like the poet's view of visiting relations:

How very nice it is to see
Our dear relations come to tea.
But nicer still it is to know
That when they've had their tea,
they'll go.

Over-painted, over-photographed, over-visited and possibly over-fished. Yet Polperro is a joy out of season. Day-trippers in conspicuous new waterproofs are thin on the ground. There is an air of self-sufficiency about the place. With the trees above the harbour bare and the holiday cottages registering a blank stare, its attractions are altogether different.

We arrived somewhat by stealth and in the dark, with rain spitting in the salty wind. Dutifully parking on the edge of town, we followed our nostrils down to the

harbour, past the Merry Mackerel and the Ship Inn and the Buccaneer, down past old smugglers' houses, artists' studios and darkened gift shops. The Three Pilchards and the Blue Peter, both "real" fishermen's pubs, still winked across the water. All the boats were in and the storm gates closed.

There are only two requirements for complete surrender to Polperro's fishy charms: a love of fish and of improbable surroundings. Staying in a studio on the harbour wall, enclosed on three sides by cottages stuck to the hills like limpets around a rock-pool, we were mesmerised by the changing scene and tides.

Excitable gulls and the grunt of engines starting up roused us in the morning. A pair of swans joined us for breakfast, visiting on the high tide under our balcony. At dusk, we were summoned to the window by the low throb of a returning boat laden with scallops. With the possibility of cliff walks along the Cornish coastal footpath, starting from our back door, and happy hours to be spent exploring the local rock-pools with a crab-line and shrimping net, there was really no reason to do anything more energetic than mess about within sight of the local boats.

Polperro's biggest fishing boat, the *Trevas* ("harvest") came in with the least sound, gliding unlit through the harbour gates like a ghost ship to unload 2,000 scallops, regarded as an excellent catch.

It would have taken extraordinary indifference or willpower not to amble around to the fish quay to negotiate for the dozen that just happened to be spare. Another evening it was a handsome four-pound sea bass from Mike Pengelley's boat (complete with its last supper, a perfect undigested sprat stuck down its gullet) and two pounds of juicy "toes" (crab claws) from the *Compass Rose.* Will fish ever taste the same again?

But for a rainy spell, we might not have prised ourselves from Polperro's cockleshell embrace and climbed out over the rim of the town into high-hedged lanes.

Nobody trusts weather forecasts in this part of Cornwall, but we didn't learn this simple lesson until we had slithered down a muddy lane to Lansallos beach a mile or two away, on a promise of sunshine, only to find a beautiful cove in monochrome. Threatened squalls on another day sent us scurrying inland, to the beautiful National Trust house at Cotehele, near Saltash, but we returned damp, to find that Polperro had been bathed in a bowl of sunshine all day.

At one time or another during the weekend, half-term holiday children inevitably made for Dobwalls Theme Park, near Liskeard, where "the only American Miniature Railroad outside North America" offered steam and diesel rides through forest scenery. Dobwalls is one vast adventure playground, except for its delightful audio-visual museum devoted to nature conservation — a refuge on wet days.

Here is a splendid collection of bird and animal paintings by the British wildlife artist Archibald Thorburn, whose pheasants in the snow grace a million mantlepieces at Christmas. Recorded birdsong accompanies children on their tour, with models and tableaux to bring the scene to life.

The only trouble with Dobwalls is its dreadful café. It should not be possible in Cornwall to run into third-rate Cornish pasties and tasteless Cornish scones, but here they were in abundance, along with soup that tasted of its packet and flaccid white sandwiches.

We compensated back in Polperro. In season and out, the town offers nourishing food at reasonable prices, and not only fish. For a treat one night, we travelled out to Nick Wainford's Victorian country manor hotel, the Well House, near Liskeard, for roast pheasant followed by toffee pudding. We were swaddled in luxury, but sitting in pullovers on our last night, eating scallops in a small, cosy restaurant in the middle of Polperro, was just as much fun and a fitting farewell.

WHAT TO DO

Walking anywhere in and around *Polperro* is rewarding for old, characterful stone cottages, odd passageways and particularly superior cats. Squelch around on the harbour bottom when the tide is out. March up the cliff path to *Talland Bay* on a clear day: the beaches are sandy at low tide and the views spectacular. For a longer walk of about four and a half miles, continue along the cliff path past *Talland Church* to the much bigger fishing town of Looe. Two towns, to be precise, *East Looe* and *West Looe*, one hanging on to each side of a steep valley.

Lansallos Beach: west of Polperro: tucked into a stretch of unspoilt beach, approachable only by beautiful cliff paths, or down a mile of leafy lane.

Restormel Castle: near Lostwithiel: a stout motte-and-bailey castle rising like a crown from a hill overlooking the River Fowey. Its two best features are its circular wall and its wide, dry moat.

Dobwalls Theme Park: near Liskeard: open all year, 11am to 4pm from October 31 to Easter, with reduced winter rates and 10am-6pm in Summer. A day ticket buys as many railroad rides as you like. Edwardian tea-rooms, souvenir shops, adventure playgrounds and "Mr Thorburn's Edwardian Countryside exhibition" (tel: 0579-20325).

Cotehele House: St Dominick: National Trust showpiece on the banks of the River Tamar. Medieval squire's house with original furniture, set in fine sloping gardens with inhabited dovecote and nearby working quay and water mill. Check if open in winter (tel: 0579-50434).

WHERE TO STAY

The National Trust, a considerable landowner in the County of Cornwall, has several cottages between Looe and Fowey, including the last house in the hamlet of Lansallos. Caretaker: Mrs S. Shakerley, Carneggan, Lanteglos-by-Fowey (tel: 072687-537). For other cottages, contact The NT Regional Office, Lanhydrock Park, Bodmin (tel: 0208-73880).

For holiday cottages in Polperro, ring Julie King (tel: 01-883 0260). She has 4 cottages along the side of the magical harbour; all sleep 5. The English Tourist Board has others (tel: 01-730 3488).

The Claremont Hotel: Polperro's biggest hotel has 9 rooms and is run by a French couple. From just £13 per person a night (tel: 0503-72241).

Mill House Hotel: Polperro: beautifully positioned pub in the centre of town, a few minutes from the harbour. Double room with shower: £27; with bath: £35. Including breakfast (tel: 0503-72362).

The Well House: St Keyne, near Liskeard: luxury living and dining. Seven individually styled rooms with bathrooms. About £70 for a double room. Ring for 4-night reductions and half-board rates (tel: 0579-42001).

WHERE TO EAT

The Sun Lounge: Neville and Elizabeth Joliffe's cheery restaurant in the centre of Polperro has some of the best seafood in town. Children not only welcome but books provided for their entertainment (tel: 0503-72459).

House on Props: 16th-century restaurant, lurching over the river on wooden props, opens at 8am for breakfast and continues in business all day long (tel: 0503-72310).

The Kitchen: more modern cooking, on the approach to town, which has won a place in many guides (tel: 0503-72780).

Isle of Purbeck

Gill Charlton

. . . .

THE BARGE carrying our car shuttled across the mouth of Poole harbour on a pair of chains and we drove off into another age. The Isle of Purbeck lies serene in a time warp, its silver-grey limestone villages free from modern housing estates, its magnificent coastline accessible only on foot. In pubs and tea-houses we were received with an old-fashioned courtesy. Down here in Dorset, rural England is alive and well.

An ideal base for exploring the area is Wareham, a small well-preserved country town on the northern flank of Purbeck — an isle which is not quite an isle any more. From Wareham all roads pass through Corfe, a couple of miles down the road, its ruined castle commanding the only gap through a solid ridge of chalk hills. Corfe Castle, a Cavalier stronghold, was blown up by a furious Cromwell for successfully holding out against him until a guard turned traitor. Despite the blowing up, however, it is a most striking place, with its 70-foot-high Norman keep virtually intact — protected now by the National Trust.

You can understand its impor-

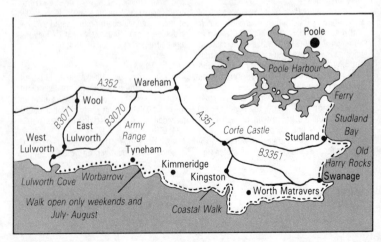

tance, and appreciate the stark beauty of the Purbeck Hills, from the garden of the Scott Arms at Kingston (perhaps the most touristy pub in the area but nevertheless a provider of good lunches). On the Purbeck time-scale Kingston, being largely nineteenth-century, is regarded as a new village, but it is popular with the makers of historical dramas looking for unspoilt Eng Lit scenery (it was the setting for the filming of *Hereward the Wake*).

Deeper into Purbeck, villages go back not just to Domesday but to Saxon, Roman and Celtic times; each a tight-knit community. The government has never been forgiven by the former residents of Tyneham for requisitioning their village and a vast tract of land stretching from Lulworth Cove to Kimmeridge as a training ground for the invasion of France and, despite promises, never allowing them to return to their homes. Now tanks and artillery rumble over Celtic fields, and Tyneham's cottages lie deserted and roofless.

It was only after considerable lobbying that the army agreed to open the whole area to visitors at weekends and during July, August, Christmas and Easter. This is one of the most beautiful coastlines in all of Britain, and the irony is that although there was much unhappiness at the way the army used to keep it completely closed off, it is thanks to the army that rare plants, birds and ancient field patterns still survive here. Exhibitions in Tyneham's school-house and church record its rich natural and human history.

We set off on a "range walk" down a muddy, wooded valley to the coast. Signs warning "Danger, Unexploded Shells" reminded us not to stray from the path, though sheep grazed unconcerned at the risk of being made mincemeat.

Chalk cliffs to rival Dover's flank Worbarrow Bay as the Purbeck Hills reach the sea. A mile further east, the scene changes completely. We looked back on the bank of limestone cliffs which we had just clambered over, and before us were the low black bluffs of shale at Kimmeridge, mined since Roman times. A lone Nodding Donkey stands on the cliff-top, still pumping oil from Britain's first onshore well, discovered by BP in 1958.

This remote Purbeck coast, with its constantly changing panoramas, is visited by only a handful of walkers out of season. The coastal path continues on to Swanage and Poole, but it would take a day or more to walk it. Instead we drove along to Worth Matravers, where pretty stone-slated cottages surround a duckpond. A path leads to Winspit, where Purbeck and Portland limestone have been quarried for centuries and used to build, among much else, St Paul's Cathedral and the Bank of England. The cliffs are riddled with caves and passageways, supported by just a few blocks of stone and unsafe to enter — unless, that is, you're a desperate smuggler, for smuggling and quarrying went hand in hand here.

Back in Worth, we made for the Square and Compass (real ale and good pasties). Like all Purbeck pubs it is a village meeting place. No *olde worlde* bar, fake beams or red velour here; the landlord serves through a hatch in the hallway, the beer barrels lined up behind him. You take your drink into one of the cosy panelled sitting rooms, unchanged for centuries, containing an odd assortment of rickety tables and chairs, old photographs of proud, whiskered quarrymen and a collection of dusty fossils.

Natives of Purbeck take a fierce pride in their history and many are indifferent to life beyond the island. A young man bemoans the lack of work but says he's bought a computer so he can start a software business from home. It's refreshing to find such a strong sense of community, created by the area's remoteness and by the powerful and paternalistic families who controlled it: the Bonds of London's Bond Street, whose seat is an Elizabethan manor at Creech; the Bankes of Kingston Lacy, landlords of Corfe

and the whole of Studland Bay until this decade when it became the largest legacy ever left to the National Trust.

It is thanks to the reclusive Ralph Bankes that the three-mile-long beach at Studland was never developed; it would have been a perfect place for a holiday camp. From sleepy Studland village with its Norman church, you walk down through pine woods to a bay of golden sand stretching from the Sandbanks ferry to the chalk stacks of Great Harry. At the height of the summer it can become crowded, though there are secret hideaways in the sand dunes behind. In winter it is a virgin beach.

The Isle of Purbeck is a corner of England which has escaped the ravages of tourism, the weekend cottage syndrome and the scarred hillsides which are the legacy of the tramping hordes. Above all, it

has retained its identity in an age when so many rural communities have lost theirs.

Fortunately I found an appropriate base for the weekend — the sixteenth-century Priory Hotel on the banks of the River Frome at Wareham, where the style and atmosphere of a rambling country home have been faithfully retained.

The bedrooms — there are fifteen, plus four suites in a converted boathouse just feet from the river — have bold country prints imaginatively made up into swirling drapes and counterpanes. It is the small touches that make this one of the best hotels I've stayed in. Window seats and comfortable chairs, bowls of fruit and flowers, novels and books on local subjects, thick towelling robes, hairdryers, toiletries and tissues.

Breakfasts are gargantuan. It's a rare place that offers porridge, kidneys, kippers and smoked haddock, wonderful buttery croissants, oatcakes and six different kinds of tea. And the orange juice really was fresh. Used to hotels which say breakfast finishes at 10am and no exceptions, it was a delightful surprise to be telephoned late on Sunday morning and asked if we would like breakfast in our bedroom — a full cooked breakfast, that is. We sat in our dressing-gowns over the Sunday papers and felt deliciously pampered. There is a restaurant in the stone cellars which, not surprisingly, specialises in English cooking. This is the place to try lambs' kidneys and sweetbreads in port, walnut and apple sauce. For the more squeamish there are steaks and excellent fish and seafood — crab prepared by a local fisherman, mussels from Poole harbour, salmon from Dorset rivers, all served with vegetables grown in a nearby market garden.

WHERE TO STAY
The Priory Hotel (Church Green, Wareham, Dorset; tel: 09295-2772): offers 2-night weekend breaks from Oct-April. Prices from £126 single, and £170-£278 for a double room, including full breakfast and 4-course table d'hôte dinner. Rooms 3, 4, 5, 21, 22 and 23 have views over the Purbeck Hills. The Ordnance Survey Dorset Landrangers Guidebook is good for historical background and suggested walks.

The Quantocks

*Julian
Critchley*

. . . .

THE QUANTOCKS divide Exmoor and the Brendon Hills from Bridgwater and the Somerset Levels. A range of hills that rises above Taunton, they run for eleven miles or so to the sea between Williton and Nether Stowey.

On the south-western flank of the Quantocks Auberon Waugh lives in his father's house at Combe Florey, on its north-eastern lives Brendon Sellick, the last of the mud-skimming fishermen of Bridgwater Bay. They are the region's celebrities: Waugh's opinions are rarely out of the newspapers; Sellick's "mud horse", which he uses to beat the tides of the Bristol Channel, rears its head in a score of television documentaries. They should meet, or at the very least, it would be nice to think that 'Bron Waugh gets the best of Brendon Sellick's sea bass, salmon and eel.

The Quantocks are gentle hills which rise to 1,200 feet above the Bristol Channel. The coast of South Wales from Newport to Barry Dock and beyond is plainly visible from the summit. The hills are less austere than the lime-stone Mendips, twenty miles to the east, and there is no Cheddar with its tat and gorge. The Quantocks are a touch genteel, their southern slopes are well-wooded, and lead the traveller down to well turned-out villages such as Kingston St Mary where every cottage has been gentrified and stuffed with an admiral's widow.

Nether Stowey is altogether more plain. There is something Irish about its long main street of cottages, its many pubs — the village was once the end of the coaching line from Bristol — and its clock tower. It is growing fast as the nuclear technicians of Hinkley Point put down deposits on starter homes.

The charm of the Quantocks lies in its hidden valleys, its combes, and its churches, many of which flaunt the elegantly decorated, pink sandstone Somerset Towers. The one at Bishop's Lydeard is the most handsome, with its carved oak pew ends, and the memorial tablets of ancient heroes.

There are no villages on the top of the Quantocks — they are on the flanks of the hills — but there are minor roads which lead up and over the moorland such as the lane from Nether Stowey to Crowcombe.

Summer is the time when pale Bristolians bare their knees and stride over the top in a kind of frenzy, bound for the Bicknoller Arms in the village of the same name or The Hood Arms at Kilve.

The natives live quietly in pretty places like Stogumber and Stogursey. They take great care to avoid travelling on the A39, the Bridgwater to Minehead road, on a Saturday morning: at one o'clock, one week ends and another begins at Butlin's in Minehead, and the coast road is packed with a convoy of nose-to-tail cars first making for the M5 at a stately pace (32 mph) and then, in reverse flow, coming down from the Midlands to Minehead at no more than one mile an hour faster ... You have been warned.

The Quantocks have their own railway. The West Somerset line runs all year round from Minehead to Bishop's Lydeard over tracks which were once the property of the Great Western. Holidaymakers trundle up and down the bosky line drawn by the pride of the West Somerset, a restored 2:8:0 locomotive which once belonged to the Somerset and Dorset Joint Railway (via the Midland).

Tourists of a solitary or ruminative disposition can do worse than spend some time at Stogumber station armed with an unputdownable book and an exquisite light lunch. The station is no more than a pretty halt, miles from anywhere, and the sunlit silence is only interrupted by the arrival of the 12.15 train to Arcadia.

The most spectacular Quantock villages lie along the western scarp of the hills: St Audries which overlooks the sea; Bicknoller; Crowcombe with its splendid manor house now renovated and turned into a retirement home, and its pinkish sandstone cottages; and Bishop's Lydeard, a stone's throw from Taunton. Here there are great houses (the kind without private zoos) such as Cothelstone, sunken lanes where the only peril is from farmers' sons driving their fathers' BMWs, and wide views over the Brendon Hills towards Exmoor.

Nether Stowey, where Coleridge wrote *The Ancient Mariner* in a cottage now owned by the National Trust, lies between the

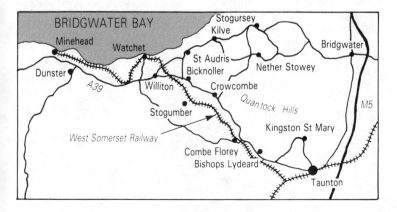

89

hills and an expanse of flat land which borders the sea. This is crisscrossed by lanes, most of which lead either to Stolford where Brendon Sellick rides his "horse", or to Hinkley Point, known to the rustic wits of Bridgwater as Chernobyl.

The area is remote, wind-swept, slightly scruffy and was once home to the young John Biffen. He was at primary school with Brendon Sellick, "Ah, he were clever".

The coast road to Minehead is slow, but pretty with glimpses of the sea and distant Wales. Watchet is a forgotten port which once shipped iron ore to Cardiff. Cleve Abbey was barely knocked about by King Henry VIII. It is Luttrell country.

Dunster is a picture-book place which is spoilt by the weight of visitors. During the summer the main street is Oxford Street as designed by the British Tourist Board, the pavements are packed with trippers moving slowly from one souvenir shop to another. Dunster is a place to be visited out of season, or, if not, well before breakfast.

In the Quantocks, as with anywhere else in rural England, the trick is to get off the main road. The hills are high but not alarmingly so, the climate can be balmy, the cream is properly clotted and the bacon, if you care about such things, is not always Danish. In the lush Quantock country, "The Green Hills of Somerset" live up to their musical reputation.

WHERE TO STAY
The Meadow House Hotel (tel: 0278-74546): in Kilve is in the luxury class with dinner, bed and breakfast at £86 per double room or £102 in *the Croft*, a detached cottage nearby. The rooms are pretty and the house comfortable. (3-day break: £284 for 2 people with dinner, bed and breakfast). Dinner is £17 per person. Meadow House is a listed building with eight acres of ground, close to a stretch of lonely, unspoilt coast. It is run with military precision by Colonel Samson, his wife and daughter.
The Alfoxton Park Hotel (tel: 0278-74211): at Holford was once the home of Wordsworth. It is a handsome house, with views over the Bristol Channel. Lunch is not catered for. Dinner is £11 a head. The food is good plain cooking although the wine list is good. Bed, breakfast and dinner and a double or twin is £37 per person. Spring and autumn break per person for a minimum stay of 2 days costs £34 for a double, £39 for a single. Closed from early November to Easter. The Coleridge cottage is open from April to September: Sundays, Tuesdays, Wednesdays and Thursdays from 2pm to 5pm. Admission: adults £1, children 60p.

WHERE TO EAT
Hikers with healthy appetites are well catered for. In Nether Stowey the *Castle Coffee House* provides home-made cream teas. *The Farm Shop* sells an excellent venison liver pâté. At Monksilver is an upmarket pub with a pretty garden. It is famous for its bread and butter ice-cream.
The Stable Cottage Restaurant (tel: 09848-239): at Triscombe, a village on the west of the Quantocks, does light lunches, and cream teas at £1.70 a head. Private parties catered for in evening.
The Town Farm (tel: 09848-655): at Crowcombe provides bed and breakfast at £10 a night. Serious eaters need go no further than to the *Castle Hotel* (tel: 0823-272671) in Taunton. Chef Gary Rhodes provides 3 fixed menus at £23, £28 and £31, the last including cheese for which the Castle is famous. The wine list is as long as a novel by Margaret Drabble and the fish is especially good. The economical would do well to have Sunday lunch; less expensive and just as good. Visitors in search of a picnic should visit the *County Stores*, the best grocer in Somerset.

The Somerset Levels

Christopher Somerville

. . . .

THE delights of the Somerset Levels, once tasted, are not soon forgotten. For ten years, two memories of Eli Scott's pub at Huish Episcopi had stayed in my mind — hens walking in and out of the bar, clucking in pools of sunlight on a stone-flagged floor; and the landlord's sweet whistling as he brought drinks to the table. Coming back to Huish, I realised for the first time that Eli's had a more official name: the Rose and Crown. Eli himself was long gone, but fondly remembered. "A sweet singing voice, too. Did you ever hear Eli sing? A dear man." Little else had changed at the pub. Dark passages gave on to cool snuggeries where cider drinkers burred long and low over the dominoes. It was still one of the most restful retreats I know, a place to sit, listen and soak up slow conversation.

From Huish Episcopi, the 500 or so square miles of the Somerset Levels stretch north and west, a world of ruler-straight watercourses, strange lumps and bumps of high ground on flat peat moors, lines of willows, winding lanes that slither away like eels into the landscape. It's a mysterious place, completely open for inspection under a wide sky, yet studded with curiosities — corrugated iron houses standing alone at the ends of long drove roads, ruins of churches perched as if solely for dramatic effect on top of hillocks called Mump and Tor and the peat diggings of past centuries like underground villages with their roofs taken off.

Looking down on the Levels from the great rampart of the Mendip Hills that enclose them on the north, the peat moors seem to stretch as flat as a floor towards the sea in Bridgwater Bay. But this is a deceptive impression. Once down there, the wide views are broken up by pollarded willows, hillocks, thickets of birch and alder, church towers, banks and ridges of hill. One great sea surge and the Levels would be back to how they were before the medieval monks arrived to drain and reclaim them — a group of dry knolls in a marshy, watery world. Every year, winter flooding puts the Levels halfway into this amphibious state.

The Somerset Levels are not picturesquely pretty, nor spectacular in any way. Shapes and colours are softened by a misty thickness in the atmosphere peculiar to the Levels. Local people are impatient of "hippy bloody ravings" about mystical vibrations of Somerset's soul, but even hard-headed tourists find something special in the air here.

It was wonderful to be back in this most secretive of landscapes. We didn't begin to enjoy it fully, though, until we had left both A and B roads and struck out on foot into one of those silent, eel-like lanes. The banks were thick with wild flowers, the fields full of drifting thistledown. Munching Friesian cows stood lower than the lane on the far side of the rhyne (pronounced "reen", a drainage ditch) from whose scummy green water a heron was stabbing out small fish. Rhynes divide up the Levels into a table of green squares edged with silver.

We climbed Glastonbury Tor to the tower on the top, windy enough to make the ears ache, to see this geometry of the Levels at its clearest. In winter the floods, viewed from up here, look like sheets of newly cut lead laid over the moors. This is one of the most stunning high-level views in the West Country, from Mendip for twenty or thirty miles into Devon and Dorset, the hill ranges and round hillocks all rooted in those miles of green-topped, level peat moor.

This is a landscape of great (though obscure) beauty and great practicality combined, a working landscape where most industries are centuries old — farming, peat cutting, shoe making, withy growing and weaving, and cider making. Almost all these industries are happy to bare their inner workings to the gaze of visitors.

For the second of our two days, as an antidote to aimless wanderings and sitting-and-lookings, we set ourselves a stern round of rubbernecking. Admirable intentions that lasted a whole morning, until Mudgley cider and a hot afternoon slammed the door emphatically on any further activity.

Withies and willows are the same thing, tough and pliable rods

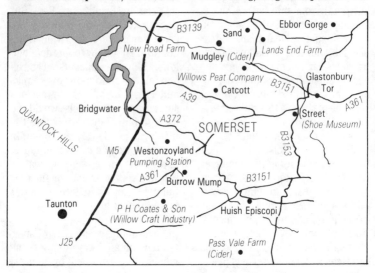

that go to make fences, baskets, trays and artists' charcoal. What is not done by hand is done by rattling, spitting old machines. At the Coate family's willow-growing and weaving centre on West Sedgemoor, down in the south-west corner of the Levels, Emrys Coate took us through the process, from planting out the withy beds to the final tying of the bundle of willow wands with an intricate "rose" of twisted withy. In the shed next door, the basket makers sat cross-legged in a rustling sea of cut withies, coaxing and bullying the whippy rods into place. Withy weaving almost died out a few years ago. Youngsters weren't interested in straining their fingers in the basket shed, or their backs in the withy bed. Setting out to interest, instruct and entertain the visitors has given the willow business a healthy shot in the arm.

Peat digging is another livelihood that people love to watch in action. At the Willows Peat Company near Westhay in the centre of the Levels, the most modern of excavating machines operates alongside the most traditional of peat-cutting tools. Peat is marvellous stuff, great for the garden or the fire, and a first-class preservative. A couple of fields away runs the Sweet Track, a log roadway built through the marshes about 6,000 years ago and perfectly preserved as it sank under generations of footsteps into the peat. The moors all around are crammed with wildlife: sedge warblers, reed buntings, ducks, swans, geese, rare marsh plants, meadows full of the kinds of plants — meadowsweet, thistles, cornflowers — that are so quickly disappearing from most of the English landscape. The historical and ecological importance of this wetland habitat, the effects of modern farming, drainage and peat cutting are all laid out in the exhibition centre run by the Willows Peat Company. All over the moors you'll see great chocolate-black mountains of machine-dug peat, side by side with long, chequered walls of hand-cut peat blocks — a treat to take home for the garden, bought at any of a hundred roadside stalls and sheds.

Outside in the peat bed I tried my hand at building the prescribed fourteen blocks of peat into a hyle, or open-sided mound for drying. Roger Rogers of the peat company eyed my collapsed failure with amusement before whisking the turves effortlessly into a perfect hyle. Then he initiated us into the secrets of unridding, benching and stooling into mumps, bearing back, winrowing the turves, ruckling and hyling. These were mysteries I could cheerfully have unravelled all day, but Roger Wilkins's cider barrels were beckoning from up on Mudgley Hill.

Buying cider from a Somerset farm is like no other financial transaction west of the Bosphorus. Lands End Farm, at the end of a lane on the hillside, couldn't have looked more traditionally English with its group of old stone buildings, farm cats and views out over apple trees. But the customs of an Oriental bazaar were being followed in the cool and fragrant cider shed.

Customers sat around on boxes reading the racing pages, or stood propping up the wall and chatting to Roger Wilkins as he went back and forth to the tall oak barrels. Everyone held a generous sampler of the cloudy, sharp and tongue-tingling product.

The taste and effect of farmhouse cider like this can't really be described, except in opposites. "Velvet-smooth, as clear as crystal, slips down without touching the sides," are three phrases that don't spring to mind. No money changed hands until the two varieties of cider — sweet and dry — had been tried neat and at various levels of mixture, with much lip-smacking and laughter. The other cider-makers transact their business in this pleasant way as well, even when, as at Pass Vale Farm under Burrow Hill, they are intent on releasing home-made calvados one fine day soon.

Time — and cider — play tricks on visitors to the Somerset Levels. The Shoe Museum at Clark's factory in Street; Weston-zoyland Pumping Station with its fully functional steam-drainage machine; a falconry display on Sunday afternoon at New Road Farm; the pottery at Muchelney — all these treats we had promised ourselves, but we never got round to them. Instead, we idled down from Mudgley Hill on to Aller Moor, found the nearest rhyne-side willow, flopped down and fell asleep to the blowing sighs of cows in the next field. That's the Levels for you.

GETTING THERE

By road: east from Junctions 22 to 25 of M5 motorway.

By rail: Bridgwater and Highbridge are the nearest stations. OS 1:50,000 Sheets 182 (Weston-super-Mare) and 193 (Taunton and Lyme Regis).

WHERE TO STAY

There are many old inns and hotels to choose from in the Levels towns — Glastonbury, Wedmore, Somerton, Langport. Under the Mendip Hills to the north are Wells, Cheddar and Axbridge. In the moorland villages and hamlets are large numbers of bed-and-breakfast places including :

The *Yew Tree Country House:* run by Ian and Elaine Corbett, at Sand, 1 mile south of Wedmore, offers comfortable farmhouse accommodation, with meals in a conservatory dining room overlooking the garden. Restaurant is open to non-residents. Children welcome. Prices: £17.50 bed and breakfast; £27.50 dinner and bed and breakfast. Tel: 0934-712520.

THINGS TO DO

Although the Somerset Levels are ideal for wandering and idling, you'll get the best out of this area if you keep a few activities in mind — and leave the cider-buying till last!

Archaeological and historical: Glastonbury Abbey and Tor; Wells Cathedral; Muchelney Abbey; Meare Lake Village and Abbot's Fish House; Wedmore and Somerton, ancient capital towns; Battle of Sedgemoor battlefield at Westonzoyland.

Cider making, sampling and buying: Roger Wilkins, Lands End Farm, Mudgley (2 miles south of Wedmore). Burrow Hill Cider, Pass Vale Farm (2 miles west of Kingsbury Episcopi).

Farm visits for children: New Road Farm, East Huntspill (3 miles south of Junction 22, M5): play areas, rare breeds, farm animals, nature-trail displays, lunches, cream teas. Tel: 0278-783250.

Shoes: this part of Somerset is famous for shoe making, dominated by C & J Clark of Street. Buy cheap shoes at Crockers in Street and Fine Shoes in Street or Wells, and visit the Shoe Museum at the Street factory.

The Willows Peat Garden Centre: Shapwick Road, Westhay (5 miles west of Glastonbury). Garden centre, tea-rooms, visitor centre with displays of archaeology, peat cutting, wildlife, local crafts. Tel: 04586-257.

Viewpoints overlooking the Levels: Glastonbury Tor (OS:512386); Burrow Mump (OS:539305); Burrow Hill (OS:414191); Ebbor Gorge (OS:520485).

Westonzoyland Pumping Station: 2 miles south-west of Westonzoyland, 3 miles east of junction 24, M5 (OS:339329). Houses 1861 Easton and Amos drainage machine, the only one in the country run by steam. Tel: 0823-412713.

Willow Craft Industry (PH Coate & Son): Meare Green Court, Stoke St. Gregory (5 miles east of Junction 25, M5). Guided tours and talks on willow industry (The Willow Trail). Walks to the withy beds. Wetland exhibition. Weaving shed. Showroom with all kinds of willow craft for sale. Tel: 0823-490249.

HOLIDAY READING

Wetland — Life in the Somerset Levels by Adam Nicolson and Patrick Sutherland (Michael Joseph).

IRELAND

Dublin

Dublin

David
Wickers

. . . .

START with the Dart. Dublin's rapid-transit train will whip you through the tedium of southern suburbs to the harbour at Dun Laoghaire. Set your sights on the distant Martello tower at Sandycove and let the sweep of Dublin Bay, reaching out to Howth Head, the distant hazy promontory, embrace your left arm. When you reach the tower — just past Forty Foot where the "gentlemen bathers only" take their naked all-weather plunge — climb its corkscrew stairway and step on to the roof.

In the opening lines of *Ulysses*, "stately plump Buck Mulligan", wearing an ungirdled yellow dressing-gown that billows in the mild morning air, steps out on to the same roof for a shave. Today, the tower is a museum devoted to James Joyce.

Dublin, one of Europe's oldest capitals, is a cradle of literary giants. With the writings of Wilde, Shaw, O'Casey, Behan, Yeats, Swift, Goldsmith and Synge so ingrained in the city's fabric, it is hardly surprising that the eloquence of contemporary Dubliners can leave you as breathless as the coldest of Forty Foot waters.

You may not be up to a Joycean breakfast of "inner organs of beasts and fowl" but a good egg and a couple of rashers in one of Bewley's Oriental Cafés will suffice. Across a marble-topped table, in front of a coal fire with a thermal yield that comes close to the face of the sun, you will meet priests and pram-pushers, Trinity College students and commuters on the last leg of their journeys to work. I even saw a poet, lost in higher scribbles, oblivious to the drippings from his buttered toast.

In the eighteenth century Dublin was the second-biggest city in Britain, chic and richly endowed with townhouses built for wealthy landowners. Today, its appeal is less tangible: in a beauty contest among European capitals, Dublin would get a slow handclap.

It is raw and poor, with even a Third World echo to the daily scenario of tinkers slumped over their horse-drawn carts, ragamuffin kids, shawled mothers begging with empty ice-cream cartons, the daily rattle of charity collection boxes and the standard issue uniform of garments too flimsy to cope with the familiar grey veil of rain or the chill winds.

You could spend a lot of time searching for Dublin's cherished atmosphere, chasing round in search of "crack" (a good time in jolly company, not a refined narcotic) but the best approach is to sit in the middle and let the city happen around you. Pubs are the best auditoriums. They are the seed beds of Dublin's loquacious conviviality, measured on a scale that may range from rosy musings between friends to a ranting diatribe addressed to all within earshot. The highest decibel delivery I experienced concerned the cooling of Joyce's "wine of the country" below lounge temperature — a new publican habit that was, the speaker bellowed, tantamount to heresy.

Pubs abound. Even Parnell's right arm points to the nearest pub from his plinth at the top of O'Connell Street. Since Dublin's pubs are not owned by breweries, they haven't all suffered from the "Edwardianisation" that has afflicted so many of their English counterparts. Each has its style, from Mulligans at the harsh and functional end of the traditional spectrum, to the almost ecclesiastical Ryans, with its polished mahogany barwork and snugs as intimate as confessional boxes.

Save a sunny, sober few hours for a stroll in a Dublin park. These are many and varied, from the bowling green trim of Trinity College to St Stephen's Green, the biggest garden square in Europe, and the tranquil heart of Merrion Square. But Dublin's real back garden is Phoenix Park — as big as London's Hyde, St James's, Green and Regent's parks, plus Kensington Gardens and Hampstead Heath put together. Walk there, following the Liffey upstream past the steaming chimneys of the Guinness brewery, with your eye on the fat needle monument to Wellington dead ahead at the entrance to the park. When he was congratulated, as an Irishman, for victory at Waterloo, his unpatriotic retort was: "Just because you may be born in a stable doesn't make you a horse." But they still put up his monument.

Dublin is both foreign and familiar. The language is English, but often it isn't. The parking meters are similar to those in New York, not London. The pound is a punt but not quite the same.

And you don't need a passport. But you might as well take it, because how else will they know you don't need it?

GETTING THERE
Aer Lingus (tel: 01-734 1212) operates up to 30 flights a day from Heathrow, Gatwick, Stansted and 8 regional airports. Other carriers include British Airways, Ryanair, DanAir and Capital. Sealink and B&I operate ferry services between England, Wales and Ireland. Several tour operators, including Aer Lingus Holidays (tel: 01-439 7262) and Trusthouse Forte (tel: 061-682 9100), feature weekend breaks, from £96 for 2 nights bed and breakfast. British visitors do not need a passport.

GETTING AROUND
Dublin, despite 1 million inhabitants, is very walkable (beyond its central core lie grim suburbs that have nothing to offer the residents, let alone the casual visitor). For short excursions, travel by Dart, the efficient Dublin Area Rapid Transport train which runs in a north-south line through the city centre, linking Howth with Dun Laoghaire, Sandycove and Bray. Taxis are expensive — about £12 from the airport (7 miles) while the bus costs £2.50. Chauffeured and walking tours can be arranged through Elegant Ireland (tel: 0001 751632).

MONEY
The Irish punt is worth roughly 10 per cent less than the pound; most shops and restaurants will take British currency (though pubs

may only offer punt-for-pound parity). Change money on arrival or at Irish banks in Britain.

KEY SIGHTS

Georgian Dublin: the best of Georgian gems are to be found in Merrion Square, with a beautiful garden at its core, and Fitzwilliam Square. Other architectural classics include the porticoed Bank of Ireland (the houses of parliament until 1800), the Custom House, the Four Courts and Trinity College.

The General Post Office: scene of bitter fighting in 1916 and reckoned to be the birthplace of the modern Irish state.

St Patrick's Street: St Patrick's Cathedral is the largest of the city's two cathedrals both of which, despite a population 95 per cent Catholic, are Protestant. Dean Swift lies buried here alongside his good friend Stella.

The Book of Kells: the gospels illuminated by monks in the 9th century and kept in the magnificent Long Room of the Trinity College Library along with rows of other ancient tomes.

Guinness Brewery: Massive 67-acre site that brews more than 1 million pints a day.

Phoenix Park: scene of the 1882 massacre of the British Chief Secretary and Under-Secretary for Ireland by the National Invincibles. More recently 1 million people stood on its vast green carpet to hear Pope John Paul.

The Liberties: Molly Malone's streets broad and narrow and the core of historic Dublin.

MUSEUMS AND GALLERIES

Chester Beatty Library: a mining engineer's outstanding collection of Oriental Art. Shrewsbury Road, Ballsbridge.

National Gallery: daunting home to paintings by Fra Angelico, Breughel, Titian, Reynolds, Murillo, Goya and lesser folk. More modern works are located in the *Municipal Gallery*.

National Museum: includes the Treasury — with brilliantly crafted Celtic gold and silver chalices, brooches and other works.

Joyce's Tower: the only Joycean museum in the world at Sandycove. Open April-Oct or by appointment (tel: 0001 808571).

Abbey Theatre: hardly a museum but still a shrine, despite its modern looks; the original, the most famous theatre in the world, burnt to cinders in a 1951 fire.

WALKS

Phoenix Park is the obvious roaming territory if it's sunny. More ambitious hikes could take in sections of the 126-kilometre Wicklow Way, the first long-distance footpath in the republic (take the 47B bus from Dublin to Clonegal; further details from the Tourist Office).

HOTELS

The Shelbourne (tel: 0001 766471): Dublin's grandest, overlooking St Stephen's Green. The Irish Constitution was drafted here in 1922. Drinks in the high profile Horseshoe Bar and discreetly charming teas in the lounge are a vital ingredient of the Dublin Society scene. Others include *Jury's* (tel: 0001 605000): a modern hotel on the edge of town (on Northumberland Road); *Buswells* (tel: 0001 764013): warm, family-owned and run, on Molesworth Street; and *Fitzpatrick Castle* (tel: 0001 851533): a sham on Killiney Bay that looks like a version of medieval Lego, except at night when floodlights make it look like Rebecca's burning Manderley.

LUNCH

Lots of coffee bars that look like gentrified transport cafés (try *Cunningham's* on Kildare Street). Up-market fish and chips, served in boxes in an oyster bar-ish ambience, from *Beshoff* (Westmorland and other branches). Also the *Winding Stair,* a 1960s-style second-hand bookshop-cum-café with a great view of the Liffey (Ormond Quay by Halfpenny Bridge). Or back to *Bewley's* (the one on Westmorland Street is the best).

DINNER

Irish kitchens have traditionally focused on making do rather than titivating the taste buds, so you won't discover any ethnic gastronomy. Even a scouring for an authentic "coodle" stew may well prove in vain. But you can dine very well in Dublin at several establishments, including: *Whites on the Green* (St Stephen's Green, tel: 0001 751975): modern cuisine, elegant setting and one of the best in town; *Shay Beano* (St Stephen's Row, tel: 0001 776384): a touch too French, pretentious and a little tight on space but good food; *Old Dublin* (Francis Street, tel: 0001 542028): looks like a pub but serves good robust dishes with Scandinavian influences; *Kitty O'Shea's* (Upper Grand Canal Street, tel: 0001 609965): named after either the mistress or wife of Parnell (a perennial debate) and one of the oldest in town, though the olde worlde fixtures are imported from other sources (banks, churches and a masonic lodge).

BEST BARS

Ryans (Parkgate): 3 generations, 4 traditional snugs and a bar that encloses an area bigger than the entire drinking room. Good soups at lunchtime — pub grub is rare in Dublin. *Mulligans* (Poolbeg Street): literary traditions, notably in the pages of *Ulysses,* perpetuated by the patronage of hacks from the next-door Irish Press. *Sheehans* (Chatham Street): busy warmth and easy conversation. *Doheny and*

Nesbitt (Lower Baggot Street): smoky, crowded and with a once-white ceiling that is now fag-stained to a deep shade of autumn. *O'Donoghues* (Merrion Row): lively student hangout, with live music — the Dubliners' fame is rooted here. *Brazen Head* (Lower Bridge Street): the city's oldest, with a subsiding floor to prove its pedigree. Note that pubs stay open from 10.30am till about 11pm. Dublin also has plenty of live music venues, including the Olympia Theatre, The Merchant, An Beal Bocht, the Cable Inn and The Four Seasons. Look locally for "sets", traditional Irish country dances that are regaining popularity with the young.

SHOPS

Not one of the weekend high spots. The pedestrianised Grafton Street and its tributaries, plus O'Connell, are the main arteries. Interesting smaller shops are concentrated in the Powerscourt Town House within the glassed-over shell of an impressive 18th-century mansion (off William Street). Other shops include Blarney for Aran sweaters and crystal glass, Kilkenny for Irish crafts, Kevin & Howlin for hand-made tweeds (all on Nassau), Cooke for antiques (Francis), Bewley's for teas and hand-made chocolates, and the House of Names (also Nassau) for armorial shields and other heraldry. Several good bookstores including Fred Hanna (Nassau) and Naughton (Marine Terrace). Biggest stores are Brown Thomas and Switzer's (both on Grafton).

SPECIAL EVENTS

Scores of happenings including street carnivals, concerts, folk festival, art exhibitions, theatre and cinema festivals. Events for Bloomsday on June 16 tend to be 11th-hour conceptions. The annual horse show takes place in August.

BEDSIDE READING

The city is weak on good guide books, so stick with *Ulysses* or museum curator Robert Nicholson's *Joyce's Dublin* published by Methuen, £5.95. Also an AA pocket guide (£3.49) plus the 95p fortnightly *Entertainment Guide* and the fortnightly *Event Guide* free sheet, distributed citywide.

FURTHER INFORMATION

Irish Tourist Board, 150 New Bond Street, London W1 (tel: 01-493 3201). In Dublin: 14 O'Connell Street. Also at Dun Laoghaire harbour and the airport.

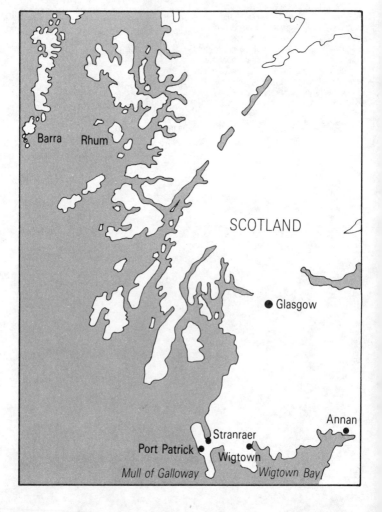

SCOTLAND

Galloway Peninsula

Barra

Neil
MacLean

. . . .

ROUTINE hardly varies. The tide retreats from the Great Shore, sucked back into Oitir Mhór and the Sound of Hellisay. Donald Beaton climbs into his yellow fire truck (Rust in Peace) to chase away any of the Eoligarry cows that may have strayed across the sand. Then, skimming low over Gighay, the Twin Otter of Loganair's island service dips its wings and drifts down on to the white sand and powdered shell of the world's only tidal airport, Cockleshell Beach on Barra.

The islanders like to say that they have the only airport runway

to be washed down twice a day. The surface is so firm that, at low tide, it is easy enough to cycle the three miles across the beach from Crannag to Eoligarry Jetty, where the daily ferry arrives from South Uist.

These days, however, it is more usual to take the road that runs the length of Barra's northern peninsula, along an isthmus collared by sand dunes, and past the ruined chapel of St Barr in Eoligarry Cemetery, last resting place of Sir Compton MacKenzie, author of *Whisky Galore*.

MacKenzie loved Barra. It's not hard to see why. The best features of the Western Isles can be found on or around its thirty-five square miles: rocky bays and inlets, vast and empty beaches, caves and sea cliffs, sheep grazing on the machair (a carpet of wild flowers and marram grass), and seals sunbathing on the rocks.

It's a good size for an island, large enough to be explored at leisure and over several visits, yet small enough for every bend in the road to become pleasantly familiar.

The peninsula joins the island's main circular thoroughfare close to North Bay, and from here it is six miles to Castlebay by the narrow east road, or eight miles if you head westwards. The post bus, which serves as public transport from the airport, will take you east, past creeks and miniature fiords, and the Norse-named villages of Bruernish, Earsary, and Skallary.

About a mile and a half before the road makes its descent into Castlebay, a gate on the right opens on to the best route to take up to Barra's highest point — the summit of Heaval (1,200 feet). From here, or from the nearby statue of the Madonna and Child, you can look out to the southern islands of Vatersay, Sandray, Pabbay, Mingulay and Bernary. On a clear day, you can see across to St Kilda far off in the west.

Castlebay clings to a hill overlooking a natural harbour — its scattering of houses dominated by the Catholic church. In the bay itself sits Kiessimul Castle, home of the MacNeils, a piratical clan which once unilaterally declared war on England.

Standing at the end of Castlebay pier, it is hard to imagine the days when you could walk to Vatersay across the decks of a 500-strong fleet of fishing boats; herring was their quarry, cured by the islanders for dispatch to St Petersburg and New York. Now the pier is only busy when the Caledonian MacBrayne ferry calls in from Oban three times a week (daily in summer).

Walking back up the short harbour road, you pass five shops and the café where Sheila McIntosh makes stovies (the stewed potatoes and onion that are Scotland's other national dish), served with fresh brown bread. You won't find a fish shop here — lobster, crab, scallops, langoustines, turbot and haddock are all bought straight from the boats, or boxed from the factory at Ardveenish. But you can buy that day's newspaper (delivered on the afternoon flight) from MacLean's the butcher's shop, which also operates the petrol pump.

The west coast of the island is flatter than the east, with large cream-coloured beaches. From

Allasdale, make your way across the machair to Seal Bay; as you walk beside the kelp, whistle or sing and soon a curious whiskered face or two will surface.

Following the road back north and inland, the small Church of Scotland at Cuier has windows on the east side only. Some say this is to stop the small congregation looking out on to the Catholics to the west. Others talk of a minister who used to bring his fire and brimstone sermons to an abrupt end when his wife signalled from the manse that dinner was ready; his angry congregation bricked up the windows so that he couldn't see her. I don't think anybody really believes it, but why spoil a good story?

HOW TO GET THERE
A weekend on Barra would need to stretch to Monday, as flights on Sundays are rare. Loganair (tel: 041-889 3181) flies from Glasgow, at low tide, and the return trip costs from £75.

WHEN TO GO
In winter the heather is the colour of chocolate cake and you can experience all 4 seasons in an hour (although there is very little snow). In spring, the machair near the airport is covered in wild primroses, a good time to visit the puffins, guillemots and razorbills on Mingulay. In summer, they cut the peat on the Dark Glen and there is a Gaelic cultural festival.

WHERE TO STAY
There are 4 main hotels on Barra. The Isle of Barra Hotel (tel: 08714-383), open from mid-May to mid-September, has a spectacular location on Tangusdale Beach on the west side of the island. The other three smaller, family-run hotels, the Clachan Beag (tel: 08714-279), the Craigard (tel: 08714-200) and the Castlebay (tel: 08714-223) are almost side-by-side, with views over the harbour at Castlebay. There is a special weekend package to either the Isle of Barra or Castlebay for £150, inclusive of flights from Glasgow, dinner, bed and breakfast.

HOW TO GET AROUND
A car can be hired from Gerard Campbell at Nask near Castlebay (tel: 08714-328) and bicycles can be hired from the hotels and the Post Office.

WHERE TO EAT
Apart from the café on the pier, the hotels offer the best option for eating out. The sea around Barra is so rich in fish and shellfish that it would be a shame not to try peat-smoked salmon at the Clachan Beag, seafood chowder and scallops *duglère* at the Craigard or clams with cream and Cointreau at the Castlebay.

WHAT TO DO AND SEE
Barra is for those who want a quiet break. The island itself is the reason for being there and if you can face 14 undemanding miles, the best thing to do is walk once around the island one way, then the next day, walk around it the other way. Alternatively, cycle. The hotels can arrange water sports (sea angling, freshwater fishing, diving, water-skiing and dinghy hire), as well as excursions to Vatersay and Mingulay. There are also boat trips to Kiessimul Castle on Saturdays in the summer. There are several sites of archaeological interest on Barra — brochs and standing stones — and an old island "black house" museum at Craigston. As well as evening entertainments in the hotels, there are often ceilidhs (informal concerts and dances) in the village hall. The Gaelic festival lasts for 2 weeks in the middle of July.

BEDTIME READING
Barra by Helen McGregor and John Cooper (Canongate Publishing, £9.95), the history and folklore of the island evocatively illustrated with black and white photographs.
Ordnance Survey Map 31 (Barra and the Surrounding Islands). Gaelic place names above are spelt as they appear on the OS map. Also contact the Scottish Tourist Board (tel: 031-332 2433) or the Outer Hebrides Tourist Board (tel: 0851-3088).

Rhum

*Christopher
Somerville*

. . . .

A
S I stood on the top deck of the ferryboat *Lochmor*, I was transfixed by the sight of the tremendous mountains of the island of Rhum, dead ahead, climbing straight out of the sea into a cloud cap 2,000 feet up. *Lochmor* had already transferred stores, mail and passengers into a tiny motorboat in a mid-sea rendezvous off the island of Eigg, and would shortly be dropping me off at Rhum in the same way. In the remote world of the Small Isles, in the Inner Hebrides, worrying about travel connections is a fruitless occupation. Once embarked on the ferry's circuit of the islands of Rhum, Eigg, Muck and Canna, you just have to settle back and go with the flow. Sooner or later — usually later — you'll get where you want to be. As an exercise in relaxation, this fatalistic journeying takes some beating.

The Small Isles form a self-contained group a few miles west of the Scottish mainland, just south of Skye. Eigg is ridged and knobbly, Canna wedge-shaped, Muck a low-lying blob. Rhum is the visual masterpiece, a diamond shape about eight miles square that rears into steep, bare mountains well over 2,000 feet high. These great peaks are cut through by glens that divide the diamond into roughly equal quarters. Stony tracks follow the glens to the coasts, winding through scenes of stunning wildness and beauty — rocky screes, wide stretches of boggy moorland speckled with flowers, chains of steely lochs, waterfalls beating down gullies in white strings of twisted water from top to bottom.

Red deer wander far and wide across the moors and mountains — there are 1,500 on Rhum. Something over 100,000 pairs of Manx shearwaters nest and breed on Rhum's mountains in spring and summer — birds that spend the rest of their lives at sea thousands of miles away off the coast of Brazil. One of Rhum's unique pleasures is to sit out at night near the summit of Hallival mountain, right in the flight path of 250,000 homing shearwaters as they come swooping all around you into their burrows. There are often ravens, less often golden eagles and very occasionally white-tailed sea eagles wheeling over the mountain tops. There are guillemots and razorbills on the cliffs, seals and sea otters on the shore, communities of alpine flowers on the mountainsides that have survived intact since the glaciers retreated at the end of the last Ice Age. Rhum is one of nature's fullest treasure chests. The rarest species here is man, a treasure in itself.

The island is jealously guarded by its owners, the Nature Conservancy Council. Much serious scientific study goes on all the year round on Rhum, carried out by the handful of full-time staff and their ever-eager volunteer assistants. Access to certain parts of the island can be restricted from time to time, especially in the north where a special study of the red deer has been in progress for decades. But I found, after checking with the warden, that there were few places I couldn't go. To be made free of all that wild and lovely landscape, to cover thirty miles on foot in two days and see nobody, was to step briefly into heaven.

For well over 100 years, up until 1957 when the NCC bought the island, Rhum was a heaven of a strictly private nature. All those thousands of acres of mountain and moorland made a deer-stalking, fishing and shooting paradise for a succession of owners, chief among them Sir George Bullough, the heir to a fortune made in Lancastrian cotton mills.

Kinloch Castle, the dream residence built by Sir George in 1901 in a commanding position at the head of Loch Scresort, makes a memorable place to stay, as much a living museum as a luxury hotel. The fabulous ornamental gardens where fourteen full-time gardeners were once employed have almost entirely faded away. But inside Kinloch Castle, nothing — almost literally nothing — has changed since it was built in flaring red sandstone by imported workmen from Lancashire, whom Sir George paid extra to wear kilts on site. Heads of stags shot by the Bulloughs stare glassily down from the walls of the wonderfully over-elaborate two-storey Great Hall, stuffed like the rest of the house with objects collected by Sir George during his many circumglobular voyages in his opulent steam yacht *Rhouma*.

On my first evening, I descended the staircase to the brassy wheezings and clashings of Kinloch Castle's orchestrion, a kind of glorified domestic fairground organ. This instrument had been ordered by Queen Victoria for Balmoral; but when she died before it could be delivered, canny Sir George took up her option. Pre-dinner drinks were served by a kilted, sporraned and be-dirked Iain MacArthur, who runs the castle with his wife Kathleen. The enormous, lake-like dining table, from which we ate five delicious courses, including fresh, locally caught lobster, was originally made for use aboard *Rhouma*, as were the dining room chairs — hence their swivelling seats and superheavy legs.

Sir George was not the man to forego life's little luxuries. One of the best things about Kinloch Castle is that, unlike any museum, every single gorgeous item is there to be used. Sir George's fine billiard cues, for example, or his shining black Steinway grand piano. If I or my fellow guests had been more than "Chopsticks" competent, we could have sat there in the Great Hall, as many visitors do, bashing out tunes to send each other eightsome-reeling over the tigerskin rugs. Sir George's bath, too: epitome of Edwardian inventiveness, with seven controls ranging from shower through wave, douche, spray, plunge and sitz to the startling "jet". I was sitting on the water-inflow hole when I operated the jet button. It felt like being coupled to an outsize enema engine. Fun, but rather too sudden. Chastened, I retired to bed in Sir George's chamber, under his canopy, all sensory terminals overloaded.

Round the back of the castle, in what were the servants' quarters, groups of visiting ornithologists, geologists, climbers and botanists were staying in hostel accommodation and making merry over DIY meals and steaming piles of drying waterproofs. I set off the following morning in the cheery company of a dozen booted and anoraked strangers; but half a mile up the glen they had all melted away into Rhum's enormous spaces, intent on their own business, and I went on alone. I stalked red deer hinds to within ten yards or so. I

climbed a mountain, up into mist and down again into butter-coloured sunlight. I saw brown trout in the lochs, orchids in the marshes, an eagle over the peaks.

By gradual stages I wandered across Rhum to the rocky bay at Harris where Sir George, his wife Lady Monica and father John lie in faintly ridiculous, more than faintly touching state, in solid tombs inside a mock-classical pillared and pedimented mausoleum. Sited here to dominate mountain and bay, the mausoleum seems just one block of stone among many at the feet of those soaring mountain slopes.

Other stones scattered on the hillside were the remnants of a farming settlement that scratched a living from the soil at Harris until nineteenth-century lairds cleared the people out and shipped them to Nova Scotia to make way for sheep.

If the weather turns suddenly nasty, as it can do in the Hebrides and did on my morning of departure, you'll find yourself marooned on Rhum until the ferry can come across for you. It's rare for delay to be longer than twenty-four hours, but not impossible. You can

plan your stay to coincide with a favourable long-range weather forecast. Or, infinitely preferable, you can extend your weekend, get round by boat to explore the islands of Eigg, Muck and Canna as well, and wave goodbye to the familiar world for a week at least. Be warned — one taste of Rhum leads to another.

GETTING THERE

By road: A380 Fort William to Arisaig and Mallaig. *By rail*: BR West Highland line, Glasgow, Fort William, Arisaig, Mallaig. *Ferries*: from Arisaig, M V *Shearwater* (Easter, then mid-May to mid-Sept, tel: 06875-224), from Mallaig, Caledonian MacBrayne's *Lochmor* (all year round, tel: 0687-2403). *Lochmor* connects with small island boats out at sea. The less luggage the better.

WHERE TO STAY

Kinloch Castle: Iain and Kathleen MacArthur, Kinloch Castle, Isle of Rhum, Inverness-shire, Scotland (tel: 0687-2037). Hotel facilities: bed and breakfast, dinner £46 (reduction for party bookings of 20-plus); specialities include venison, salmon, sea trout, lobster, catch your own dinner of brown trout in one of the lochs (fishing permits from NCC chief warden at White House, Kinloch). Hostel facilities: self-service bed and breakfast, £7 with a bistro available.

The Nature Conservancy Council's self-catering *bothies* (isolated, simple huts) and *campsites* at Kinloch are cheaper still. For details and permission, apply to the chief warden, White House, Kinloch, Isle of Rhum, Inverness-shire PH43 4RR (tel: 0687-2026).

THINGS TO DO

Residents at Kinloch Castle don't need permission for the ordinary moorland *mountain and coastal walking* that Rhum offers, but check first, in any case, at White House, a quarter of a mile from the castle. Residents also have free run of the castle's games, musical instruments and large library. *Guided tours of castle* for non-residents, Tuesday and Thursday afternoons.

Rock climbing, botanical and *ecological study, bird* and *deer watching*: obtain information, advice and, where necessary, permission in advance by writing to the chief warden.

There is often a *ceilidh* or other social get-together at weekends in the village hall at Kinloch (you may well be called upon to contribute to the evening's entertainment!).

WHAT TO BRING

OS 1:50,000 Sheet 39 Rhum & Eigg, a good compass, bird and flower books, binoculars. Walking boots and waterproofs are essential — Rhum's terrain is rough, its climate wet. The island's midges are a force to be reckoned with — Jungle Lotion and Shoo are thought to be the best deterrents. Rhum's single Post Office/shop at Kinloch sells basic goods as well as whisky and canned beer — but no other luxuries. Bring extra cheques, or cash, in case the ferry is delayed for a day or so by bad weather.

HOLIDAY READING

Bare Feet and Tackety Boots — a Boyhood on Rhum by Archie Cameron (Luath Press), on sale in Mallaig and Fort William bookshops. Many booklets and leaflets available by NCC, available from the chief warden. For children, the *Katie Morag* books by Mairi Hedderwick.

The
Solway Coast

Neil
MacLean

. . . .

MY FIRST history textbooks were full of pictures — line drawings of wild woolly mammoths, Queen Boadicea, her chariot wheels armed with curved swords to carve her enemy's shins, a gang of Vikings beating up a monk and that mellifluous trio of woad, wattle and daub.

Each elementary vision eventually took its place in the sepia world of damp, woollen school blazers, grass-grazed knees and third-of-a-pint bottles of milk, lodged in my mind's museum, dusty and forgotten.

Until last weekend, when I came face to face with woad.

Actually, it took archaeologist Simon Lee some time to find it. "It's here somewhere," he said, searching his office absently. "Ah, looking a bit sick and dry, I'm afraid. I think I'd better give it some water." What I like about this contemporary breed of archaeologist is their chummy rapport with ancient history. Surely there can be no more practical example of bringing the past to life than casually watering a thirsty pot of woad.

The Whithorn Dig, where Simon trowels, is proving a huge attraction for visitors to south-west Scotland — although this seldom means more than 100 visitors a day.

The Machars and The Rhins are the last two peninsulas on the Solway coast. The first name means a flat marshland; the second, a point or headland. They are both rich farming lands, part of Dumfries and Galloway, famous for dairy products and beef, and less well known for the narrow, empty roads, banked by wild flowers, deep green pastures, and gentle hills, offering views across the retreating Solway tides and over to the coast of Ireland.

It is fine touring country between seaside villages and peaceful country towns. Every mile or so, a smaller track crosses the road and it is generally worth the digression to follow it.

The road round The Machars and The Rhins has recently joined the Solway Coast Heritage Trail which starts at Annan in the east and ends at the ferry port of Stranraer. It is a well-signposted trail that highlights historic buildings and ancient monuments, gardens, forest walks and pic-

111

turesque harbours along the way. In particular, the trail marks the story of Scotland's Christian heritage, starting with the arrival of Saint Ninian, probably in the late fifth century, and his first Christian community at Whithorn.

It is in the shadow of the Whithorn priory, possibly itself built over Ninian's own church, Candida Casa, that the archaeologists are peeling away the postmedieval, Viking and Anglian layers, right back to the early Christian settlement. This might sound as dry as ancient dust, but they are making a considerable effort to involve visitors in their work.

The woad, for instance, is grown not as a horticultural curiosity but to be used, along with gorse and nettles, as a dye for local wools. These are then spun and woven to make authentic "Dark Age clothes" for local schoolchildren to wear while they are Vikings for a day in the Viking house built by an intriguing combination of the Dark Age Society and the Manpower Services Commission. By next summer, children invading from other parts of the country should also be able to join.

Apart from learning ancient dress codes, the children find out how the Vikings lived at Whithorn, as well as Viking fighting skills.

So far the archaeologists have unearthed about 1,200 skeletons at Whithorn. These prove a great attraction for visitors on the aerial viewing platforms although, after the first few hundred, they have ceased to be quite so fascinating for the archaeologists, however respectfully they may dust them off.

Rather more interesting is the midden or rubbish heap of the Anglian monks, which has yielded gaming pieces and coins, as well as the remains of excellent cuts of meat and the first evidence of domesticated chickens and geese in Scotland. They have also found

Merovingian glass from a cone beaker, holding three-quarters of a pint. It had, however, no base so that your three-quarters of a pint of wine had to be consumed before you could put your glass down.

It certainly seems that the Anglian monks fared better than the Vikings, whose daily diet consisted principally of four pounds of bread and two pounds of onions. "We think they ate a lot of onion soup," said Simon.

My dinner that evening was not onion soup. It was a delicate fish consommé with saffron and strips of monkfish, preceded by a quail thigh and slivers of quail breast with an oak leaf and curly endive salad, dressed with a warm vinaigrette infused with herbs. This was followed by fillet of John Dory with a lobster sauce and gar-

nished with shrimps. I think I will spare you a description of my dessert. Suffice to say it was not, perhaps, what you would expect near the source of Scottish Christianity.

However, there are few parts of the world where you won't find a Frenchman feeding the natives with a missionary zeal, converting barbaric tastes to haute cuisine. Marcel Frichot is one. When he talks about Scottish boiled potatoes, he has the expression of Ninian beholding a Pict latrine.

The hotel, which he runs with his wife Corinna, is called Knockinaam Lodge. In 1988 and 1989 the AA awarded it two red stars and two rosettes, an unprecedented combination north of the border. The red stars are for the hotel and the rosettes are for its food, which the AA suggests is

the best in Scotland. I wouldn't go that far, but it is certainly startling to find such sophisticated cooking so far off, or rather along, the beaten track.

Knockinaam Lodge sits in a small valley between cliffs many lengths of string from Portpatrick (it's not easy to find), with a shingly beach, a boat house, a croquet lawn with a mole and a view of Ireland beneath its sunset.

When I arrived, the receptionist walked halfway down the drive to greet me. I was led to the room called The Croft — a misnomer, it was in fact the loft — with all the personal touches that I still sucker for.

After floating in a cumulus of bathfoam, I tried the huge, monogrammed bathrobe. I looked like Joe Bugner. I put it back on the chair.

Dinner was the main event. Marcel has imported three French chefs to tickle the palate and he personally advises on your choice of wine. The only change I would make would be to introduce Merovingian beakers to the dining room.

The climate of the south-west is milder than you would expect due to the influence of the Gulf Stream, and at Port Logan on the western shore there is a garden, an out-station of the Royal Botanic Gardens in Edinburgh, where they grow exotic plants from around the world.

As well as eucalyptus trees, the gardeners of Port Logan tend cabbage palms, passion flowers, enormous tropical ferns, a fourteen foot flowering spike (*Echium Pinniana*, I am assured) and a Brazilian plant (*Gunera Manicata*), like rhubarb, with leaves that seem to be as wide as a rowing boat.

It is possible to spend a whole morning at Port Logan, fingers green with envy, wandering round the Walled Garden and the Woodland Park, strolling up the stone steps, flanked by Chinese palms, to the ruined tower house and round the impressive, landscaped, carp-filled lagoon.

Back at Knockinaam Lodge, I relaxed in the drawing room with a book from the mantelpiece called *The Highways and Byways in Galloway*, described as "a district which has remained unknown to the world longer than any other part of Scotland with the possible exception of Rockall".

The book was written in 1916 and not much has changed except that the Vikings are back, the French are spreading *l'essence de truffes* and Brazilian rhubarb is growing by the sea.

HOW TO GET THERE

By car: the A75 from Carlisle or the A77 from Glasgow. *By train:* nearest station is Stranraer (direct trains twice daily from Euston and regular service from Glasgow) where you can hire a car.

WHERE TO STAY

Knockinaam Lodge (tel: 077-681 471): Portpatrick: twin room, breakfast and dinner from £57 per person per night. *Corsemalzie House Hotel* (tel: 098-886 254): Port William: twin room, breakfast and dinner, £42 per person per night. *Creebridge House Hotel* (tel: 0671-2121): Newton Stewart: twin room, breakfast and dinner £39.50 per person per night.

WHERE TO EAT

If you are visiting the dig, go on to the Isle of Whithorn and try the lobster at the *Steam Packet Inn* (tel: 098-85334) on the pier.

PLACES TO VISIT

Apart from the *Whithorn Dig* (tel: 09885-508), the *Solway Coast Heritage Trail* will lead you to *Wigtown*, a quiet market town; to the pastel fishing village of *Garlieston*; the picturesque harbours of the *Isle of Whithorn* and *Port William*; and past west coast beaches to *Glenluce* with its abbey and motor museum. The promontory of the *Mull of Galloway* is Scotland's own Land's End with some of the most impressive cliff scenery in Scotland. As well as the Botanic Gardens, there is a fish pond at *Port Logan* with tame salt-water fish like cod, hand-fed by their keeper. The popular seaside town of *Portpatrick* used to be a Gretna Green for young couples from Ireland; now it is busy with day-trippers from Glasgow.

FURTHER INFORMATION

Contact The Dumfries and Galloway Tourist Board in Dumfries (tel: 0387-53862) or the sub-office in Stranraer (tel: 0776-2595).

115

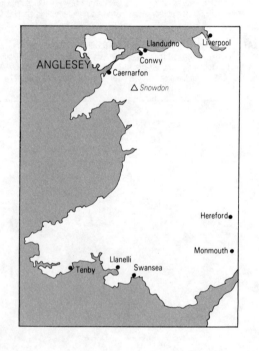

ANGLESEY

Llandudno
Liverpool
Conwy
Caernarfon
△ Snowdon

Hereford●

Monmouth ●

Llanelli
Tenby ● Swansea

WALES

Swallow Falls

Gower

Sharon Maxwell Magnus

. . . .

RETURNING home to Gower I am constantly astounded by the sheer variety in this fourteen-mile-long peninsula jutting out into the Bristol Channel close by Swansea. There are meadows so full of buttercups that the pollen coats your shoes, rolling hills tipping like the waves just visible in the distance and smooth honey beaches unspoilt by litter.

It is the sort of countryside that Enid Blyton would have chosen to set an adventure in: ruined castles, small secluded bays which might be used for smuggling, chatty village stores where they still sell ginger ale, and lots of heather for our hardy hero to bed down in.

You need a spirit of adventure to enjoy Gower as it is wonderfully, hopelessly uncommercial. Signposts lead you down winding country roads almost hidden by tangled hedgerows of wild flowers and long, burnished grasses. Muddy paths through the fields suddenly taper out and on some of the remoter beaches such as Mewslade or Pwll-du (pronounced puchdee) you may find yourself sitting alone on the soft sands with only the swish of the sea and sound of the gulls for company.

The most gregarious part of Gower is The Mumbles, known as the Gateway to Gower, a bustling little village on the curve of the bay, brimming with bed and breakfast accommodation, cafés and sea-view pubs. Seen from a distance it looks like a lakeside Swiss village with its squat stucco houses gazing out at the sea and the masts of the yachts on the front jangling like cowbells. On a summer's day, the front is thronged with people, strolling, jogging or watching the red sails of the dinghies bobbing on the sea.

At high tide the waves spray these promenaders, but at low tide they recede so far that the sea is almost invisible, leaving a long, gloomy tract of muddy sand. One family who arrived at dusk when the tide was in, woke up the next morning to find that their sea view had disappeared. It took the landlady ten minutes to persuade them that they had not been moved in the night.

It is fun to go shopping in the local stores where you can buy fresh fish, laverbread — a Welsh speciality made from seaweed — local cockles from Penclawdd and sweet Welsh cakes, baked on a griddle.

The Mumbles is cosy and quaint, with its fairy lights, ancient crazy-golf courses and carefully tended flower beds. It is a good place to eat and to shop. But if you want to enjoy the thirty or so bays along Gower, you have to drive on or take the cliff path that links the bays.

The most spectacular view is at Rhosili. Sheer green cliffs, their lines as rigid as if they had been cut from the rest of the land by some almighty scissors, gaze down on sand remorselessly clawed by the sea. Looking down into the void from the safety of the cliff walk one has a feeling of almost limitless space.

On most Sundays you can see hang-gliding enthusiasts leaping from the cliffs, casting themselves into nothingness and then floating down like falling handkerchiefs until they get lost in the backdrop of grey waves billowing up to meet them.

The sea always seems to be slate grey at Rhosili. At Oxwich Bay, a few miles back along the coast, it is more welcoming, a mild, green sea that tentatively licks the sand, like a small, friendly dog. This is the ideal family beach; a place for exploring rock-pools and playing games on the sand. In summer, the car park end of this three-mile beach gets crowded as families plop themselves down and anchor their windbreaks, picnics and children to a convenient plot, before they rush down for a quick dip in the tingling cold sea.

Oxwich is a good place to try out watersports — ideal for apprentice and expert windsurfers or even water-skiers — although most people confine themselves to building sandcastles and swimming.

If you are a surfing fanatic, you will find much more to occupy you on Langland Bay's long beach. Here the waves are wilder than in Oxwich or Horton bays and give the surfers more scope. Indeed, surfers are so enthusiastic that even on Christmas Day you will see them lying on their boards in the bay like basking whales waiting for the perfect wave to carry them in.

One of my favourite walks is from Parkmill down to Three

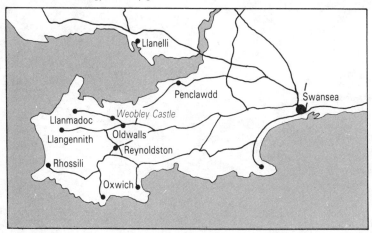

Cliffs Bay through a valley where the river meanders lazily in wide, snake-like coils to the sea. For an even more spectacular view, one can climb to the ruined castle at the top of the hill and see valley, wood, river and sea mistily merging into one.

You need to enjoy exercise to get the most from Gower. If you don't like the outdoor life there is little else to do. Nightlife is extremely limited and most people choose to stay in self-catering lets, caravans or secluded country hotels. Besides, after a day spent hiking, pony trekking, gathering strawberries in one of the many pick-your-own farms or merely dozing on the beach, even the most ardent socialites tend to find that they feel exhausted by eight o'clock.

But if it is quiet here, it is not lonely. There are friendly little villages dotted throughout the peninsula, each with a mix of old farmhouses, thatched cottages and modern, often flashy, bungalows. This is Wesley country, for the famous preacher stayed at these small villages, as he brought the word to the people, although it seems that even his fiery oratory disturbed the peace only a little.

For the enduring charm of Gower is its air of calm and serenity. It is one of the few places left where people still stroll instead of trot and always have time for a chat. As you gaze out at the sea and the still, silent meadows, the hurly-burly of Monday morning seems a long, long way off.

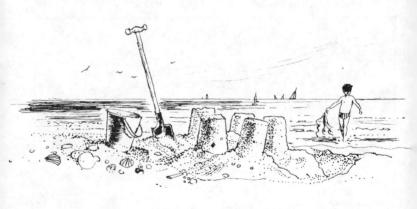

GETTING THERE

By car: from London, take the M4 to the end, then the A48 to Briton Ferry. From Briton Ferry, take the A483 to Swansea and the A4067 to The Mumbles or A4118 to the heart of Gower. Alternatively, take junction 47 off the M4 and follow the signs to Gorseinon, Gowerton and then the B4295 for North Gower. From the north, take the M6 to Birmingham and the A465 for a picturesque route.

By rail: the nearest railway station is Swansea. The journey from London by direct route takes just under 3 hours and a standard single fare costs £30; return £60; white saver departing Friday £38.

GETTING AROUND

A car is advisable as the buses are expensive and infrequent. Alternatively, you can hire a bicycle in Swansea at Wheelies, 34 Uplands Crescent, from £5 per day (tel: 0792-472612). Bike hire is sometimes available on the promenade in Southend, The Mumbles, during the summer months. You could also try a pony trekking holiday or day ride at Parc Le-Breos, Parkmill (tel: 0792-371636).

WHERE TO STAY

Fairyhill Residential Country House and Restaurant: Reynoldston: is a restored country house set in its own beautiful grounds, complete with lake and trout stream. Rooms are large and luxurious, service friendly and helpful. Prices from £59 (2 people, bed and breakfast) for a double room with en-suite bathroom, telephone and TV. Dinner not included. (tel: 0792-390139). *The Osborne:* Rotherslade Road, Langland Bay (tel: 0792-366274). Perched on a cliff with majestic views over the sea. Modern and comfortable with bars and restaurant. Prices from £36 per person on weekend breaks, including breakfast and dinner. *The Oxwich Bay Hotel:* Oxwich (tel: 0792-390329). Basic, clean accommodation by the sea and in one of the larger villages. Meals available. Bed and breakfast from £19.95.

Self-catering information available from Swansea Tourist Information Centre, Singleton St, Swansea (tel: 0792-468321). For spur-of-the-moment accommodation, scour the seafront in The Mumbles.

WHERE TO EAT

Widest choice of restaurants is in The Mumbles. Try *La Gondola:* 590 Mumbles Road, Southend. Closed Monday (tel: 0792-362338). Popular Italian restaurant with wide range of dishes and children's portions available.

The Artful Dodger: 602 Mumbles Road (tel: 0792-367309). Anglo-French cuisine in quaint surroundings. Prices about £8 for three courses. Not open for Monday or Sunday lunch.

Fairyhill: mentioned above, has an excellent restaurant, serving French food in lovely surroundings. Prices from about £17 for dinner, not open at lunchtime apart from Sunday lunch at £10.50.

Britannia Inn Gaslight Restaurant: Llanmadoc (tel: 044127-624). Cosy, family restaurant serving traditional English food. Sunday lunches from £5.

Langland Court Hotel: Langland Court Road, Langland, The Mumbles (tel: 0792-361545/6). Dinners and Sunday lunches. Seafood specialities and local cuisine. Egon Ronay recommended. Dinner from £12 for 3 courses.

TEA

Several tea-rooms at Rhosili including *Thomas's* tea-rooms overlooking the cliffs. *Oxwich Bay Hotel,* Oxwich, *The Hollies Guest House and Restaurant,* Horton, reasonably priced teas (dinner also available). The *Woodside Restaurant,* Guest House, Oxwich, Relais Routiers recommended.

PUBS

The Greyhound Inn and Restaurant, Oldwalls. Popular, with good bar food. *The Gower Inn,* Parkmill. Pretty setting.

THINGS TO DO

If you tire of sitting on the beach or looking at the beautiful views, you could explore the ruined castles at *Weobley* or *Oystermouth Castle* in The Mumbles which has a good view over the bay. Information, also available from The Mumbles Tourist Information Centre, Oystermouth Square, The Mumbles (tel:0792-361302).

Gower Festival: July, chamber music and poetry all over Gower. *Watersports:* windsurfing available at Port Eynon and surfing at Llangennith throughout the summer. *Windsurfing:* by qualified Royal Yachting Association instructor at Oxwich Bay (tel: 0792-390774).

Snowdonia

Martin
Collins

. . . .

SNOWDONIA — Eryri to the Welsh — assumes a sterner countenance during the months of winter. Not only do dramatic light and weather animate the hills, they restore chastity to a landscape debauched by holiday-season crowds. Gone are traffic queues, fast-food vendors and the press of fellow humans. What winter visitors forfeit in daylight hours and amenities is amply compensated for by the chance to gain an authentic sense of Eryri — its Welshness, its history and its pervasive grandeur.

Revived by a new breed of entrepreneur, slate caverns, quarries and mineral workings in the hills open up for summer trippers, but pickings are seasonal, gone with October. Only Eryri's great castles, evolved from the ages-long conflict between England and Wales and strung in a defensive ring around its mountainous heartland, provide enduring echoes of man's presence here. Within twenty years, during the late thirteenth century, Edward I initiated the construction of no fewer than seventeen castles. Those in North Wales represent some of the finest ever built — fortresses the audacity of which is admired even by our own generation, inured to monolithic architecture.

When Snowdonia finally fell to Edward's English armies in 1283, Conwy Castle was begun under the great military architect James of St George. Within nine years the work was completed: lime-washed and with conical roofs atop its eight battlemented towers, the fortress stood sentinel over the entrance to the Conwy valley.

Public interest in Conwy's medieval structures over the past 150 years has ensured their preservation and restoration, even though, until the new road tunnel under the estuary is completed, Conwy's discomfiture with A55 traffic will persist. The all-dominating castle, eminently explorable and complemented by some of the most intact town walls in Europe, nobly transcends the goings-on around it.

From the B5106 Conwy valley road, which leaves the town to the south, views extend to the lumpy, whaleback summits in the Carneddau range, falling north to the Irish Sea. Sinuous lanes above Trefriw village lead to twin forest-fringed lakes, Crafnant and Geirionydd; both can be walked round and a knobbly hillside path connects their northern ends.

At Betws-y-Coed, numerous forest trails lead up to unseen lakes, and a string of craft galleries, eating places and those ubiquitous woollen shops part summer hordes from their cash. Even in deepest winter, any reversion to the sleepy, grey-stone village it once was is only grudgingly conceded. The A5 is its lifeline, joining other roads and a confluence of angling rivers at Snowdonia's threshold.

But first, a five-mile sidestep south-west on the A470 will bring you under the stark square tower of Dolwyddelan Castle, reached on foot from a roadside car park. It was the fall in 1283 of this strategically crucial Welsh stronghold, built by Llewelyn the Great in about 1200, that gave Edward I command of the Conwy valley. The castle's upper parts were robustly reconstructed during the nineteenth century, and the gaunt cliff-top ruin still exudes impregnability. There are fine views from the battlements, and an exhibition is housed in the tower.

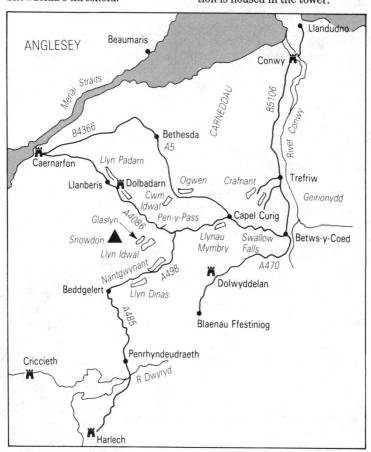

On the slow climb past Swallow Falls to Capel Curig, a majestic view of Moel Siabod is quickly surpassed by comprehensive panoramas over the region's highest tops. Capel Curig's equipment shops and friendly café serve the year-round outdoor fraternity, while just down the road, on the banks of Llynau Mymbyr, Wales's National Centre for Mountain Activities runs courses in more than fifty different activities.

Five miles ahead, beside Thomas Telford's London-to-Anglesey highway between the Glyder and Carneddau massifs, lies Llyn Ogwen. From the fisherman's path on the northern shore of this lake, the rearing bulk of Tryfan peak is seen to its best effect.

Before plunging down the Nant Ffrancon valley to the coast, park near the youth hostel at Ogwen Cottage and take the rocky path to Cwm Idwal, Wales's first National Nature Reserve. Few short walks are as richly rewarding (though in 1778, Thomas Pennant considered it "a fit place to inspire murderous thoughts, environed with horrible precipices"). You may care to continue on round the lake and moraines, a popular nature trail; Eryri's glacial origins are seen to theatrical effect, from Idwal Slabs to the towering cliffs of Twll Du (Devil's Kitchen) and Y Garn's rugged eastern face.

Wriggling from the mountains' grasp, the A5 delivers you through dour Bethesda; named after one of many slate workers' chapels, it might as readily have been christened "Jerusalem" or "Siloam". Flat lands are reached bordering the Menai Straits, and Caernarfon stands a few miles south-west along the B4366 — an unremarkable market town but with a castle of rare quality.

Designed partly as a fortress for Edward I's second Welsh campaign in 1282-3, and partly as seat of government and official residence, it has been in Crown ownership since its foundation and is the nearest thing to a palace in the entire principality; in July 1969, it saw the investiture as Prince of Wales of HRH Prince Charles. Extensive restoration was begun in the 1840s, intensifying for the investiture of young Prince Edward in 1911 and accounting for today's impeccable state of repair.

From Caernarfon, the A4086 heads back for the hills. Largest of all Eryri's lakes, Llyn Padarn is ringed by a two-hour walk, one of several trails in Padarn Country

Park. Adjacent Llanberis loses its raison d'être with the winter closure of the Snowdon Railway and other attractions.

Across the valley, 700 acres and 2,000 vertical feet of Elidir Fawr mountain were hacked away to satisfy the nineteenth century's burgeoning appetite for roofing slate. Today, invisible behind the naked quarry terraces, a cavern complex of science-fiction dimensions accommodates Europe's largest pumped storage power station.

Thus, Dolbadarn Castle presides over a tract of Welsh landscape more ravaged and reshaped by man than William Turner would have imagined possible when, in 1800, he sketched and painted the 40-foot tower silhouetted against a lowering sky. Once

serving to control the overland route between Caernarfon and the Conwy valley, Dolbadarn Castle's influence is now confined to its grassy knoll. Put up by Llewelyn the Great, its impressive round tower matches those of the southern marches, more English than Welsh.

Grey crags and beetling cliffs beloved of rock climbers hang suspended above skirts of scree and boulders in the Llanberis Pass. Exploration by car inevitably inhibits experience of wild country, but climbing Snowdon in winter conditions is a serious proposition, an option for the experienced only. A compromise, which nevertheless requires respectful attention to the elements, is a foray — two or three miles each way — on the Miners' Track from

Pen-y-Pass car park, which will yield breathtaking views of Yr Wyddfa, Eryri's loftiest summit. The path to Glaslyn, the upper lake, is steeper and increasingly overshadowed by the Stygian east face of Yr Wyddfa; you will get no closer on any footpath without scaling the heights.

From the Pen y Gwryd Hotel, convivial climbers' haunt for more than a century, the A498 descends to the verdantly picturesque valley of Nantgwynant, where a path meanders through woods on Llyn Gwynant's northern shore. Llyn Dinas, further on, featured in the film *Inn of the Sixth Happiness*, and an especially scenic path traces its southern slopes.

Beddgelert was named after Llewelyn the Great's faithful hound, Gelert, mistakenly slain by its master after saving his child from a wolf. There is a suspicion, however, that the story, riverside grave and all, were concocted by a local hotelier to drum up custom. Plentiful accommodation, including an all-year Forestry Commission campsite, make the village a likely weekend stopover.

By following the prettily tortuous A485 to the Pass of Aberglaslyn and thence to Penrhyndeudraeth, you can cross the vowelless Dwyryd River by toll road and sweep south-west along the foothills of Eryri towards the very epitome of medieval military architecture.

Along with those at Beaumaris, Caernarfon and Conwy, Harlech's castle forged the southern link in Edward I's "iron ring", designed to deter all future Welsh resistance. Smaller than Conwy Castle, where this itinerary began, but bearing all the same hallmarks, Harlech's fortress squats massively on a hilltop crag 200 feet above the sandy Morfa.

Today the sea sulks behind dunes a full half-mile away, but during the castle's construction and early role in Welsh history — notably its seizure by Owain Glyndwr in 1404 — sea level was appreciably higher and the garrisons were victualled by ship; access steps still climb from the base of the cliff. Defiant, heroic in conception, Harlech Castle fits our childhood fantasies of knights and derring-do and is remembered when others are forgotten. Eryri, distant now, is a fitting backdrop.

WHERE TO STAY

Bodysgallen Hall Hotel (tel: 0492-84466): off the A470 between Llandudno and Conwy. A luxuriously appointed medieval manor house set in formal gardens and rambling grounds. Full of timeless elegance and superbly equipped, but with homely and comfortable touches too. High season dinner, bed and breakfast, £77 per night for a 3-day stay.

Pen y Gwryd Hotel (tel: 0286-870211): near the A4086/A498 junction 4 miles west of Capel Curig. An informal, down-to-earth mountain hotel, frequented over the years by many climbing and mountaineering celebrities. A welcome refuge, but no frills — strong on atmosphere and used to muddy boots! Open Friday am to Sunday am only during Jan and Feb and closed from Nov-Dec: bed & breakfast £15 per person, dinner £9.50.

WHERE TO EAT

Y Bistro: High Street, Llanberis (tel: 0286-871278). Open 7.30pm to 9.30pm Tuesday to Saturday. Good traditional cooking and many creative dishes too. Facilities for the disabled. Menu about £15. *The Moelwyn Restaurant:* 27/29 Mona Terrace, Criccieth (tel: 0766-522500). Superb local seafood and all facilities for children, from babies upwards. Beautifully situated above Cardigan Bay. Open 12.30pm to 2pm, 7pm to 9.30pm from beginning of March. *Pinnacle Café:* Capel Curig (also Post Office/stores). Warming food and drinks, much patronised by walkers. Open every day 8.30am to 5pm.

WHAT TO DO

By a combination of driving and walking, the winter splendours of Eryri are readily sampled. None of the walks described above is difficult, lengthy or far from roads, but mountain weather is gloriously unpredictable so appropriate clothing and footwear will be needed when following footpaths. Always obtain a forecast (tel: 0286-870120) before venturing into the hills, and err on the side of caution. *Castle Opening Hours:* from October 15 to March 14 the castles open Monday to Saturday 9.30am to 4pm, Sundays 2pm to 4pm; from March 15 to October 14: 9.30am to 6.30pm, Sundays 2pm to 6.30pm. Free entry to all historic sites in the care of CADW for members of Heritage in Wales — details from PO Box 38, Swansea, SA1 1BT, or call Cardiff (0222)-465511. Other nearby castles worth visiting are Criccieth (A497 west of Porthmadog) and Beaumaris (A545 north-east from Menai Bridge on Anglesey).

For residential courses on a wide range of subjects, contact the Snowdonia National Park Study Centre (Plas Tan-y-Bwlch, Maentwrog, Blaenau Ffestiniog, Gwynedd, LL41 3BR; tel: 076685-324) or The National Centre for Mountain Activities (Plas y Brenin, Capel Curig, Gwynedd, LL24 OET; tel: 06904-280/214).

● **Glossary:** *Cwm — a mountain hollow or combe; du (or ddu) — black; eryri — a high land; fawr — large; garn — an eminence; llyn/llynau — lake/lakes; moel — a barren hill; morfa — flat seashore; nant — a brook; pen — a peak or top; twll — a cavern; y (or yr) — the (definite article)*

ACTIVITY HOLIDAYS

Clay Pigeon Shooting

Neil

MacLean

. . . .

WE'LL have you breaking clays in no time," Iain Miller told me. I wasn't quite so sure. My only experience of shooting had involved pulling the trigger of a grease gun pointed at the wheels of an old Morris 1000. As essential maintenance goes, it worked well enough, until the day the car turned right and the wheel went left. I had probably mis-aimed. My eyesight relies on glasses for an accurate focus, but my glasses slide down my nose at moments of intense concentration.

I looked up to Iain Miller. I had to — he's six feet six inches — and when he says it's time to break clays, you gird your loins, or in my case you borrow a pair of green wellingtons and cotton-wool earplugs, and set off with a sense of determination in a spirit of discovery.

A Range Rover was idling purposefully nearby and the staff at Cromlix House (who kept telling me that everything would be all right and would I like another drink?) had packed a Pickwickian hamper, just in case we felt peckish.

Iain's son, Keith, was operating the trap. "And this is a clay," said Iain. I was introduced to a black Frisbee, four inches in diameter, made of coal dust. I understood that I was to hit this with a thirty-inch pattern of shot within forty yards, or my name would be mud. I started practising my new autograph.

Iain showed me the hollow in my shoulder where a twelve-bore is meant to nestle and handed me his gun, while a crowd of bullocks gathered round to watch. The gun seemed extremely heavy, but Iain said a lighter weapon would have a nastier kick, so I pushed my glasses up, pulled the gun in tight, pressed my cheek against the stock, transferred my weight on to the front foot, aimed the thin end above the Ochil Hills — and shouted: "Pull."

The clay flew faster than a Scottish summer. I was meant to follow its line, quickly and smoothly, and strike when it was obscured from view by the barrels of the gun, before it reached its high point. "If you can see the target when you squeeze the trigger, you have missed it," Iain said. He was right.

Something, somewhere, made a

very loud noise and smelt like fireworks. I stood, dazed and disappointed. They say that every bullet has its billet, but my shot was lodged in heaven. I turned to see Iain's eyebrows angled like a teepee and twenty-one bullocks still munching carelessly behind us. By the second shot, the right side of my mouth felt as if I had been to the dentist and the bullocks were bored. "You're snatching at it, Neil," said Iain. Then — "you're stopping on the shot. You have to follow through."

But the sixth shot was like the end of a planet, as tiny asteroids flew in all directions. I felt a lump in my throat and a heavy thumping between my shoulder blades. It was Iain. "Well done now, well done. You did that nice and smoothly." I didn't like to tell him I had closed my eyes.

birds. To Iain, the teal rising was a duck from the marsh. To me, it was a circle of coal dust that danced provocatively in the sky before hiding in the long grass. Like many other people, I am quite content to leave it at that, without graduating to anything that actually squawks or lays eggs.

A driven grouse came over the hill like a flying saucer, while I stopped and started and fired and missed. It seemed I had to reconcile the concepts of taking my time and firing more quickly. To demonstrate, Iain broke the gun, loaded, called "pull", took a casual puff on his cigarette, snapped the gun, raised it, fired and broke the clay as it was rising.

But I chipped away (sometimes literally) and after half an hour, I broke five clays in succession. Iain clasped my hand and shook it

The eighth clay went from dust to dust, and the eleventh flew out in a crazy pattern. "No clay," Iain shouted, which made me jump and blow the rest of the errant target clear out of the sky. I began to warm to my task.

"Now, we'll try the driven grouse," said Iain. The trap discharges clays in ways intended to imitate the flight of different

warmly. "I'm standing in a cow-pat, Iain," I said. "Well, they do say it's lucky." Then, to stop me from becoming over-confident, he called for pairs — two together, like an invasion from Mars.

"Now I know what you'll do here, Neil," he said. "You will miss the first and break the second." I shouted "pull", fired and broke the first. In my surprise I relaxed my grip on the gun and fired the second shot. Something hit me on the shoulder like a sledgehammer. I never saw the second clay as I spun round and round on my cowpat, cursing. "Now, you *know* what you did there," said Iain, and I glared at him, both barrels blazing.

Whoever said you should get back on a horse after you have fallen off, should have kept her opinions to herself. Iain made me reload (gingerly), move forward (hesitantly) and shoot away (in pain), until I was back into the swing of things, hitting one clay out of four. Not brilliant, I admit, but at least I finished on an upbeat — a particularly satisfying hit that tattooed the sky with

parabolas of shrapnel.

Iain grinned and handed me a clay engraved by the Clay Pigeon Preservation Society. A little cruel, I thought, but looking round, the hillside *was* studded with enough virgin clays to build a dovecote.

Back at Cromlix House, I ran a bath filled with what looked like herbal tea bags and lowered myself, gently, to the point of my chin. I had enjoyed my clay pigeon shooting, and, although I had a bruise on my shoulder the colour and the size of an aubergine, I felt a sense of elation and utter peace.

It was ten minutes before I found that I still had my ear plugs in.

HOTELS

Cromlix House (tel: 0786-822125) one of our best country-house hotels. Part of an estate that stretches north of Dunblane for about 5,000 acres, the house was built in 1880 and much of it remains unchanged. There is a recently renovated Edwardian conservatory for afternoon teas and a comfortable old library, with leather chairs and velvet cushions, for post-prandial contemplation. The young chef, Mark Salter, creates some inspired dishes, while the rest of the staff make you feel that nothing could be too much trouble. A single room with private bathroom, morning tea and Scottish breakfast costs £75 per night, and a double room costs £110. The 6-course dinner costs £30.

Many other hotels offer clay pigeon shooting weekends. *The Watersmeet Hotel*, Mortehoe, Woolacombe, Devon (tel: 0271-870333) advertises a shooting weekend of 2 nights, dinner, bed, breakfast and shooting in spring and autumn. *The Wildercome House Hotel*, Ilfracombe (tel: 0271-62240) offers 3 nights for £67 per person, shooting £10 per 100 clays, and at the Gleneagles Hotel, Auchterarder (tel: 0764-62231), it costs from £220 per person.

For more information, contact the *Loch Lomond, Stirling and Trossachs Tourist Board* (tel: 0786-75019) which has a comprehensive list of hotels, guest houses, farmhouses and cottages.

SHOOTING

Clay pigeon shooting isn't cheap and has to be booked in advance. At Cromlix, individual instruction is by the hour (inclusive of trap, 100 clays and cartridges) costs £45 and is organised by *Kingfisher Field Sports* (tel: 0786-814805). Group shooting at Cromlix costs £824 for a full day for 10 people and includes tuition, morning coffee, lunch, wine and tea. Most people have their first shot at clay pigeons in a club. There are more than 1,000 clay pigeon shooting clubs in Britain. To find your nearest, contact the *Clay Pigeon Shooting Association* (tel: 01-505 6221), the *Scottish Clay Pigeon Association* (tel: 0877-31323), the *Welsh Clay Target Association* (tel: 06462-3076) or the *Ulster Clay Pigeon Association* (tel: 0247-463153).

RESTAURANTS

Broughton's: near Blair Drummond; features local specialities and home-grown produce. Dinner (veal and apricot pâté, perhaps followed by lamb in a lemon cream sauce and a dessert) costs a reasonable £16.25, while Sunday lunch is a downright bargain at £9.15.

EXCURSIONS

Stirling Castle: a famous landmark — seat of the Stuart kings and BBC's *Colditz*. Down the hill, in Broad Street, there is a medieval market during the summer, and at the *MacRobert Arts Centre*, within the university campus, there is a year-round programme of concerts and drama. The *Smith Art Gallery* is also worth a visit. You can see seven famous battlefields from the top of the *Wallace Monument*, including Bannockburn, where there is also an excellent heritage centre. *Bridge of Allan* was a popular Victorian spa town, and now hosts the *Strathallan Highland Games*. Further north, Scotland's smallest city, *Dunblane*, boasts a 13th-century cathedral and the Dunblane Hydro Hotel, where you can jig an eightsome reel to Jim McLeod and his Dance Band.

Fly-fishing

*James
Adams*

. . . .

IT IS a perfect, balmy evening, the kind that brings with it a brief glimpse of the long, languid summer to come. The dying rays of the sun glance through the branches of the trees overhanging the river and in the orange light reflected off the water, insects dance — appetising morsels for the passing swallows.

Under the branches of an overhanging willow, a large fish lurks. Every few minutes its shape can be dimly discerned as it rises, with a gentle flick of its tail, to pluck out of the surface film an appetising fly. For the brown trout, this is the busiest time of day, when it must pack away a full evening meal before night falls.

The line curves back from the fishing rod in a perfect arc. The rod flexes and then, in a masterpiece of co-ordination between hand, eye and instinct, the forearm brings the rod back at the exact moment that its power can be used to push the line out and bring the fly at its end to land perfectly, without a ripple, just upstream of the waiting trout.

Suddenly, the fish bites, the rod bends and the line streams out from the reel as the fish dives deep. Several minutes later, after a struggle between man and fish that requires the skill of experience to outweigh the excitement of the moment, the fish lands in the net and is brought triumphantly back to the bank.

Well, that is how I had always been told it should work. But here I was standing in the river with no fish visible. My perfect co-ordination had resulted in a line tangled in the branches of a tree above my head and the second of my flies was about to join the ravel of lines already tied in the same branch. But, above all, there was the rain, slanting across the water, cutting visibility to a few yards and trickling down my neck to invade every pore of my very cold body.

Clearly, I had discovered the other side of fishing that, for some reason, fishermen never seem to talk about.

This was all part of my attempt to join the 750,000 anglers — out of a total four million in Britain — who prefer to fish with the fly rather than a lure such as maggots or worms. To its proponents, fly-fishing is close to an art form and other fishermen are referred to, rather disdainfully, as "coarse fishermen".

In the past, fly-fishing has been an elitist sport. Nearly all British rivers are private and the privilege of their fishing rights has been restricted by landowners to their friends or those with fat cheque books. However, in recent years there has been something of a revolution among fishing folk. The growth of fishing clubs and, in particular, the development of reservoirs as a resource has allowed a broader cross-section of society to join the fly-fishing fraternity. At the same time, more women are fishing.

To meet this demand, several special courses have become available. Like so many sports, fishing is surrounded by arcane rules, a new language and a complicated technique that few master — even after years of practice.

Undaunted, I chose a course run by the Arundell Arms, in Lifton on the edge of Dartmoor in Devon. The hotel has more than twenty miles of fishing on nearby rivers, as well as a three-acre lake. Two instructors — Roy Buckingham, a former Welsh Open Fly-Fishing Champion who has taught more than 8,000 anglers, and David Pilkington, his assistant — provided the tuition. The author and journalist Conrad Voss-Bark, whose wife Anne runs the hotel, lectures about fishing lore and provides early lessons on safety.

My course began with an alarming piece of information: apparently, three people were killed in Wales last year when their lines caught in overhead power cables (the new graphite rods are excellent conductors). Most valuable of the early instruction was how to remove a fly-hook from flesh without pain (press down hard on the hook, loop a piece of string around the curve and pull hard).

The principle of fly-fishing is to send a line (the cast) out on to the water with a lure (the fly) on the end; the latter will, with luck, land near the circle of water that marks the spot where a trout has come to the surface to eat (the rise).

With his flies, the fisherman will attempt to imitate the stages of a fly's life from the nymph, on or near the river bottom, through the hatch and back to when the fly returns to the water once again to lay its eggs. That final moment marks the beginning of the fishing season, the end of the winter fast for the fish and the moment when the water can literally boil as the fish fight for the mayfly. This highlight in the fisherman's calendar should occur sometime in May.

The two most common forms of fly-fishing are wet, when the fly sinks to just below the surface film, and dry, when the fly sits on the water. It is the latter that is the most difficult as it requires precision casting of the fly to a particular fish. Also, because the best dry-fly water is frequently a chalk stream, it is gin clear and the slightest disturbance can scare the quarry. Imagine, then, casting a line that weighs practically nothing, with a fly on the end about an eighth of an inch long and weighing even less, in a perfect line to land about thirty feet away in a circle the size of a soup plate. It is not easy.

The goal is to catch either a brown or rainbow trout. Both my instructors made the movement of the rod and line appear as one fluid motion. But for the beginner, the line invariably lands with a lumpen splash several feet short of the target, sending a thunderous vibration through the water to scare off even the most insensitive of fish.

During the four-day course, the pupil is taught not only how to cast but also the various knots needed to attach fly to line. In addition, a brief introduction is made to the colourful world of the artificial fly, of which there are dozens of varieties with such wonderful names as Bloody Butcher, Woolly Bugger and the Pale Watery.

My fellow course members were a mixed bunch that included a butter maker from Wales and a coarse fisherman and his wife who wanted to try something better. After the first day the stories in the bar began: in fact, as much time seems to be spent in reminiscing on what might have been and talking of what is to come as on actually fishing.

By the second morning huddled figures could be seen sliding off in the morning mist to try and catch the breakfast.

My weekend away coincided with dramatic events in various parts of the world, but they disturbed not one jot the even tenor of our pleasure. At the start of the weekend, the prospect of several days flogging the water presented a challenge in simply surviving the boredom. In fact, hours pass in what seem like minutes, the world telescopes into a simple competition between angler and trout.

At last, after hours of thrashing the water to a froth, scaring the fish and catching the trees, the cast begins to resemble a more skilful movement, if not the caress it is supposed to be.

The cast that finally won the fish was not noticeably different from its predecessors and the fly was just one of several tried that afternoon. The strike took me totally by surprise. Suddenly the rod came alive as the fish – a record weight, surely — first dived deep under the surface and then leapt out of the water in an acrobatic display that both thrilled with its beauty and terrified with the prospect that it might break the line. The rod, designed to flex under strain, bent at the top as I wound in to take up the slack and then allowed the fish to draw out the line as it wanted. The fight, so often a triumph for the wily fish, was eventually won and a magnificent three-pound rainbow drawn into the net.

I have already reserved my fishing days for the summer. The monster awaits.

PLACES TO GO

The Arundell Arms: Lifton, Devon PL16 0AA (tel: 0566-84666). Beginners; river/lake; 4-day trout fly-fishing course; £165 for adults and £110 for children under 16, including VAT. Hotel charges excluded.

The Rod Box: Winchester, Hampshire (tel: 0962-61561). Individual lessons in dry-fly and salmon fishing; £25 for 2 hours.

Wessex Fly Fishing School: Lawrences Farm, Tolpuddle, Dorset DT2 7HF (tel: 0305-848460). Non-residential or residential course at £7 per hour plus VAT, or from 1 to 4 days (1 day course costs £62).

The Royal Hotel: Llangollen (tel: 0978-860202): has a fly-fishing weekend with instruction on May 6-8 for £159 per person for 2 nights, including half board.

The Tweed Valley Hotel: Walkerburn, Borders, Scotland (tel: 089687-220). Guests may buy permits to fish for brown trout and grayling on more than 30 miles of the river and its tributaries. Salmon beats are also available. *Trout:* April-end Sept. *Salmon:* Mar-June and Sept-end Nov.

Pony Trekking

*Justine
Picardie*

. . . .

MY FRIEND Neill vehemently protested: "I'm not going pony trekking with you, and that's final. The last time I went, I was thirteen, and a vicious pony tried to kill me on the Black Mountains." The murderous beast in question "leaned" on him as they were trudging up a hill together — or so he claims. But spurred on by the memories of happy equine excursions during my childhood, my will prevailed — and we set off for a jolly weekend in Abergavenny.

We arrived late one Friday afternoon, and were welcomed by a rainbow over the River Usk and a host of daffodils on its banks, and in time for a walk around the town which is called "the gateway to Wales". Its main attraction is the ruined Norman castle, where wicked William de Braose murdered his fellow Welsh chieftains in the twelfth century.

Then we settled into our hotel, the Angel, a comfortable old coaching inn in the town centre. After dinner (large quantities of homely food served by motherly waitresses who urge you to eat your vegetables before they produce delicious puddings), we adjourned to the Foxhunter Bar, where the barmaid is also last year's mayoress. (Abergavenny, being an egalitarian town, has just elected the Angel's day porter as mayor.)

Encouraged by horsey decor in the bar I took the precaution of reading *Pony Trekking for All* by J. Kerr Hunter, in preparation for the following day's exertions. Apparently the author coined the phrase pony trekking — which started in the early 1950s — after being inspired by a South African friend singing happy Afrikaans trekking songs.

Neill, however, remained unconvinced: "I think I'll go for a walk instead." (He was, nevertheless, interested in the chapter entitled An Icelandic Interlude, which revealed that the Icelanders ate their ponies if they were not sturdy enough for trekking across frozen wastes.)

On Saturday morning we ate grilled kippers and poached eggs, and then poked around Abergavenny's many junk shops. Back at the hotel at noon we met the manager, a charming gentleman from Cork, Frank MacCarthy, who escorted us the fourteen miles

137

from Abergavenny to the Grange at Capel-y-ffin, where the Griffiths family have organised pony trekking since 1957.

Clearly, with the hotel manager in attendance — not to mention a photographer and sixteen schoolchildren about to go on separate expeditions — there was no going back. "I want a quiet horse," said Neill, "one that doesn't lean on me if I lead it up mountains." He was duly allocated Wildfire, a placid bay with very large feet, and I was introduced to Lemon, a solid-looking piebald mare. And after capable instructions from nineteen-year-old Marieanne Griffiths, we mounted our steeds, without getting on backwards or slipping off the other side.

There was a rather strange swaying sensation to begin with, as the ponies set off in line like a camel train. Lemon picked her way up the side of the hill with practised guile, leaving me free to enjoy the scenery of the Vale of Ewyas.

All went well until one little girl in our party of six fell off her pony, Peggy (probably because she screamed and dropped her reins when the pony started moving faster than a stately pace). But she was scooped up, unhurt, by Marieanne and put back in the saddle without further mishap. (There have been no serious accidents at the Grange, although some time ago one poor man was knocked unconscious while still mounted, when he leant forward at the same time as the pony threw its head back.)

The ride took just under three hours across the sweeping hills of the Black Mountains, passing spectacular waterfalls and undulating swathes of heather. We had an occasional trot, and, reverting to my teenage enthusiasms, I was allowed a quick canter while the others stood sedately to one side. Everyone looked happy — including the girl who had said she hated horses, much to her mother's dismay, at the start of the ride — and Neill declared the whole experience to be "wonderful", even though Wildfire had stepped on his foot.

Back at the hotel we ate an enormous cream tea, and I promptly fell asleep until dinner, when it was time for more food. The nice thing about pony trekking is that you don't have to walk anywhere, but it is energetic enough to make you feel virtuously healthy; large dinners are, therefore, entirely justified.

On Sunday morning, the rain cleared to reveal another beautiful rainbow, a perfect half-circle over the River Honddu that runs through the Vale of Ewyas. My mother had decided to come pony trekking too, but with even more reluctance than Neill had shown.

"I prefer my pet sheep," she said, looking at the ponies with some doubt. "And if I manage to get on a horse, I don't want it to canter. It's simply got to walk." And walk it did, stolidly, up the ridge of Darren Llwyd. This time we went out trekking with another family, who had come for the weekend from London, obviously for the benefit of their little girl: her face shone with enthusiasm throughout the ride, but her dad Barry was not so keen. "I'd prefer it to have a steering wheel and a hand brake," he said. His wife was more enthusiastic, even after her pony decided to have a roll on top of the Twyma mountain before she had time to get off.

The wind blew hard, but the sun was out, and the views magnificent across to the Wye valley and the Brecon Beacons. Marieanne fortified us with peppermints and I crooned quietly to Lemon about the joys of spring, while she flicked her ears back in a friendly way. Even Barry looked cheerful, and my mother announced she was definitely returning.

It is not difficult to see why pony trekking at the Grange is so popular: the forty-odd ponies are obviously well cared for and the treks are gentle enough for the most timid beginners while offering more experienced riders the chance to canter across beautiful countryside.

"We get people here from all walks of life," says Dai Griffiths, a stalwart of the Pony Trekking and Riding Society of Wales. "One chap comes here from London regularly. He works for a sausage factory — and he loves pony trekking, because it's so different."

And it is not just an eccentrically British pastime: one week last summer, recalls Mr Griffiths, "We had two Chinese, seven Greeks, a couple of Danes, a Dutchman and a Californian chap — as well as a family from Kuwait, who said they had a lovely holiday in the mist and rain, because it was such a change." The Grange also caters for a wide age range: from five-year-old children whose ponies are led on short rides, to elderly people who have never been riding before, including an eighty-two-year-old woman who came with her three daughters. I would happily go again; and in the meantime I am investigating the possibility of riding in Hyde Park. Either that, or selling up and returning to the Black Mountains with a horse named Lemon.

● Further details from The Pony Trekking and Riding Society of Wales, 32 North Parade, Aberystwyth, Dyfed, SY23 2NF. Also from the British Horse Society, Stoneleigh, Kenilworth, Warwickshire, CV8 2LR. Pony trekking weekends are available from Trusthouse Forte's *Angel Hotel*, Cross Street, Abergavenny from £106 per person for 2 nights, including accommodation, breakfast, dinner and a minimum of 2 hours of pony trekking a day (tel: 0873-7121). There is also accommodation at the *Grange* in Capel-y-ffin, tel: 0873-890215. Two nights' accommodation, breakfast, dinner and 2 full days trekking for £61 per person. THF runs trekking weekends in other parts of the country. For information tel: 01-567 3444.

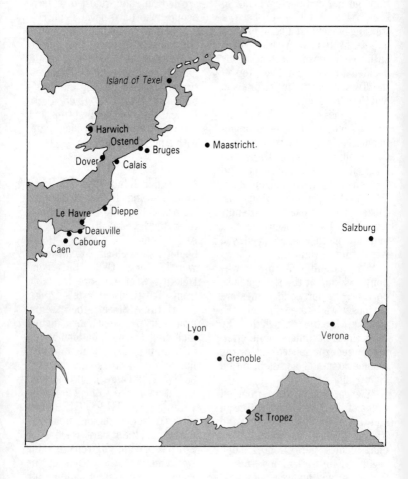

Island of Texel •

Harwich •
Ostend
Dover • • Bruges
Calais

• Maastricht.

Le Havre • Dieppe
Deauville
Caen • • Cabourg

Salzburg •

Lyon •
Verona •

Grenoble •

St Tropez

ABROAD

Salzburg

Bruges

David
Wickers

. . . .

WEEKEND or not, you won't sleep late in Bruges. At 7am the baritone chimes of Notre Dame, along with lighter more orchestral peals from the Belfry, penetrate even the downiest of hotel duvets.

But there is plenty to get up for. Bruges is the best-preserved medieval city in Europe and the obvious way to put your mind in a Middle Age mood is from the back of a horse-drawn carriage, swaddled under a blanket.

Let the bowler-hatted driver, his face a hybrid of Benny Hill and a bulbous root vegetable, guide you beside lime and willow-shaded canals, over hump-back bridges and along cobblestoned alleyways lined with fine gabled houses, merchants' mansions, ornate guildhalls and other spoils of the city's ancient trade.

Today's high state of preservation was not a deliberate act of mothballing. In the twelfth and thirteenth centuries Bruges was the most important commercial centre in Europe, its harbour a vital crossroad between the Mediterranean and the Baltic. The gradual silting up of the River Zwin spelt commercial doom. With the dramatic decline in their income, the city burghers could not afford to refurbish. Little did they realise their unintended neglect would prove the city's greatest asset.

Today, Brugeans can't even put a lick of paint on their front door without getting a chitty from the town hall.

Bruges is a small town packed with big-town distractions, all of which lie within an easy stroll of each other. The heart of the city is the Belfry, a medieval skyscraper that looks down on the Grote Markt like a gangly adolescent. For a full assault from the Belfry's forty-seven-bell carillon, climb to the top of its 366 steps and watch the gnome-like campanologist thrash out Vivaldi, Mozart and Bach on a wooden keyboard. The floor vibrates, your eardrums retreat to the inner sanctum of your boots and you half expect the town below to gyrate about the Belfry's base like a giant glockenspiel.

Architecturally, Bruges is one of the richest cities in Europe. From the Markt walk down Breidelstraat through a gauntlet of lace shops and into the Burg, a surprisingly harmonious square despite its catalogue of architectural styles, ranging from twelfth-century Romanesque to twentieth-century shopping arcade. They call Bruges the Venice of the north (though Brugeans would argue that Venice is the Bruges of the south) on account of its girdles of silent, lacquer-black, tree-shaded canals. In fact the gabled houses make it more a miniature Amsterdam, while other parts imitate the grace of the Cambridge Backs.

Save time, in between strolls, for indoor Bruges. There are several museums on the Dyver: the most interesting are the Gruuthuse, which shows what life was like for the well-fed merchants of old, and the Groeninge, which houses works by Memling, Van Eyck, Breughel and Bosch. Many more Memlings are displayed in the thirteenth-century St John's Hospital whose retired wards also exhibit a gruesome display of early surgical instruments.

At night, beyond the floodlit squares and grander edifices that burn like bonfires, the medieval fairy-tale takes an eerie turn.

Down crooked passages lurk imagined evils and grotesque deformities. You dive into a bar, a cosy, candlelit haven warmed by a pot-bellied stove and order a beer. "Which one?" the stocky barman wonders. "We have 265 varieties."

Time for dinner. There are some thirty Michelin-rated restaurants, more per square mile than any other provincial city in Europe. A longer holiday may seriously damage your health.

HOW TO GET THERE

By air: scheduled services from Heathrow (also Gatwick, Luton, Stansted, London City and Manchester) to Brussels (50 minutes, cheapest fare from £81 plus £5 Belgian tax). Take the shuttle train to Brussels's miserable Central Railway Station (15 minutes, half-hourly service) then change for Bruges (1 hour, half-hourly service).

By sea: via Calais, followed by a 1½-hour drive. Zeebrugge, the nearest port, is served by North Sea Ferries from Hull, and P&O from Felixstowe and Dover. Jetfoil runs from Dover to Ostend.

Packages: Travelscene (tel: 01-935 1025) has 2 nights from £109 to £220, depending on hotel and whether you opt for ferry, Jetfoil or flight. Other mini-break operators include: Belgian Travel Service (tel: 0920-461171), Winter Inn (tel: 065382-741) and Time Off (tel: 01-235 8070).

HOW TO GET AROUND

The railway station is a 5- to 10-minute taxi ride south of the centre (£4). Horse-drawn carriages can be hired from the Burg (£8 for 40 minutes) and take up to 5 people. Open boats cruise the canals March-October picking up from 5 points (£2 for 35 mins). Sit-up-and-beg bicycles and tandems for hire at the railway station and from Het Koffieboontje beside the Belfry (about £4 a day). If you go to Bruges by car you won't need it in town since everything is within walking distance. There are 4 modern underground car parks, well signposted.

WHAT TO SEE

Burg Square: a span of interesting buildings including a 12th-century Romanesque basilica housing the "relic of the Holy Blood", a fragment of cloth once soaked in the blood of Christ and brought back by one Derick of Alsace on the Second Crusade. The Town Hall has a remarkable Gothic Hall.

Grote Markt: Bruges is Belgium with a Flemish accent thanks to its two heroes, Jan Breydel and Pieter de Coninck, who sent the French packing at the Battle of the Golden Spurs and whose statues have pride of place in the Markt. Belfry carillons can be heard on Wednesday, Saturday and Sunday in winter (Oct-June) around 2pm-3pm; 9pm-10pm on Monday, Wednesday and Saturday in summer.

Church of Our Lady: on the Dyver, the church contains Michelangelo's white marble Madonna and Child, a rare example of his work to leave Italy.

Beguinage Convent: crenellated, Munchkin-like houses, the home of Benedictine nuns who scurry across the daffodil lawns to chapel dressed in 15th-century habits.

WHERE TO STAY

Navarra: Napoleon nearly slept here (they built a fancy swan staircase for the occasion but he didn't show up). Formerly a 17th-century palace of princes, restored in 1983. Central but quiet and characterful. Moderate prices. St Jacobsstraat (tel: 34 05 61). *De Orangerie:* hard on a canal and one of the best in town. Breakfast on the terrace. Expensive. Kartuizerinnenstraat (tel: 34 16 49). *Pandhotel:* old burgher's house. Moderate. Pandreitje (tel: 34 06 66). *Astrid:* simple clean rooms in quiet family house. Inexpensive. Stalijzerstraat (tel: 34 07 52).

LUNCH

Even the chips, topped with a blob of mayonnaise and sold from a pair of green potting sheds on wheels in the Markt, are a gastronomic experience. Breydel de Coninck on Breidelstraat is the place for mussels brewed in an onion and celery sauce and brought to the table in a cooking pan the size of a bucket. With beer, salad, chips and coffee. £8. Bruno's Passage on Dweerstraat is arty and alternative with good Flemish specials, including *hutsepot* (hot pot). Inexpensive.

DINNER

Two brave newcomers on the crowded scene, opened within the last year and still awaiting their (inevitable) Michelin accolades are: Huyze die Maene, the "house of the moon", owned by chef Jean Dante. Highly elaborate dishes and a magnificent view of the floodlit Markt. About £45 a head with wine (tel: 33 39 59); and Patrick Provoost, with an excellent menu de saison for £25 including wine, a gastronomic at £40; superb wine list.

Ezelstraat (tel: 33 64 65). Others include 't Bourgoensche Cruyce, an ancient canalside building, Wollestraat (tel: 33 79 26); De Visscherie in the fish market specialises in *waterzooi*, fish stew (tel: 33 02 12).

BARS AND NIGHTLIFE

One and the same, the loudest being around the Eiermarkt. Several feature music, ranging from wandering minstrels at Bruno's to wall-to-wall Sixties records and renegades at De Doordrinker on Oostmeers. More cosy and candlelit retreats include De Garre, down a shoulder-width passage off Breidelstraat (try a "white of Bruges" on tap with a head as tall as a topper). 't Brugs Beertje on Kemelstraat is the one with the 265 varieties, and Jantje van Pardoens on the Walplein a Flemish Rovers Return.

SHOPS

Irresistible chocolate shops including Sukerbuyk ("Sugar belly") on Katelijnestraat, Sweetvaegher on Philipstockstraat and Venerande on Steenstraat, the main shopping artery. The place for lace is Breidelstraat, with 10 shops, as well as De Mulder Danneels on Wollestraat and the Lace School in Santa Anna — however, since lace is mostly imported from the Orient it is important to look for the yellow star, the authentic Belgian trademark. Other interesting shops include Retro, full of Flemish attic oddities, on Eekhoutstraat; Marie Brat for thick kaleidoscopic sweaters and hand-spun wool, on Walstraat; Deldycke, the best deli, on Wollestraat; and Anne Perneel, a potter on Genthof. And don't forget the Dyver, a fine-weather weekend market for bric-à-brac. Currency: roughly 60 Belgian francs (BF) to the pound.

EXCURSIONS

The surrounding polder scenery is dull beyond belief. Ostend and other seasides are only 30 minutes away by car. Canal boats to the pretty village of Damme, north of Bruges, operate May-September (5 trips a day). Or cycle along the towpath (or skate along the canal in the worst of winters).

BEDSIDE READING

Bruges Inside Out: on sale in hotels, restaurants, shops, packed with info, 250BF (about £4). Plus two free sheets: *Agenda* from the tourist office and *hitkrank*, the "alternative" version, from bars.

INFORMATION

Tourist office can be found in Burg Square. In the UK write to Bruges Tourism News Bureau, PO Box 172, Petham, Canterbury, Kent CT4 5SZ.

Cabourg

Alan
Tillier

. . . .

MIDWAY between the D-Day beaches in Normandy and the Paris-by-sea that is Deauville, there stands one of France's most incongruous "palaces", as the French call their grand hotels.

It dominates the small (3,300 inhabitants), pleasantly somnolent resort of Cabourg. At any time of the year, one can sit in the large hall, which runs the length of the hotel from the main door to the beach promenade, and watch an extraordinary parade of ancient counts and faded duchesses from the enfeebled but still existent French aristocracy. "*La voiture de madame la duchesse est avancée,*" announces the doorman-cum-car parker.

Meanwhile, young Parisian yuppies, some newly wed, anxiously ask if room 414, fourth floor, *côté mer*, is free. Earnest American professors sit in the easy chairs clutching thick tomes. This summer Esther Williams was invited by the town "as a symbol of romanticism". She asked for the lights above the reception desk to be dimmed — out of consideration.

What we were witnessing, here in this little town, was the birth of a tourist "industry" which exists by kind permission of a ghost, that of the great French writer Marcel Proust, whose gargantuan novel, *A la Recherche du Temps Perdu*, has come to be regarded as one of the century's masterpieces and who used Cabourg and its pre-1914 society of often atrocious aristocrats as the model for the mythical town of Balbec in the book.

Proust was fascinated by the Grand Hotel at Cabourg, although his fascination sometimes took the form of a love-hate relationship. The hate part, based on Proust's abhorrence of noise (waiters tiptoed past him), has been conveniently pushed under the carpets by the Pullman-Wagons Lits group which leases the Grand from the town.

The room Proust normally occupied and where he spent his days in virtual darkness, writing usually in bed, venturing out to the casino at night, was redone in 1988 and is now heavily booked with prices ranging from £74 a night in the low season, November 1 to March 30, £87 in the so-called middle season, March 31 to June 15 and September 17 to October

145

31, and £100 in high season, June 16 to September 16.

The room today is not exactly as it was in Proust's time, namely the summers between 1907 and 1914. Proust had the maids pin the curtains in such a way that not a chink of natural light entered the room (for four summers he practically never left the hotel, dining late and alone in the huge, ornate restaurant and then playing heavily at baccarat in the adjoining casino).

Today, room 414 is somewhat brighter than his sombre world as he wrote the symbolic story of his life. Still, the overall style and atmosphere have been recaptured — the mauve and violet decor, the big *début de siècle* bed with its ornate, copper-topped headboard lined with material painted to resemble wood, *belle époque* bedside lamps, Proust's writing table and parquet flooring.

As for the clients, the manager of the Grand divides them into two categories: "There are the true *nostalgiques* of Proust who want to plunge into his world and the decor of the past and those who, perhaps, have not read Proust but who want to tell their friends, 'I slept in Proust's bed.'"

Anyway, Cabourg, which has had considerable swings in its fortunes as a resort since it was built by two Paris financiers in 1853, is playing the Proust card to the full. What is exploited is a nostalgia tinged with the romanticism attached to the writer who was normally dressed even in the height of summer in a thick cape with violet lining and who wore several pullovers under his dinner jacket. The town has also organised a romantic film festival. It seems to have captured some of the romantic business of neighbouring Deauville which exploited the romantic angle for years in the wake of the Claude Lelouch film *Un Homme et Une Femme*, but which has now decided to give itself a touch of Atlantic City with its newly installed slot machines.

Proust first went to Cabourg as a child of ten to alleviate his asthma. At that time, just before the turn of the century, Cabourg was an unreal spread of villas grouped in a semicircle around the Grand Hotel. Today, the pattern is the same, although there is now a busy little main street and a mile-long Marcel Proust Promenade.

When Proust returned in later years to remember and write ("those seaside holidays when grandmother and I, lost in one another, walked battling with the wind and talking"), he likened the Grand Hotel to a vast aquarium filled with strange fish. He often complained, but never chose to stay anywhere else.

As Proust's biographer, George Painter, points out: "Throughout his life it was only in the theatrical but intensely real environments of a luxury hotel, a society drawing room or a great restaurant that he could feel at ease away from his own bedroom ... for around him was the delightful and appalling spectacle of Alfred Edwards, the gross, shady, Anglo-Levantine proprietor of *Le Matin*; his mistress, the lesbian actress Lantelme; his fifth, recently separated wife, Misia Godebska; a previous wife, Mme Ralli; the Antarctic explorer Charcot, ex-husband of another ex-wife of

Edwards; and Misia's first husband Thadée Natanson, one of Proust's editors, all pretending not to notice one another's presence. One evening the heartening rumour circulated that Misia had shot Edwards stone dead; but next morning, alas, he was to be seen in the best of health. Proust watched the menagerie around him with relish and entered into its curious pleasures."

Today's newspaper proprietors pale by comparison and this world of Proust's was swept away by the First World War. Still, when there's a Proust celebration, a highly unusual crowd takes the Friday night train from Paris (the only direct connection: otherwise it's Paris-Caen and then a bus). There is a worldwide Société des Amis de Marcel Proust and the members give the impression that they had tea with Proust last week. Its president is the Marquise de Puységur (born Dominique Mante-Proust, a branch of the great man's family although obviously not a direct descendant of the homosexual writer). There are Maurice Schumann, former French foreign minister and now in the Académie Française, the Duchesse Edmée de la Rochefoucauld, the Comte Jean d'Ormesson and other aristocrats, plus a heavy contingent of American scholars. When these people gather at the Grand ... well you can feel that Marcel himself might step through the door.

Today, the hotel still has only sixty-eight rooms and two suites. It has a good, no frills restaurant (Proust normally would descend at 9.30pm when the place was empty) with *turbot braisé aux poireaux et aux pommes, matelote au cidre, canard aux fruits.* Menus from £15 to £21.

THE HOTEL
Grand Hotel: Cabourg, Calvados (tel: 31 91 01 79). Prices range from £52 low season to £160 high season for a vast suite. Breakfast £6. Dogs: £9.

GETTING THERE
Britanny Ferries (tel: 0705-827701) from Portsmouth to Ouistreham, less than 10 miles from Cabourg. Crossing: 6 hours.

THINGS TO DO
People watching: Bruno Coquatrix, late owner of the Olympia music hall in Paris (the French Palladium) and promoter of Edith Piaf, was mayor of Cabourg and rescued it from near oblivion after the war. The town is still favoured by French show business stars who want something quieter than the bright lights of Deauville 12 miles to the east. The impresario had a mania for "twinning" Cabourg with towns all over the world, including Salcombe, and his Maison des Cités Unies is a kind of hotel-cum-cultural centre filled with tourists and artistes from all over.

EXCURSIONS
Right next door is Dives where William the Conqueror embarked with his army in 1066. The one-time port is now silted up, but in the Notre Dame de Dives Church is a wall bearing the name of William's companions. Many have a familiar ring. Bayeux and its famous tapestry is some way to the west as are the D-Day beaches with the D-Day Museum — and the remains of the artificial Mulberry port — at Arromanches. The city of Caen, 20 miles inland from Cabourg, now has its own D-Day and Peace Museum, Un Musée Pour La Paix, to which British and Americans contributed money, which was opened by President Mitterrand last June 6, D-Day. The museum covers world events before, during and after the Second World War and is rich in films, photos and music. It's open daily (in the summer to 10pm, the winter to 7pm with later opening Friday to 10pm. Entrance: 30 francs).

Deauville is packed with Parisians during the season. Whereas Cabourg is still banking on quiet elegance and literary nostalgia, Deauville has just installed 240 one-armed bandits in the opulent casino and imported English lady croupiers.

Dieppe

Lailan Young

. . . .

O
F ALL the French Channel ports, Dieppe is the most welcoming, the most intimate. The ferry boats are not berthed a wasteland away from town, but are allowed to slip right into the urban heart and tie up alongside a quay full of cheerful restaurants and brasseries, in view of the town arcades, and at the mouth of the principal shopping street.

Dieppe is not only a passenger and fishing harbour (specialising in sole, scallops and the finer sorts of fish) and a commercial port (importing bananas, exporting timber) but also France's oldest seaside resort, the beach closest to Paris. It has appearances to keep up.

The harbour entrance is hidden away at the eastern end of almost a mile of steeply banked pebble beaches and a grassy esplanade. Flimsy vans sell *croque-monsieurs*, ice-creams and bright plastic windmills along the boulevard du Maréchal Foch. The hotels and apartments are on the parallel boulevard de Verdun, set back behind a 100-yard-wide lawn where people stroll, walk poodles,

fly kites, or play impromptu beach games.

A modern casino squats beside the medieval towers of fourteenth-century town defences. There is little uniformity along the shore, and it is difficult to imagine that it was here that Canadian commandos were pinned down by murderous fire in the disastrous raid of August 19, 1942. Now the fifteenth-century castle, keeping watch from its cliff-top to the west and dominating the scene, presides over leisured tranquillity.

Within its walls is a museum where delicate ivories carved by Dieppe craftsmen of the past are casually displayed with a Renoir portrait, a Pissarro view of the port and two Sickert scenes (the artist lodged with a local fishwife). There are few labels — the curator encourages visitors to guess what they are looking at.

Below the castle, a monument with a flower bed designed as a maple leaf commemorates the Dieppe raid. People stop to admire it and those who are really interested, or have children with a taste for rusting tanks and armoured cars, will drive along the white cliffs towards Pourville, where, opposite Dieppe golf course, a military museum re-counts the story in painful detail.

Towards the sea from Canada Square, a thalassotherapy centre will train a therapeutic saline water cannon on you as if you were a South African clergyman or a demonstrating student. Other saline cures and less forceful treatments using mud imported from Brittany are also available to those in need of less invigorating types of ill-treatment.

There are few hints on the sea-front of the thriving and industri-ous commercialism that prospers in the town behind. Dieppe is blessedly free of seaside amuse-ment arcades and tawdry knick-knackery. Instead, it has more than its fair share of hard-work-ing, practical and enterprising town shops.

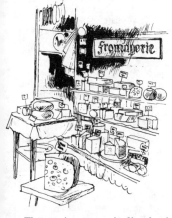

The main street is lined with clothes boutiques, gift shops, groc-ery stores, charcuteries, and cake shops in vivid variety. On Satur-days, the air is full of the scents of fresh food and flowers and it teems with crowds jostling from stall to stall in one of the finest street markets north of Paris.

There are van-loads of delicious cheeses, barrows of fish, and stalls strung with garlands of onions and plaits of the new season's garlic. Carts of dried fruits, tables buried under piles of mushrooms and long counters weighed down with fresh fruit and vegetables start to empty by mid-morning.

Almost half the stallholders are country people, come to offer a few skinned rabbits (they always leave the socks on), live chickens, garden flowers, bunches of herbs, packets of hand-made butter cut from the freshly churned block and tasty fresh farm cream ladled from big buckets.

The market spills down the side streets. The front of the Place Nationale is filled with flowers and potted plants. Behind them are clothes, shoes and hardware. Around the foot of the gothic jumble of St Jacques church there is food again, and the food stalls continue up the rue St Jacques to rejoin the main market at the Puits-Salé Square by the Café des Tribunaux, town meeting place for 200 years.

The stalls are set up at 7am, busy at 9am, and mostly gone by 1pm. Promptly, mechanical street-cleaners do a whirligig about the place, and by 2pm it's as if the market had never been.

Freshly cooked, succulent shrimps are sold by fishwives at covered stalls next to the ferry terminal. In town, the best fish shop, at the corner of Place Nationale near the church, has walls decorated with anatomical drawings of shellfish, their parts so intimately detailed that anyone who distrusts oysters will discover why an oyster should be swal-lowed in one, never bitten. Not, of course, that this has ever been a problem for the French.

Dieppe is not all prosperity. The tongue of land between the seafront and the ferry harbour is a picturesque but impoverished quarter of crumbling houses and courtyards. These were the atmospheric back streets Georges Simenon had in mind when he wrote *Newhaven-Dieppe*, a thriller full of the menace of sea mist, poverty and secret crime.

The area was once known as Petit Veules, because it was here that the fisherwomen of Veules, a village sixteen miles along the coast, settled after a storm had drowned their husbands. Today, Veules, cheerfully renamed Veules-les-Roses, is a happy resort on the white-cliffed Alabaster coast. It has white cabins on the seafront, the shortest river in France, an antique church, some beautiful cottages and a splendid Michelin-starred restaurant called Les Galets. Victor Hugo spent holidays in the village.

The countryside around Dieppe is filled with verdant valleys, bubbling trout streams, timbered manor houses and thatched cottages topped with iris and saxifrage. Turn a winding corner and the view will be of fields of soft blue flax or sulphur-yellow rape. An elegant château or a picturesque farm hides around the next twist of the lane. Patch-eyed, brindle-coated Norman cows browse in fields dotted with bright red poppies.

WHERE TO STAY

Univers: 10 blvd de Verdun (tel: 35 84 12 55). Rooms: 250F-395F (the exchange rate is roughly 10 francs to the pound). Half board: 335F-500F a person. Friendly, family-run. Good hotel dining room.

Présidence: blvd de Verdun (tel: 35 84 31 31). Rooms: 220F-460F. Modern. Grill room.

Aguado: 30 blvd de Verdun (tel: 35 84 27 00). Rooms: 284F-350F. No restaurant.

Plage: 20 blvd de Verdun (tel: 35 84 18 28). Rooms: 230F-265F. No restaurant.

WHERE TO EAT

La Mélie: 2 Grande Rue Pollet (tel: 35 84 21 19). On far side of harbour from the main town. Stylish, fishy dishes earned a Michelin star. Menu 140F-190F. Closed Sun eve and Mon.

Le Sully: 97 quai Henri IV (tel: 35 84 23 13). Closed Tue eve and Wed. *Fruits de mer*, mussels, grilled fish. Menus: 52F-115F.

Armorique: 17 quai Henri IV (tel: 35 84 28 14). Closed Sun eve and Mon, June 1-15 and October 15-31. Excellent fish. Must book. A la carte only.

Marmite Dieppoise: 8 rue St-Jean (tel: 35 84 24 26). Closed Thurs and Sun eve and Mon. The *marmite* is fish, shellfish and cream. Menus: 100F-170F.

Les Tourelles: 43 rue du Commandant Fayolle (behind the casino) (tel: 35 84 15 88). Closed Tue eve and Wed. Good value; 3 courses for 55F.

EATING OUT OF TOWN

La Bucherie: at Vertus, 3.5km on Rouen road (tel: 35 84 83 10). Closed Sun eve and Mon. Menus 160F (weekdays) to 240F.

Auberge du Clos Normand: Martin-Eglise, 6.5km from Dieppe (tel: 35 82 71 01). Closed Mon and Tue. Classic, unpretentious cooking in 15th-century inn. A la carte: about 190F.

Auberge du Dun: Bourg-Dun, 17km west of Dieppe (tel: 35 83 05 84). Closed Sun eve and Mon. Good value, imaginative, small. Menu: 81F.

Les Galets: Veules-les-Roses, 24km west of Dieppe (tel: 35 97 61 33). Closed February, Sunday evenings in winter, Tue eve and Wed. Very refined, distinguished cooking by Maître Cuisinier de France. Menus: 200F, 310F.

SHOPS

Grande Rue: No 186, *Geneviève Lethu* for gifts: pretty items for kitchen, bedroom, dining room; 56 shops in France and planning to invade England soon.

No 115, *Ratel*, for chocolates.

No 138, *Divernet*, for *salon de thé*, pastries.

Rue St Jacques: No 16, *Claude Olivier*, for 100 cheeses, 350 wines, fine groceries.

No 6, *Millau*, for leather bags.

13 place St Jacques: *Aux Aromes de Provence,*for pure vegetable soaps.

Sainte Cathérine area behind St Jacques church: Former fishermen's *quartier* renovated as apartments and small shops. Visit *l'Atelier du Vannier*, 9 rue Pecquet, for baskets made from Norman willow by Jean-Claude Creignou, graduate from the National School of Basket-making near Dijon.

1 rue du Bel, *Arques-la-Bataille*, 7km south of Dieppe, where Monique Schmeltz decorates white Limoges plates, lamps etc in a rustic studio in a picturesque village with old castle and fine forest. Open 7 days.

Mammouth hypermarket, 4km out on the N27 Rouen road. Food, wines, camping/picnic equipment, furniture, boutiques. Coffee is a good buy. Open Monday to Friday, 9am-9pm. Saturday, 8.30am-9.30pm.

GETTING THERE

Sealink Dieppe Ferries take 4 hours between Newhaven and Dieppe. There are up to 4 sailings a day. Apex fares start from £135 for a car and 4 passengers, bookable 28 days in advance for certain sailings.

Excursion fares include 60 hours for foot passengers (£22 return adult, £12.50 child) and 5 days (£28 adult, £17 child). Bookings by telephone: 0273-512266 or 0223-47047.

Personal applications and train information (to Newhaven): Travel Centre at Victoria in London; principal BR stations and Travel Centres; AA and RAC travel offices.

TOURIST OFFICES

Excellent maps and booklets on Dieppe and Normandy are available free from the Office de Tourisme, blvd Général de Gaulle, Dieppe. In London, the French Government Tourist Office is at 178 Piccadilly, W1.

Lyon

Adam Hopkins

. . . .

EVELYN WAUGH, asked why he wrote travel books about distant countries which he obviously detested, replied that he was saving Europe up for later.

Personally, I have taken the same attitude to France, passing through often, speaking the language a little, but never making the kind of contact that allows British francophiles to engage in that easy, slightly condescending patter about French wine and cheeses, medieval art and contemporary cinema.

But Lyon, France's second city, seemed to offer two mutually exclusive possibilities. One was the Beaujolais region, north and a fraction to the west. The other was in the opposite direction, the great massif of the Vercors on the edge of the Alps in the south-east.

Our departure on a Friday was bright and early as we headed out of Lyon's Satolas airport and north past the city through fearful motorway traffic. Soon, though, we were calmed by the appearance of hills with rectangles of beige and sultry green like living Cézanne landscapes, somewhat displaced.

In no time at all we were in Villefranche-sur-Saône, one point of entry to the Beaujolais district. It was delightful, truly delightful, to have left home in south London that morning and to be lunching on a restaurant balcony among geraniums in a small French town.

The sun picked out the stonework opposite as we experimented, variously, with snails and proper *coq au vin* and *quenelles de brochet sauce Nantua* (poached mousse of pike in a creamy sauce with crayfish).

During our brief stay we sampled more different dishes, more cheeses and wines than we could hope to bore our friends with in a year. They ranged from the phenomenal Burgundian cheese named *époisses* — thunder and lightning would be a better name — to the simple wholesomeness of *gratin dauphinois*.

That first afternoon we climbed into the hills of the central Beaujolais district, finding them surprisingly well-wooded, like a slightly large-scale Shropshire, with vines among the woods where meadows might have been.

At Vaux we stopped to visit a wine "cave" or "dégustation" and found it so tarted up we left at once to wiggle northwards through sleepy, less wooded little places with more familiar names ... Morgon, Fleurie, Juliénas. At Fleurie, at the local Cave Coopérative, we found a serious *dégustation*, tried two vintages and bought three bottles of the one we liked the best. By now we were getting to be real experts.

That night in Mâcon, we were humbled but still lucky. We had pre-booked, a little sniffily, in a chain hotel just out of town — the Altea-Mâcon. Now we discovered every room in town was taken and, exhausted, we were delighted both to stay and to dine in an atmosphere of peaceful modernity — except for a family of Dutch children who had been cooped up for three hours in a motorway tailback. It was here that I met my own *époisses*. Here, too, we walked the river banks in darkness, admiring the darker reflection of the tall trees opposite and the stillness and comfort of the night.

By late afternoon the next day we had entered a different world. From far away, as we headed down towards Grenoble, we had seen two mighty bluffs of rock rising in front of us, each virtually a mountain range in itself except that each appeared to be a single monolith of stone. The great crag to our left was the Chartreuse massif, to the right was our destination, the Vercors.

The Vercors is twenty miles

wide and thirty long. It is, indeed, a single mighty lump of rock but, once on top, one discovers it is full of its own mountains and high valleys, with gorges, flower meadows and dark forests pierced by brilliant sunshine.

We stayed in the little resort town of Villard de Lans, in a hotel called the Christiana. Its restaurant dining room yielded up trout poached in gamay and ravioli stuffed with mountain mushrooms. Coming out in the morning into the freshness of the all-but-alpine air, you see the wide arc of the mountain meeting the sky in a single great grey cliff, hauling itself clear of the morning mist.

The nearby Gorges de la Bourne is a knife-slit of stone broadening finally as it descends to reveal great slabs of rock stacked in recession further down the valley. Pausing on the road, you hear nothing but the distant sound of water.

At the small village of Vassieux, which is entirely modern, there is a cemetery and a building which is a cross between a war memorial and a shrine, with a deeply moving tape and slide show to commemorate those who died in July 1944 when the Germans burned down the village, killing the inhabitants — women, children, even the animals — as well as the Resistance fighters holed up there. It was not until this action that Germany finally subdued the fierce *montagnards* who had made the Vercors a centre of resistance throughout the war.

We saw all this because of industrial action which halted Monday flights and gave us an extra day in the Vercors. One day would not have been enough; and even two, we felt, gave us merely a first impression. But with an early flight on Tuesday, we headed back to the airport hotel at Satolas and found it comfortable and civilised, not at all the anonymous venue of our imagination. Definitely on the list for next time, we said sagely to each other, obliquely acknowledging a new commitment.

GETTING THERE:

Weekend with Air France Holidays (tel: 01-568 6981). From £119 per person you fly by scheduled Air France flights, and have use of a small car from Hertz (Renault 5 or similar — we took a Peugeot) for Friday to Monday breaks in nine destinations — Lyon, Paris, Strasbourg, Nantes, Bordeaux, Toulouse, Montpellier, Marseille, Nice (£15 supplement). The price includes unlimited mileage on car, collision insurance and local tax. Hotels are then up to the individual.

WHERE TO STAY:

Prices per night in hotels we used were as follows, based on two sharing: *Altéa-Mâcon*, 300F to 480F; *Christiana*, Villard de Lans, 380F with mountain view, 305F with views of village; *Sofitel Satolas Airport*, 520F. If one could be certain of a room, the Vercors would be most agreeable for a weekend, or when diverting from route south towards the coast, to stay in a small village hotel. Villard de Lans itself, however, has all the holiday amenities — bicycles for hire, swimming, tennis, riding and good access for walking, excellent for holidays with children. As a winter resort (offered for the first time by Air France in 1988) it is unusual in offering both downhill and cross-country skiing with the possibility of staying either in village or purpose-built resort.

FOOD AND WINE:

We travelled through three very different gastronomic zones. The Lyon area offers fine ingredients — poultry, freshwater fish, mushrooms — with a formidable collection of well-known restaurants in Lyon itself. At Mâcon, we were in the southern extremes of Burgundy — much cookery with wine, such as *coq au vin*. Other pleasures: *boeuf en daube*, smoked duck, *époisses* cheese matured in marc brandy and tiny round goats' cheeses — trouser buttons or *boutons de culotte*. The Dauphinée (Vercors and surrounds) — the calmer *gratin dauphinois*, thinly sliced potatoes baked in milk and butter with other ingredients, depending on the chef. In Vercors itself, mountain products such as hams, sausages along with a tradition of ravioli, allegedly brought long ago by Italian refugees. There were local cheeses everywhere.

In Villefranche-sur-Saône we ate at *La Colonne*, 6 place Carnot; 75F for lunch. In the *Altéa Mâcon*, 26 rue de Coubertin, we paid 175F each for an excellent Burgundian dinner with delicious white mâcon. In Crémieu we ate at the *Auberge de la Chait*, cours Baron-Raverat; 75F each. In the hotel *Christiana's* restaurant *le Tétras* we ate historic Dauphinois and Vercors specialities from 130F to 250F.

Wines included, of course, beaujolais, then mâcon and burgundy generally. In the Vercours area, local reds and whites from the fringes of the massif, less distinguished but fun because they are local.

INFORMATION:

Michelin Rhône-Alpes sheet 244 for detailed navigation. Guide-books: rather than buy the 3 French-language only green Michelin guides we would have needed for this trip, we invested in the AA/Hachette guide to the whole of France, which has brief coverage of history, sights, hotels, restaurants, all in one volume. Seemed trustworthy.

TOTAL MILES:

Too many. Best stick either to Beaujolais and southern Burgundy or to the Vercors. Doing both in one weekend is madness.

Istanbul

Denis Herbstein

. . . .

NOT even the most devious preparation can make the trip a surprise. There is Tom to be farmed out to his aunt, the cat's first litter is imminent and even if we manage to fly from Heathrow "destination unknown", my wife Patty will surely look out the window and wonder at the abundance of minarets in Cork. So the secret is out — we are going to Istanbul to mark her fortieth birthday.

It is late May — a bank holiday weekend of four nights and three days and we are to be lodged in a comfortable pension in a cobbled street separating the Topkapi Palace from the Ayasofya Mosque. "The traveller feels as if he's in his own house," the brochure predicts. "Only a knave welcomes him." But there are few knaves in a city where taxi-drivers, gently prodded, will drive half an hour for the equivalent of thirty bob, with the meter on.

We chose Istanbul as much for its living history as for the cuisine, both of which I remembered from a youthful visit as second only to Paris. For the culinary kick-off, hotel reception suggests a tavern, "not touristy, and good seafood". On arrival, we sit down and a lad runs in to find out which hotel has sent us. The network in action. Excellent fish kebab, but expensive. They send us home by taxi on the house.

The Old City has enough in a square mile to occupy the tourist for a week. We remove our sandals at the Blue Mosque and get down to work. The guide-book notes that discarding footwear is not so much a religious rite as a sanitary measure for the reclining Muslim worshipper as he touches the ground with his head. Hereabouts, the floor is covered by coach-loads of Germans. Still, the blue-glazed tiles which give the place its name direct your eyes up to the heavens. We retrieve our sandals and are hailed by a gentleman anxious to direct us to his uncle's carpet shop. I ignore him. He persists. "Are you English?" "No, Scottish," (jokingly). ""AaaahHAH," he rejoins, "what is your name?" I point to Patty, "Mrs Thatcher." He, quick as a flash: "I do not like the north of England because I cannot get a job."

The rugs will have to wait since we are to devote ourselves to a leisurely and inexpensive steam up the Bosphorus to the Black Sea. It is hackneyed, but so is the ascent of the Eiffel Tower. The routine is to buy the tickets early, then cross the bridge to the Spice Market for pistachio nuts, dried apricots, sickly pastries, maybe *aphrodisiaque de Sultane* (honey with spices).

The ferry zigzags intercontinentally across the Bosphorus. We drink tea out of hot glasses, and shell nuts. A Turkish professor, home for the summer from an American campus, points out the passing parade. Palaces and mosques wind by, restaurants hover on stilts over the water and a Russian freighter bound for Odessa passes under a British-built bridge linking Europe and Asia. Later we climb to the ruined Ottoman fortress at Anadolu Hisar, whence Sultan Mehmet prepared the attack that was to topple the Holy Roman Empire in 1453.

The sun comes out and Patty's sandals don't fit. I make an ill-judged remark about *"dames d'un certain âge",* and she says she hopes this isn't going to be a silly piece. Blue fish, grilled gently, with a tomato salad and crusty Turkish bread, restores equanimity. I read Wilfred Thesiger on the way home. As a young man he had walked the whole of Istanbul's ancient city walls.

We rise early on Sunday and proceed directly to the Cagaloglu Turkish baths, built by a sultan three centuries ago but latterly privatised. Florence Nightingale and Kaiser Wilhelm abluted here, presumably separately, for there are "him" and "her" entrances. I change into a fetching gingham loin cloth. I am persuaded that

the "assisted bath" is not to be missed. Massage? Not today. In the marbled inner sanctum, held aloft by finely decorated pillars, an attendant jumps on the outstretched back of a patron.

The steam room is gentle: Lagos on a cool day. I worry more about athlete's foot than Aids, but the place is spotless. The assisted bath routine is as follows: I sit on a stone slab, the attendant drenches me with hot and cold water, soaps me, rubs me down with a rough glove. The wrap stays round your waist at all times. Nothing butch about the Cagaloglu, whatever the sultan got up to in the side "chapels".

Had the Ayasofya not beckoned, I would gladly have lain in my cubicle for an hour sipping tea and reading. But there is touring to be done. Minarets pierce the Istanbul skyline like missiles from a launch pad. Half a dozen mosques are worth a visit, but we are not on a pilgrimage. We limit ourselves to the Ayasofya, soaring sixth-century basilica of the Roman Emperor Justinian and later conquered by the Turks who converted it into the mosque. But it jars, this mix of early Christian and Islam.

The gilt-engraved extracts from the Koran hanging from the walls have the same effect as that cathedral which a Spanish king built inside the magnificent mosque at Cordoba.

And so to the palace of the film. Topkapi is Istanbul's Buckingham Palace. To be sure, the London building doesn't have a harem, nor eunuchs for that matter, no circumcision chamber, nor the equivalent in Christian terms of a tooth and a hair from the beard of

Mohammed. But from both locations mighty empires were held in sway, the one celebrated for brass bands, the other for shish kebab.

I remembered Topkapi as a haven of reflection, and no doubt it still is on a cold Thursday in January. On a summer weekend, when even the Turks inspect their heritage, the coach tailbacks almost to Kennedy Caddesi, the ubiquitous queues, the stampedes for the Treasury or the Holy Relics, constitute the worst of modern tourism.

But the harem is worth a wait. Don't believe the guide, who attempts to deflate our fantasies. "There were 600 to 800 girls, but many were the children of concubines or half-sisters". By my calculation that still left a good few legally deflowerables. When the sultan died, the girls were turned out, with no redundancy, and the new fellow brought in his own team. Lunch on the terrace of the Topkapi restaurant. The food is nothing particularly memorable, but you do have a seat and a view of several seas.

In one ferry bound, we cross the Bosphorus (for 8p) to Üsküdar, night sister Nightingale's "Scutari", and the hospital, now a military headquarters, where she nursed the remnants of the Light Brigade. Her rooms are a museum, a "lamp of the period" on her desk. I sign the visitors' book below Mrs Thatcher's stirring entry. We walk to the *Ingiliz mezarligi* (English gravestones) to complete the late afternoon patriotism.

The pace is relentless. What sort of a refreshing break is this, we ask ourselves over coffee and a shoeshine. A call to prayer echoes from the mosque. Let's take it easy from now on. A pedlar offers "genuine Turkish antiquities". Thanks, no. We order more coffee and *maden suyu* (mineral water). "A leather coat for the lady?" No! We are not "seeing" Istanbul. "A sponge?" No!! Let's go somewhere quiet for supper tonight, just the

158

two of us. "You wanna taxi?" YES!!! Oh, I am sorry.

At last we cross the Golden Horn, a strip of water the width of the Thames, once pronounced clinically dead from pollution, now being revitalised. The "new city" is for shopping and business hotels. Americans and Japanese stay here. On the Hagi Baba restaurant terrace, Istikal (Independence) Street, the elderly waiter has the air of having battled all day in languages he cannot speak. We ask for fish. "Feeneesh." he smiles, waits. Dolmades? "Feeneesh," resignedly. I suppose you're going to tell me you have no shish kebab. "Feeneesh." He is consumed with sadness. All around us diners are de-skewering lamb onto their plates. Our waiter returns with meatballs and chops. I create a scene, march through several rooms of heavily laden tables and catch the prop. "Shish kebab? No problem. I'll bring you all you want." I can recommend it.

The solution is *bakarim*, Turkish for "I am looking". The Turks have a reverence for food rather like the French. You should leave your table to inspect the fare, sniff appreciatively into cooking pots, ask to nibble the *imam bayildi* (stuffed aubergines translated as "the imam swooned" or, less invitingly, "the priest fainted"). Ask for recipe. "Bakarim." Then no "feenesh". But I was. I didn't hear the heavy storm that night and snored for the first time ever.

We plot our last day. The covered bazaar has so many alleyways and shops you fear you might never get out. A fellow announces 15,000 jackets in fifty styles, and many will be cribbed from Italy. Another is "official supplier" to Pan Am crews. You must be thick-skinned and flexible, humorous and willing to drink several cups of apple tea, and know the rates of exchange of the main currencies. I can remember ploy by ploy the kelim bought at this bazaar twenty years ago and which now lies on my study floor. It might not

be "antique" and I am sure I did not drive the seller and his family into penury, but it gives me pleasure still.

We sit on a café bench half-listening to Marius Goring recount the *son et lumiére* story of the Blue Mosque. The menu offers "cizburger" or "kokteyl sandovic". We taxi down to the Marmara for farewell mezes of taramasalata, tuna fish, mussels stuffed with rice and pine nuts, yoghurt salad, carrot fritters, pastry filled with goat's cheese and spinach, all washed down by arak. By now we've had just about enough of the good eating life — bring back bran breakfasts and macaroni cheese.

On the morrow we fly back to London to recuperate. We'll go back on her fiftieth, see some more mosques, bit of belly dancing, some grease wrestling, maybe a trip to Troy. By then the Turkish empire will have fallen to the wooden horse of European tourism.

HOW TO GET THERE

British Airways (tel: 01-897 4000) and *Turkish Airlines* (tel: 01-499 9240) have daily scheduled flights to Istanbul. BA offers a longer stay as the flight leaves in the morning and returns in the evening, but it is heavily booked during early summer. Turkish Airlines leaves Heathrow in the afternoon, arriving early evening, and leaves Istanbul early, arriving Heathrow before lunch.

We booked through *Metak Holidays* (tel: 01-935 6961) on Turkish Airlines on a 4-night "flight only" special, price £155. Metak also has less expensive week or fortnight trips, as does *Delta Sun* (tel: 01-935 9535), with late-night departures from Gatwick on Thursdays and Saturdays. It offers flight-only prices of £140 return and accommodation in 3-star hotels for £10 a night bed and breakfast; or a package including 3-star hotel accommodation at £199 for a week or £268 for a fortnight.

Sunquest Holidays (tel: 01-749 9933) is another agent specialising in holidays to Turkey, and is mentioned in a Holiday Guide, available from the Turkish Travel Office.

WHERE TO STAY

We stayed bed and breakfast at the *Ayasofya Pansiyonlari* (tel: 010 901-513 3660) in the Old City for US$90 a night per double room. In sterling, it came to barely £200, including calls to England and an excellent meal in the hotel restaurant. Istanbul hotels range in price from £10 a night 1-star to £120 for the most superior 5-star. A list is available from the Turkish Travel Office.

WHERE TO EAT

Restaurants are cheap by European standards. The best one we went to was *Pandeli*, a turquoise-tiled wonder above the Spice Market. The *Yengec* in Kumkapi offered excellent fresh fish but cost £25 for 2. We got wise immediately and never paid that much again. Our hotel restaurant, the *Sarnic Taverna*, in a restored Roman cistern, is touristy but again good food. We ate well at lunch and supper, but could have gone to more modest restaurants for the equivalent of less than £8 for 2.

GETTING ABOUT

Transport in Istanbul is best by taxi. You can ride virtually anywhere within reason for less than £2. Beware of the similarity between 1,000 and 10,000 lira notes. After a short ride, I paid a driver with the larger denomination, thanked him for the ride, and he was gone before I realised my mistake. The Turkish Travel Office has details of guided tours, as do several tourist offices dotted around Istanbul, the main one being near the Galata bridge.

PLACES TO VISIT

The trip up the *Bosphorus*, visits to *Topkapi Palace*, the *Ayasofya* Mosque, the *Blue Mosque*, the *Cagaloglu Turkish baths* and the wonderful restored *cistern* (water reservoir) of *Justinian*, opposite Ayasofya, were the highlights of our weekend. The last 5 are in walking distance of each other, within a mile-radius in the Old City. They are run by the states and will cost from 1,000 to 5,000 lira. ""Assisted" Turkish baths cost about £3.50, including entrance fee.

SHOPPING

The *covered market* in the Old City, of course, for kelims, leather goods, jewellery (always, always bargain); the *spice market*, where *Aphrodisiaque de Sultane* turns out to be honey with spices; and for conventional shopping, *Istiklal Caddesi*, known locally as Beyoglu, for Oxford Street's equivalent. Things are cheap, but getting expensive.

WHAT TO EXPECT

The language is full of strange sounds, though a surprising number of Turks get by on basic English. To avoid tourists, visit during the early spring and the autumn when the crowds — and heat — are absent. It snows occasionally in winter. The exchange rate depends on the strength of sterling and hovers round 2,430 lira to the pound. I changed money at Heathrow, but there was a rather better rate in Istanbul. One other boon is that you seem to get the same rate when changing money in a hotel as in a bank. Black market rates, slightly better than the official, are advertised in the newspapers.

FURTHER INFORMATION

Get in touch with *The Turkish Travel Office* 170 Piccadilly, London W1 (tel: 01-734 8681/2). For some background reading, I used Fodor's *Turkey* which is excellent. The French writer Pierre Loti lived and wrote about Istanbul in the last century, but you may find it difficult to obtain copies of his titles like, *Asiyadé*, in English.

Maastricht

Lewis
De Fries

. . . .

A short drive from Maastricht, Holland's oldest city, the forest road winds gently up through silver birch, pines and beech glades to the roof of the Netherlands, just 1,000 feet above sea level. At the summit, a stone pillar marks Three Countries Point. There's a strange compulsion to ape the local children: you put your left foot in Germany, your right foot in Belgium, while the rest of you stays in Holland.

Yet Maastricht itself needs no mere frontier post to symbolise its own internationalism. Both the city and its province, Limburg, live up to the title the Dutch have given them: the Balcony of Europe. At first sight nothing could be more removed from the Briton's conception of Holland than Limburg: not a canal, not a windmill in view, but green rolling hills more reminiscent of Dorset or Hampshire, dotted with pinnacled French and solid German-type châteaux and sturdy white timber-framed farmhouses which look transplanted from Alsace Lorraine. There's even a chairlift. And to complete the illusion, there are vineyards drowsing on the sunniest of those so rare Dutch hillsides.

The Maas — the Meuse as it becomes across the Belgian border — flows through Maastricht's heart, spanned by a bridge which has stood since the twelfth century. It has been a blood-red river in its time; the city has seen twenty-one sieges as Romans, Franks, Spaniards, French, English, Germans and the Dutch themselves have fought over it.

There is a honeycomb of underground casemates to be explored on guided tours, forts and lofty ramparts on which to bask in summer or for brisk windswept winter walks. Maastricht has known Charlemagne, Spain's grim Duke of Parma, Louis the Sun King, the musketeer D'Artagnan — who died fighting for it alongside the English in 1673 — and Napoleon, who shut down its vineyards, the only ones in the Netherlands.

Today D'Artagnan is commemorated by a modest statue at the spot on the ramparts where he fell and Napoleon — last French master of the territory before the Dutch finally repossessed it after his fall — by the very fact that there are only three vineyards and one "wine garden" still operating, compared with the dozens which existed in the more distant past.

The rarest wine in Europe is Limburg's modest annual production of about 25,000 bottles of riesling, auxerrois and müller-thurgau and the 100 or so bottles of red produced in the minute wine garden run by an enthusiast in the city's heart. You're more likely to be offered Limburg wine in a private home or in a first-rate Amsterdam hotel than in Maastricht.

Take your pick of the two reasons the locals give for Napoleon's part in the wrecking of what was once a thriving wine industry. One is that he did not want Dutch wine to compete with the French — because it was too good. The second is that the quality of Dutch wine so appalled him that he closed the vineyards. Whatever the truth, the local growers were so fed up with the damage done to their soil and crops by successive wars that they could not be bothered to start yet again.

Successive conquerors and the simple fact of geography have left their mark on Maastricht. The locals have a unique dialect — a mixture of German, French, Dutch and Flemish. Bargaining in local markets is done in three languages and three currencies. The outstanding buildings in the city range from romanesque and gothic to pseudo-renaissance, classical, French and boulevard styles.

The oldest buildings are the churches of Onze Lieve Vrouwe and St Servaas, acknowledged to be two of the most beautiful romanesque structures in all the Netherlands. When their Spanish masters were expelled, Maastricht took on typical Dutch Calvinistic architecture; the town hall is Dutch classicism at its best. By the eighteenth century French baroque and rococo had taken over.

The miracle of Maastricht is that despite its mixture of styles and cultures, its stormy history and its position as essentially a border city, it presents a picture of an integrated, unique whole. Everything seems to slot smoothly into place.

It is a handsome city, with its gabled houses, wide windows, filled with flowers in true Dutch style, its water-wheel which grinds a city baker's corn as it has for centuries. The heart of Maastricht is the great square called the Vrijthof, overlooked by the soaring Basilica towers of St Servaaskerk, named after the city's most venerated bishop who died in 384. But the Vrijthof itself is anything but solemn. The city's most popular pavement cafés are there, and the square is a blaze of light well into the night.

Around the Vrijthof, too, you can relax over coffee and the province's famous fruit pie, the vlaai, disconcertingly pronounced "fly". Purists will tell you that the best vlaai filling of all is of real Limburg cherries — and cherries in Limburg, like the local asparagus, are unbeatable. But a vlaai can come in many different versions, made with rice or sweet carrot as well as other fruit. Only the crust must be roughly the same for all types: similar to a sweet pizza dough.

The heartiness of midday snacks — more than sufficient to

tide you over until dinner (or the afternoon *vlaai* hour) following a breakfast of mixed breads, egg, very satisfying creamy Limburg cheese — is typically Dutch. Only at night does the French culinary influence come into its own. The most rewarding — and priciest — of all restaurants are French: about Limburg, Michelin is appropriately enthusiastic.

But if you prefer to eat French meals in France and regard a Maastricht weekend break as essentially a Dutch occasion when it comes to eating, you can feast yourself on a multi-dish Indo-nesian *rijsttafel*, imagine you are in Amsterdam — and save yourself pounds.

The carillons ringing across stately squares, the cyclists, the flowers and those wide Dutch windows will add to the illusion — even if you are a long way from the nearest canal, windmill or hump-backed bridge.

Maastricht is still Holland — but with a difference. And maybe after all, the best way to enjoy it for a weekend is to accept the unique mixture of cultures, cuisine and atmosphere the Balcony of Europe offers.

GETTING THERE:
Flights: daily to Maastricht from Luton by Virgin Atlantic for £78 return. The KLM subsidiary NLM flies twice daily, Mon-Fri for £195 return from Gatwick. By European Saver ticket from British Rail London-Harwich-Hook of Holland to any Dutch rail station for £50 for 5-day return.
By car: the most direct route to South Holland is via Olau Line (tel: 0795-666666) from Sheerness to Vlissingen; twice daily service. Single journey: adult fare £22 until the end of 1989; (day sailings only); children 4-13, £11. Cars from £35 single on a day sailing outside peak season to £50 night sailing between mid June and mid September. Night accommodation from £2.50 to £58. Maastricht is about a 2½-hour drive from Vlissingen. Time Off (tel: 01-235 8070) has short breaks in the city leaving from Luton with 2 nights and air travel starting from £109, in a 1-star hotel, low season. Transalpino (tel: 01-834 9656; 041-334 0800; 031-557 3140) weekend breaks start at £114.

GETTING AROUND
Any distance by bus within the city, hourly valid ticket 64p. In summer it is possible to use a horse-drawn carriage; £3.45 per person for 45 minutes.

SIGHTS
Basilica of Our Lady: on the Onze Lieve Vrouweplein; focal point is the 15th-century Virgin and Child known as The Star of the Sea. The treasury has the gown of St Lambert, the last but one bishop of Maastricht, assassinated in 720, and the Belt of the Virgin. The church of *St Servaas* on the Vrijthof is famous for its treasury filled with gold, including the golden and silver bust of St Servaas, presented by the Duke of Parma. He was our would-be conqueror, fortunately let down by the 1588 Armada.
Bonnefanten Museum: Dominikanerplein 5, open every day except Monday, 11am-5pm (weekdays 10am-5pm). Italian and Flemish medieval art collection, including several works of Breughel the Younger. There is a fascinating *Son et Lumière* display with the aid of a huge model of the city as it was in the 18th century.
There are *guided tours* of the casemates, old mining galleries used in times of siege; *Fort St Peter:* complete with shellproof chambers, and a superb view of the city and surrounding countryside from the heights; the *Caves of Mount St Peter:* an enormous labyrinth of more than 20,000 passages. In winter these tours operate only on Saturday and Sunday. There is a boat trip every Sunday on the Meuse which can be combined with a visit to the *Zonneberg Caves.*

WHERE TO STAY
The Derlon Hotel: 5 stars, on the Onze Vrouweplein (tel: 010-31-43 216770). Superb modern luxury hotel, expensive, built on top of a recently discovered Roman temple, still to be viewed in the cellar. Beneath the temple, a stretch of pre-Roman road. *Le Roi* is a reasonably priced, cheerful, relaxed little 3-star at Maartenslaan 1 (tel: 253838), as is the *Hotel Stijns,* 2 stars, at Stationstraat 40 (tel: 251651). Both these hotels average about £30 for a double room with breakfast.

LUNCH
Choose one of the *brown pubs* now competing with quick service restaurants to provide

unpretentious, truly Dutch-style dishes. Locals clink genever glasses at the bar beside your table. Typical example: *Cafe Sjiek*, Sint Pieterstraat 13. Speciality of the house: an *uitsmijter* — huge open sandwich with cheese, ham, peppers, mixed vegetables topped with three eggs. Follow this with a big slice of cherry pie. With coffee and beer the meal is under £5.

DINNER

Le Bon Vivant: Capucijnstraat 91 (tel: 210816). Romantic 300-year-old candlelit former brewery cellar — specialises in coquilles St Jacques, sole, Ardennes quail, wild pigeon, hare with cherries, venison. Can be pricey if eating à la carte, but a choice of pleasant fixed menus for about £22.

City outskirts: *Château Neercanne:* handsome old castle at Cannerweg 800 (tel: 251359), where you can walk through the wine cellars or through the back gate into Belgium. Four courses with wine: £36.

For the ultimate in dining out: take the train (15 minutes, just over £1 return) to the resort town of Valkenburg and the *Princess Juliana Hotel Restaurant:* Broekhem 11 (tel: 010 31 4406-12244), 2 Michelin rosettes. Charges the same as Neercanne for its Menu Alliance including 2 wines. Round off the evening with a visit to *Valkenburg's* casino, the only one in Limburg.

BARS AND NIGHTLIFE

Cafés and brown pubs, mostly with recorded music, as background, but you can dance at the *Café des Artistes* in the Vrijthof. In the café *Troubadour Chantant* in St Amos Plein, you're welcome to do your own thing on stage — singing, dancing, monologue, no one minds. Jazz sessions around the city centre, a few places offer romantic piano music.

SHOPS

Brudsje Stols in Maastrichter Smeden Straat, for fabulous local chocolates; a huge selection of genever and other potent Limburg spirits at *Thiessen* in Grote Gracht. Delicate porcelain figures — local speciality — from *Schoonbrood*, in the Spilstraat.

INFORMATION

Tourist Office: VVV Maastricht, Het Dinghuis, Klein Staat 1, NL6211 ED Maastricht (tel: 010-31-43 252121). Also, read *A Walk Through Maastricht* by Mary Maclure and Derek Blyth, available from the tourist office at £5.62.

Manhattan and Boston

*Askold
Krushelnycky*

. . . .

ISUCCESSFULLY resisted the Filofax, I can't afford a convertible VW Golf and I don't wear designer clothes. But there I was, a diligent opponent of yuppyism, hurtling at 30,000 feet in a Jumbo jet towards what must surely be the newest symbol of the genre — a long weekend in New York.

The strong pound and competition between airlines means that a flight across the Atlantic must be cheaper than ever before. My trip began with a Virgin Airways flight from Gatwick on a Thursday afternoon.

The aircraft was clean and comfortable, with adequate leg room even in the economy seats. The service was friendly and efficient, and the food (choice of two dishes) good.

Feeling fresh and excited, I reached Newark Airport in New Jersey — just a 40-minute, $5 bus to the Port Authority terminal on 34th Street in the centre of the Big Apple. I enjoyed the city from the moment I stepped off the bus. Noisy, humorous, bustling, sleazy,

taxi-horn-blaring New York is like a vast film set where everyone acts a part in the movies.

The policemen swagger along with guns and billy clubs, criminal-looking groups of men hang around street corners, the "respectable" inhabitants are always in a rush and the Bowery bums really do swig their drinks from bottles touchingly hidden in brown paper bags.

I took a yellow cab to my friend's apartment on West 119th Street near Columbia University and we later took the subway into Manhattan. The trains were surprisingly free of graffiti but still had their full complement of loonies.

Eating out is a way of life for New Yorkers, and interesting restaurants with food for every palate and prices for every purse abound in Manhattan. We kicked off our evening with Cajun cuisine (about $40 for two, wine included) in Greenwich Village.

On Friday I took the subway into Madison Avenue. I knew from the movies that it was the proper time to have coffee and a doughnut in one of the hundreds of little eateries where people dive in for breakfast and the newspapers.

Armed with a wallet full of dollars, I wandered through the clothes departments of Bloomingdales, emerging with a colourful track suit, a couple of stylish shirts, lots of smart socks and a pair of novelty boxer shorts at about half the price I would have paid in London.

A quick turn around Central Park for fresh air and a cigarette (frowned upon in most US enclosed spaces) and I went to meet a friend for lunch in the East Village on the periphery of fashionable Greenwich Village. A trendy bistro with a south-east Asian Bladerunner feel to it, the No Ho Star, swallowed a mere $20 of my hard currency (meal and drinks) from a menu which spanned everything from massive hamburgers to the popular Cajun and offered a variety of beers following

the recent popularity of small NY breweries.

Next day, catching up on the cultural programme, I went to the Metropolitan Museum of Modern Art. It was just like the last time: grey canvasses fifty feet long with a line through the middle. Very expensive. Very laughable. You know — art.

More meetings in restaurants in the lower streets of Manhattan — fairly impoverished until a few years ago when the middle class started to infiltrate. Now, colourful restaurants and shops are moving in. There's even South Street Sea Port, an Atlantic-side Covent Garden yuppy pleasure dome.

The weekend continued in a blur of elegant and interesting cafés, restaurants and bars where I felt my Thatcheresque sterling reverse the conventional image of mendicant Europeans. Cameras and electronic equipment are ridiculously cheap and can pay for the trip in savings.

Monday — my last day in New York — and I am a bit tired. A souvenir-hunting expedition is followed by a two-hour meander through the city to meet a friend at the Twin Towers (World Trade Centre), Manhattan's tallest building. I take the lift to the observation tower for one of the most impressive man-made views in the world.

Flying out, the airport is efficient and civilised. Aboard the plane I sit next to a Rasta with the longest dreadlocks I have ever seen. He spends the first part of the journey working out his expenses on a Psion Organiser. He is a yuppy too.

● Weekend packages including return air fare, accommodation and US airport departure tax are available from: American Vacations, Suit 19, 4th Floor, Morley House, 320 Regent Street, London W1R 5AD (tel: 01-637 7853).

Boston

Stephen Davies

. . . .

IT WAS the advertisements that tempted me. A weekend in America for just £359 — three nights in a decent hotel and return air fare all included.

My colleagues were sceptical as I announced I was flying off to Boston on Friday morning but would be back in time for an appointment the following Tuesday. They all knew I was keen on the US but wasn't this taking things a bit far?

But I was undeterred. Six hours and forty-five minutes on the flight, thirty minutes clearing unusually swift customs and immigration formalities, forty-five minutes in the cab — and I was unpacking my bags at Howard Johnson's Motor Lodge at Fenway Park, near the home of the famed baseball team, the Red Sox.

It was mid-Friday afternoon, I was tired and the hotel desk clerk had an attitude to service that was positively un-American. As he spent what seemed like hours shuffling through reservation forms, I discovered one truism about weekend breaks in faraway places: when your time is limited, so is your patience. Waiting to be shown to your room can be a

chore even if you are settling in for a two-week stay, but when the clock is ticking away on your seventy-eight hours in Boston, the smallest delays become a major irritation.

Eventually, I reached my room, a typical motor lodge affair — huge, clean, uninspiring but very comfortable. I wanted to sleep but the clock was ticking ... I had decided I would not bother with the tourist sights, some of which I had seen on a previous visit anyway: the splendid red brick buildings of Harvard University, the reconstructed site of the famous Tea Party in Boston harbour, or the old stamping grounds of Paul Revere, hero of the War of Independence.

Instead, I would relax and soak up some of the things I enjoy about American cities. These include — culture snobs will be horrified to note — watching sports such as basketball and ice hockey, going to the movies and shopping in malls.

For movie fans (that is, those of us who go to be entertained, amused or moved by a good story, not those who go to study art house conversations in Serbo-Croat) America is Mecca. I took the chance to sit in proper cinemas with large screens, crystal clear sound and no advertisements and watch films that will not be released in Britain for months, if at all. In Boston, the cinemas across the Charles river in Harvard Square next to the university are particularly recommended for comfort and quality.

Boston is also a paradise for shoppers and the home of some of America's best restaurants, belying its nickname Beantown, earned in the days when the only cuisine the city was famous for was baked beans.

Down by the waterfront at Faneuil Hall/Marketplace there are hundreds of shops including three brick and stone warehouses that have been converted into malls. You can eat in a hall serving about forty kinds of ethnic food, plus beer and cocktails. Complete Greek or Chinese meals cost less than ten dollars and snacks range from kosher Russian to Thai.

The marketplace is also ideal for visiting shops that cannot be found in London — The Sharper Image specialises in executive toys and you can try everything in the store — or Banana Republic, which sells good-looking, inexpensive safari-type clothing.

I also enjoyed Copley Place in Back Bay. Here there are two hotels, a nine-screen cinema, Neiman Marcus (America's answer to Harrods but, in my opinion, not as good) and enough stores to keep the most dedicated shopper happy. It also features one of those touches that make mall-haters grind their teeth — an atrium with a sixty foot waterfall, sculpture and pink marble floors. Great fun.

Close by is a branch of Barnes and Noble, the bookstore chain that is so cheap it offers supermarket trollies to carry away your purchases.

Boston has all the attractions of a big city, including good bars (visit the Bull and Finch in Beacon Street, the inspiration for the TV series Cheers), but it has more of a "town" feel about it than New York and Los Angeles and you can get around most of the places by foot and subway in the space of a weekend.

But is it worth going for just a weekend? By the time I had arrived back in Britain on Tuesday morning I had spent eighteen hours travelling (door to door) for what amounted, deducting three nights sleep, to fifty hours in Boston.

I enjoyed myself, but on balance there was simply not enough time. For those like myself who hate flying, the ratio of travel time to leisure was a bit too high. Boston is a great place for a short break, but take four or five nights rather than just the weekend.

● *The package included return airfare, accommodation and US airport departure tax; from American Vacations, Suite 19, 4th floor, Morley House, 320 Regent Street, London W1R 5AD (tel: 01-637 7853). Weekends in other US cities are also on offer all year round.*

Reykjavik

Neil
MacLean

. . . .

THEY say that if you can sit in a Reykjavik hot pot long enough, you will hear all the gossip about everybody in the city. We had already failed the test. Besides, we didn't speak Icelandic.

The hot pot is a communal outdoor bath, beside the swimming pools. The water, like Reykjavik's homes, offices and even some of its streets, has arrived from mountains and springs, already hot from geothermal energy. Then it is cooled from 90°C to a simmering 40°C. To sit up to your neck, cooking like a lobster, while snow freezes your brain, is to understand the psychology of a baked Alaska. The release is exhilarating.

Like a hot bath in the snow, a short stay in Reykjavik offers the purest form of hedonism. It is as refreshing a travel experience as I have had in years.

Although the population of Iceland began on Austurvöllur, the grassy square beside Parliament House, it is the Tjörn, or lake, that is the magnetic centre of Reykjavik. Here small crowds gather to feed the ducks, wild geese and swans; to skate; or just to walk beside some of the oldest buildings in the city.

In the north-eastern corner, by the Tjörn, sits a theatre (a red house with a blue roof called the Idno or artisan's centre) and an old white ice-house, beautifully restored to serve as the new National Gallery of Art. From this corner, a stream runs down to the sea, under the street called Laekjargata.

Because of a lack of natural building materials, timber or stone must largely be imported so Reykjavik's builders have made much use of corrugated iron and now concrete. Knowing this does not, however, prepare you for the colourful gingerbread charm of the houses and shops.

This can be appreciated in the small streets that run above the south end of Laekjargata, from the old Grammar School and the giant outdoor chess board (the game is an obsession).

From the square and the lake we wandered up through this patchwork of houses — the weak northern sun a pale reflection on the windows — to Hallgrimur's church on the hill.

From the top of its spire, Reykjavik stretches out in clean and colourful lines. Because of the

171

geothermal energy, it is one of the world's least polluted cities.

The best shops are on the narrow Laugavegur. There you can buy knitwear, jewellery, delicacies such as caviar and *gravadlax* and all kinds of books. Few countries boast such a high level of literacy or standard of education. The great Icelandic sagas were, and are, read by the whole population, and, for most people we met, English is a comfortable second or third language.

We turned into Hverfisgata, and paused before the dark façade of the National Theatre, with its columns modelled on the basalt pillars of Svartifoss waterfall. There, too, are the Opera House, the National Library, and the statue of Ingolfur Arnarson, a Viking, who was the first settler, at the prow of his ship.

HOW TO GET THERE

Icelandair has a special Breakaway Weekend, packaged through 11 British tour operators, that includes return flight, airport transfers, 3 nights' accommodation, bed and breakfast at any one of four hotels (*Loftleider, Esja, Saga* or the *Holiday Inn*) and discounts on shopping, tours, internal air travel and car hire. The price for departures is from £274, flying from London on Thursdays and Fridays, and from £210, flying from Glasgow on Saturdays. For information on Icelandair tour operators and agents, contact Icelandair in London (tel: 01-388 5599) or out of London (tel: 0345-581111).

WHERE TO STAY

The *Hotel Loftleider* is also the airport terminal for the city, enabling one to make the maximum use of the short time available on a weekend break. The *Esja* is near to the most popular of the outdoor swimming pools. Both these hotels are run by Icelandair. The *Hotel Saga* is the best appointed of the hotels available through the Icelandair package. For independent travellers, the *Hotel Borg* has bags of character and charm, and costs about £60 a night for a double room in low season.

WHEN TO GO

Because of the Gulf Stream, Iceland's climate is milder than one might expect at that latitude. In winter, the cold can be fierce; but there are also temperate days of clear blue skies. The arrival of the Arctic tern in May signals the beginning of summer. In June and July there can be as many as 21 hours of daylight, with light enough for a midnight stroll or a round of golf.

MONEY

The main unit of currency is the króna, which can be divided into 100 aurar. Unfortunately, you need a lot of these to enjoy yourself in Reykjavik. In an ordinary supermarket, cornflakes will cost £2.40, a tin of beans

£1.20 and bananas as much as 50p each, There are about 82 króna to the pound.

GETTING AROUND

Reykjavik's bus service is good and efficient. There are 2 local bus terminals, one right on the Laekjargata, and 20 bus routes. Each bus follows a circular route that would eventually take you back to where you got on. There is a flat-rate fare of 40 króna. All the sights in the old town are within walking distance.

FOOD AND DRINK

Icelandic cuisine proves that cold-water seafood is the best of all. Over the past few years, the preparation of food in Icelandic restaurants has undergone a revolution, with the return of chefs trained in Scandinavia, some of whom have also been greatly influenced by the kitchens of France and the postnouvelle cuisine style. The result is that Reykjavik has some of the best fish restaurants in the world. Eating at the top restaurants can, however, set you back as much as £50 per person. There are plenty of bars and nightclubs where you can get a drink. The national drink is a sort of schnapps called *Brennivin*, also known as The Black Death.

LUNCH

Vid Tjörnina is a relaxing, stylish restaurant beside the lake. A typical menu includes shrimp soup à la crème and fresh butter-dried plaice with a cheese sauce, Kr880. *Hotel Loftleider* offers a buffet of Icelandic specialities. As well as some excellent, more orthodox, fish dishes, this includes some traditional tastes, such as raw cured trout, shark, dried fish and smoked lamb. *Laekjarbrekka* is a wonderfully friendly restaurant in one of Reykjavik's oldest houses in the centre of town. The brilliant young chef prepares Icelandic caviar with blintzes and fillets of flounder with lobster.

DINNER

Hotel Saga: the penthouse grill room has a magnificent view over Reykjavik, and the seafood gratin is the speciality of the house. *Vid Sjavarsiduna:* by the harbour. The fish could hardly be fresher, and the Icelandic lamb is excellent. Three of the city's best chefs offer sea perch with mustard and tarragon and fillet of lamb stuffed with blue cheese and apple sauce. *Arnarholl:* beside the Opera House. Iceland's most influential chef, Skuli Hansen, created miracles in his famous restaurant: dishes such as crab pâté in madeira jelly and lightly roasted breast of guillemot.

CULTURE

The new *National Gallery of Art,* beside the lake, is definitely worth a visit. There are many sculptures and statues throughout Reykjavik, and one of their most talented creators was *Asmundur Sveinsson.* His house and gallery can be visited at Freyjugata near Hallgrimskirkj. The *Icelandic Symphony Orchestra* offers concerts in the university concert hall, and the excellent *Icelandic Opera* performs at Ingolfsstraeti. The *Icelandic Dance Company* performs at *The National Theatre* in Hverfisgata, and manuscripts of the famous Sagas are displayed at *Arnagardur* near the university.

OUT OF TOWN

Reykjavik Excursions offers tours to *Gullfoss* (the Golden Waterfall) and *Strokkur,* the world's most active geyser; to the lava fields of *Reykjanes Peninsula,* and to the fishing town of *Grindavik* and the amazing *Blue Lagoon.* You can also fly to the *Westman Islands,* scene of the famous 1973 eruption.

BEDTIME READING

Iceland: The Visitor's Guide by David Williams (Stacey International, £12.95). It's the most practical guide available and an excellent introduction to the country. *Iceland Saga,* by Magnus Magnusson (Bodley Head, £7.95). Magnusson's own specialist subject, the Sagas, is brilliantly linked to the living landscape of today. *Reykjavik Within Your Reach,* by Vigdis Finnvogadottir and Magnus Magnusson (Nal Og Menning, Kr198) is an extremely useful walking guide with a map included.

Salzburg

David Wickers

. . . .

PRINCE Archbishop Wolf Dietrich von Raitenau dressed as a soldier, kept a mistress called Salomé, had fifteen children and persecuted both Jews and Protestants who had the misfortune to live within his domain, the sixteenth-century German-speaking world. On the plus side, he happened to be one of history's most stylish town planners.

We have Raitenau to thank for Salzburg. Raised in Italy, the son of a Medici mother, he was appointed, at the age of twenty-eight, Prince Archbishop of Salzburg, then a dark, foreboding medieval place. He tore it down, even digging up the churchyard and tossing the bones into the river, and set out to build a Rome of the north.

His achievement can still be relished today. Despite its middle-European climate, Salzburg is a light, airy, playfully baroque city of graceful squares, statues, fountains, gardens, belfries, alleyways, weathered-green copper domes and courtyards. Stallion-sized frescoes and equestrian statues turn even a horse trough into a richly monumental work of art.

Salzburg's good looks have been preserved partly because of its declining fortunes — the discovery of sea salt led to the economic collapse of the "white gold" mines which gave the city its name — and partly because of its romantic attachment to nineteenth-century poets and painters which helped stave off pressures to bulldoze and build with the times. A print, dated 1791, is used by the tourist office to show where places of interest can still be found.

The town's seventeenth-century core, built on a lozenge of land bordered by the River Salzach and the sharp cliffs of the Mönchsberg (the monk's mountain), makes for easy familiarity, perfect in scale for a weekend affair. What you see today is more or less the Salzburg in which Mozart was born — his statue in Mozartplatz is one of the few structures in Salzburg that he never knew.

Although not appreciated in his home town during his lifetime (he left for good at twenty-five after a row with one of Raitenau's successors), Mozart's birthplace now tops the sightseeing menu.

Among the memorabilia are his first infant-size violin, a first edition of a violin primer written by his father Leopold (still a hot seller), locks of the wunderkind's hair and a portrait of him when he was aged six and chubby.

The town has spared its visitors by labelling very little as a Mozart this or that. Other than his home, which could hardly have been called anything else, there is just a square, a footbridge, a chocolate (which didn't exist in Mozart's lifetime) and a café on the city's main shopping street, Getreidegasse, famous for its ancient hanging signs. Most date from illiterate medieval times, except for the golden 'M' in the heart of wrought-iron twirls that stands not for Mozart but McDonald's.

Salzburg is as famous for its music as its beauty. Tickets for the summer festival concerts can cost as much as £175 each, and that is the official rate; the black market price is much higher.

There are performances all over town, starting with a 7am glockenspiel rendition of *The Magic Flute* and ending with chamber music in baroque salons where Mozart performed. In between you can hear the petal voices in a choir of Benedictine nuns in the 700-year-old Nonnberg convent or the barrel organs and Dylan-esque drawlings of a score of itinerant minstrels.

Don't miss a night at the opera in the rococo Marionette Theatre, an uncanny performance by two-foot-high prima donnas (there are strings attached, including the prices — about £15 for a seat).

This may be Mozart's city but the tourist office says more people ask about following the footsteps of the Trapp family rather than those of the illustrious composer.

Where did Julie Andrews do "Do Re Mi"? Where exactly did Gretel drop her tomato on the pavement? And what's the grid reference for "Sixteen Going On Seventeen"?

The town as well as its surrounding hills are filled with *Sound of Music* locations. You can tour them by coach on any day, morning or afternoon, and listen to the soundtrack in between "gee it really happened right here?" stops. On my bus, hands shot up smartly when the guide asked who has seen the movie more than a dozen times?

Salzburg's wooded, voluptuous countryside lies at the end of most streets, close enough for visitors to see hang gliders floating from summits like confetti. On Sunday, after the 10am Mozart mass in the cathedral, take bus 55 to Hellbrunn, but only if it's warm and sunny.

Built as a "villa suburbana" for one of the archbishop princes, Hellbrunn is a 400-year-old theme park, famous for its trick fountains that strike visitors mercilessly from behind bushes, out of the orifices of statues and even from a chair just as you are about to rest your wet feet.

After several dousings, pick up another 55 and continue to St Leonhard and take the cable railway to the 6,000-foot alpine plateau of Untersberg for a stunning view of the Salzburg basin. (Stick to the paths, wear sturdy shoes and carry a sweater and rainwear, for it may even snow in summer.)

What of the weather? Locals say you will need only two sets of clothes, a fur coat and a swimming costume. But to be sure, check with the cherub on top of the fountain on Residenzplatz. If the water is splashing on his face the news is good, if it's being blown by a westerly and is running down his back it's bad. If there is no water at all it's very cold indeed — though snow-flaked Salzburg looks like everyone's dream of a white Christmas.

Any hint of sunlight immediately puts Salzburg in a festive mood. The coachmen fold back their carriage hoods and the café crowds shift outside. Kaffeehaüser are a vital part of the Salzburg experience. There are 759 registered with the Salzburg chamber of commerce, ranging from the stand-up-and-sip Eduscho shops that also roast and trade in beans, to Tomaselli's, Austria's oldest (eighteenth century, as seem some of the waiters). Tomaselli's, a shrine to caffeine, very nearly didn't survive the war as billeted GIs turned it briefly into a "Donut and Snack Bar". Today, the marble-topped tables, inlaid wooden wall panels, chandeliers, newspapers on sticks and brass coat-stands, bare in summer like stags' antlers, loden-laden in winter, are back where they belong.

GETTING THERE:

Weekend breaks can be arranged through Austrotours (tel: 0727-38191); Canterbury Travel (tel: 01-206 0411); Travelscene (tel: 01-427 4445); Intasun (tel: 01-851 3321); Austrian Holidays (tel: 01-439 7108). Prices from about £220 for 3 nights, including bed and breakfast accommodation. For independent travellers Austrian Airlines has a direct scheduled service 3 or 4 times a week. There are even services to Salzburg on the Orient Express and Concorde. Maxglan airport lies 3 kilometres west of the centre. Some Salzburg operators use Munich airport, a 2-hour train ride away.

GETTING AROUND

Virtually everything of interest can be reached on foot, mostly along pedestrian-only streets and squares. Romantics may like to hire a "fiacre", a horse-drawn carriage, from the Residenzplatz. Bicycle hire from *Krois*, Ignaz-Harrer Strasse, 88 (32263) and others. Buy trolley-bus tickets from *Tabak Trafik* shops, the tourist office or automatic machines before boarding. Tickets from the driver are dearer. Sightseeing guides cost about £30 for 2 hours for 1 to 25 people (arrange through the tourist office). Best walks include the dappled beech-wood paths on top of the *Mönchsberg*. Best bike rides are along the river, all the way to *Oberndorf* where Silent Night was first played, in one direction, the salt mines at Hallein in the other.

KEY SIGHTS

Hohensalzburg fortress: an impregnable, harshly functional stronghold and symbol of power of the prince archbishops, built between 1077 and 1681 on a rock 400 feet above the river. *The cathedral:* a baroque giant, contains the romanesque font where Mozart was baptised. *St Peter's:* where Mozart's C Minor Mass was first heard, with an ancient cemetery containing grand tombs and catacombs. *St Francis:* an interesting blend of romanesque, gothic and baroque. *Mirabell Palace:* built by Raitenau for Salomé, with delightful formal gardens.

EXHIBITIONS

Archbishop's Residenz: conducted tours of the state rooms plus a gallery of 16th- to 19th-century paintings. *Mozart's birthplace* on Getreidegasse — head just for the third floor, the original family apartment, which also has the best exhibits (the Mozart House, on Mkart Platz, is less interesting as only the music room, now a museum, survived bombing). Other museums worth considering include the *Carolino Augusteum*, showing the history of the city, with an annexe devoted to dolls, puppets and toys, and the *Haus der Natur*, an excellent natural history museum.

WHERE TO STAY

The best of the central hostelries are the *Goldener Hirsh* (AS1,400-AS4,500 per night) on Getreidegasse, with an excellent restaurant noted for its soufflé-like Salzburger Nockerln (tel: 010-43-662 848511) and the *Österreichischer Hof* (AS1,055-AS3,290) which overlooks the river (tel: 72541). *The Elefant* (AS560-AS2,200), a townhouse in a quiet central alley and an inn for 400 years, is also a good choice (tel: 843397). The 5-star ivy-covered *Schloss Mönchstein* (AS2,200-AS3,600) on top of Mönchsberg surrounded by gardens, is an ideal town/country compromise (tel: 848555). In the surrounding mountainside are *Fondachhof* (AS850-AS2,950), an old manor furnished with antiques at the foot of the Gaisberg (tel: 209060) and the *Kobenzl* (AS1,050-AS3,950) (tel: 21776). Exchange rate: £1 = AS21.95.

EATING OUT
For views: the glasshouse restaurant of *Café Winkler*. For atmosphere: the open *Stifts Keller* in St Peter's, open for business since 803 when it was the guest house of the monastery. For duck: the *Goldene Ente* (Golden Duck) with real creamy Czech Budweiser beer on tap. For good traditional cooking: *K & K*, an ancient house with several small dining areas and a tank of live trout. For company: any of the *"imbiss"* stands, open till 3am or 4am. The only thing they have in common, apart from sausages, is customers with a reason for not going home.

Meals tend towards the meat and 2 veg, dumplings optional, though there's more variety than the usual Teutonic fare, drawing on the days of empire for inspiration and subtlety.

COFFEE HOUSES
Apart from *Tomaselli*, in the Alter Markt, the best include *Fürst* on Brodgasse, famous for its Mozartkugeln chocolates, made according to an 1890 prize-winning recipe; and *Bazar*, an actors' haunt where Max Reinhardt is said to have plotted the first summer festival.

WHERE TO DRINK
The highest density of bars, clubs and discos are to be found in the so-called *Bermuda Triangle* (enter on a Friday evening and stay lost till Monday morning) just north of the Staatsbrucke. *Chez Roland* is the trendiest bar. On Steingasse, there's even a house with a Maison de Plaisir sign. *The Stieglkeller*, *Stern* and *Augustiner* beer halls, with gardens or terraces, each form part of a brewery. The

Augustiner is usually the rowdiest in the summer with a supping and swilling crowd of young Americans; Stieglkeller has a weekly folkloric night (Wednesdays, mid-May to mid-September).

MUSIC
Salzburg's main festival, held between the end of July and the end of August, is one of the most important and oldest musical events in the world. Others include *Mozart Week* at the end of January, Herbert von Karajan's *Easter* and *Pentecostal Festivals*, budget-price concerts in October and the *Advent Carol Concerts*, held from November to December. There are in all some 1,500 "manifestations" throughout the year, held in the various venues.

SHOPPING
Wood carvings of Worzel Gummidge lookalikes; pipes with lids, some as big as saxophones; *petit point* embroidered handbags and cushions; Mozartkugeln chocs; ski equipment and hiking boots; fancy candles; porcelain; dried and hand-made flowers, perfumed with spices and called Gewürzstrausschen; dirndls and lederhosen.

Note that locals tend to catch the number 4 bus to *Freilassing* in Germany, a 5-minute ride away, where prices are much cheaper. On Saturday morning go to the *Green Market* on Universitätplatz where the women shop in the best dirndls while the men sit at tables in the middle enjoying beer and sausages with their chums.

INFORMATION
Austrian National Tourist Office, 30 St George Street, London W1R OAL (tel: 01-629 0461). City tourist offices: Mozartplatz, the railway station and the Stadtverkehrsbüro head office on Auerspergstrasse 7.

St Tropez

Adam Hopkins

. . . .

THE air was sharp in the early morning, perhaps with a touch of frost, but now I sit in shirtsleeves on a balcony above the harbour. Boats jiggle below me in crystalline water. One or two are moving slowly under sail along the gulf. If I walked 200 metres up to the old citadel, a larger view would unfold, out across the red-rocked Esterel massif and ending where the milky Alps give way to hard blue sky.

The place is St Tropez, the season deep mid-winter and I am heir to a long tradition of British winter-visiting to the Riviera.

Not, of course, that there was in the beginning a Riviera as we understand it — just a stretch of mind-bogglingly beautiful coast with cliffs and plains and mountains, and a history of political divisions and marauding conquerors. Vines, pines, cork oaks and olives flourished. Except for such coastal fortresses as Nice and Monaco, Antibes and St Tropez, settlements were defensive positions perched inland on crags.

The novelist Tobias Smollett came to Nice in 1763 and wrote two volumes on his travels, grumpy about men and manners but unable to conceal his delight at weather and vegetation. He went sea-bathing and his shaky health improved. Lord Brougham, English lord chancellor, "discovered" Cannes in 1834. Queen Victoria was a frequent visitor to a series of resorts. What with the British, the Russian aristocrats who joined them, and then a wave of American millionaires, the Riviera was launched.

Now here I am on my balcony in St Tropez and hardly a winter tourist to be seen — at least on this western end of the Riviera. At noon today, in the interior of the Maures massif, another local range of mountains, I was the only visitor to the marvellously positioned Chartreuse de la Verne, a monastic site since the twelfth century and now being restored in bits and pieces.

The workmen were there, though, having their lunch behind an open window, a flask of wine just visible, a generator running somewhere above birdsong and the men's voices drifting out across the courtyard. The previous day a friend and I had been the only visitors — the *only* visitors

— to the Roman amphitheatre in Fréjus.

The basic reason for the emptiness, of course, is that the winter season on the Riviera — regarded for 100 years or so as the whole point — collapsed after the Second World War. By the 1950s and 1960s it was the sun-seekers who were in occupation, and this part of the coast, increasingly described as the Côte D'Azur, was famous for its summer crowds, voluptuary yachts and jolly traffic jams.

Just lately, the pendulum has begun to swing a little. People have come to realise that Nice offers big-city pleasures all year round (not to mention the Carnival just before Lent). Monte Carlo proffers posh shops and razzle dazzle, and Cannes has been so overcome by its success with the film festival that it puts on congresses and conferences all winter.

But further along, by St Raphael and Fréjus, Ste Maxime and St Tropez, locals are a bit bemused to see you. Attractions and festivities are laid on over Christmas and the New Year. But from January to March, as in November and the first half of December, you will probably be asked, in tones of polite surprise, what you are doing here. Enough hotels and restaurants stay open, however, for the traveller to be reasonably confident.

I was filling in on part of the coast I had known in summer and which I thought looked promising for a winter mix of outdoor visiting and strolling in the sun, if I was lucky with the weather, and indoor sightseeing, French food and local wines even if I wasn't.

What I got was all these and a few unexpected extras. The weather was brilliant, literally brilliant, all through my stay. The sights, indoors and out, were even better than expected: and, best of all, I actually had a few real conversations with French people. Hotel staff seemed, I swear it, actually pleased to see me and sometimes even allowed me to practise my French on them.

Let me just mention a few of the sights, running east to west and starting after Cannes. The Corniche d'Or, the coast road round the Esterel massif, with red rocks plunging into a blue abyss, is just about the most beautiful thing on the whole of the Riviera. Three stars in Michelin and three from me.

The first big resort is St Raphael where, to be honest, there is nothing much to look at — a serious old romanesque church of the kind the local folk found useful for defence, and one or two pretty pastel-shaded streets behind the front. It would be pleasant enough to stay here, but, for those passing through, just a quick look would be enough in winter.

Fréjus Plage, the coastal strip that follows St Raphael, is fairly dire bereft of its summer throng. But Fréjus itself, a mile or so back from the sea, is another thing entirely, a little Provençal town with ancient streets and market, busy with its own activities. Here I laid up in the Hôtel les Résidences du Colombier behind the town and dined beside a fire set on a huge hearth at thigh height. In daylight, I explored the ruins of the largest Roman town on the Riviera — founded by Julius

Caesar and under Augustus a great naval port — and visited the very early Christian baptistry, fifth century or so, and the lovely cloisters of the small cathedral.

Then on to St Tropez. Since it was early December, I was able to stay in the Sube Continental, the only hotel on the port. Prices were running at just over half their summer level. There was another enormous fire and up in the first-floor bar, with harbour views and under the genial presidency of New Zealander Bryan Southcombe, there waited a crowd of Tropezian regulars ready to ensure a visitor would not run short on human cheer and gossip.

Will this be next year's fashionable watering hole? I learn that mine hostess, Annie Bolloré, has just made refurbishments which have earned a third star for her wonderfully creaking old hotel — an event celebrated in poetic prose in the latest Gault-Millau guide.

I venture out to see not just the Chartreuse de la Verne but also the wild Maures mountains, shaggy with cork oak and chestnuts, vines in the few broad valleys. In St Tropez itself I wander the streets, revealed as truly beautiful when largely empty of the Beautiful People, and visit L'Annonciade, an art gallery in a spacious former chapel on the harbour front.

French painters, from about 1880 to the Second World War and beyond, have given an even more vivid account of the Riviera than is found in Smollett or Scott Fitzgerald's *Tender is the Night*. Some of the lightest and loveliest of all this southern work, much of it done in St Tropez itself, is gathered in L'Annonciade.

The upstairs windows look out on the harbour, offering a view

of the soaring three-masted schooner *Shenandoah*, all 150 feet of her, her main deck hidden as she undergoes a winter refit.

Back at the cheerful Sube, directly above the *Shenandoah*'s berth, I am able to observe that smart Tropezian dogs — poodles, Yorkshire terriers and even the better class of mongrel — are still wearing scarves and bandanas round their necks, just like they did last summer. Lots of laughs in St Tropez, even in mid-winter.

HOW TO GET THERE
Scheduled air services to Nice or Marseille: Air France (tel: 01-499 9511) and British Airways (tel: 01-897 4000), starting at £146 return with obligatory stopover Saturday night and some other restrictions. Dan-Air (tel: 0345 100 200) has scheduled flights every day except Tues-Wed.
Packages/inclusive holiday breaks: In winter, these are mostly to the east end of the Riviera — Nice, Cannes, Monte Carlo. Euro Express (tel: 01-748 2607), a company specialising in the south of France, can fix a weekend stay anywhere along the coast, though pointing out it's perfectly easy to stay in Cannes and day-trip to Fréjus or St Tropez. Air France Holidays (tel: 01-568 6981) offers a flight-only deal for 3 nights (Mon-Fri only) to Nice, plus car, for £153. There are other packages for longer stays. Other companies: Cresta (tel: 0345-056511) and French Travel Service (tel: 01-568 8442).

WHERE TO STAY
Cannes has masses of hotels. *The Hôtel Les Résidences du Colombier* 3km from Fréjus, Route de Bagnalo (tel: 94 51 45 92), now Scottish owned and open all winter, has 62 rooms in pavilion-style hotel — i.e. terraces of rooms (very comfortable) in gardens. Winter price, F350 (£35), 1- or 2-person room with bath. At St Aygulf, just past Fréjus going west, *Hôtel Plein Soleil* (tel: 94 81 09 57) is small, attractive and open all winter, rather more expensive (F650 for a double room). In St Tropez, the *Sube Continental* (tel: 94 97 30 04), F550 (£55) for two on harbour front, F395 (£39.50) behind, is open all winter. So is the attractive residence *La Maison Blanche* (tel: 94 97 31 98) in the central and entertaining place des Lices. Other hotels open and shut to please themselves. There is everything from the film-star standard *Byblos* (tel: 94 97 00 04) to tiny inns in outlying villages.

GETTING ABOUT
Many package deals include cars and, compared to summer, it is a pleasure to use the roads (much faster, too). For independent travellers, cars are readily available at Nice airport, in winter sometimes on special offer. There is also an excellent rail service which shuttles up and down the coast, convenient and in parts extremely scenic. Probably not worth getting a special rail pass just for a short stay on the Riviera, but some good deals for longer stays and longer journeys (details from travel agents or British Rail). It's good fun, too, to travel down by sleeper-supplement, about £20). No railway to St Tropez, though, down on its own peninsula. This means catching the bus just behind St Raphael station, horrible in summer but reasonably quick and convenient in winter.

WEATHER
When it rains, it rains buckets, then usually cheers up. Can be windy, with mistral blowing out of clear skies. More often, crisp morning and evening, warm as English early summer at midday.

FOOD AND DRINK
The underlying cuisine is Provençal with an emphasis on olive oil, tomato and garlic. But choice extends well beyond. Lots of fish, with excellent fish soup in almost every restaurant. Wines: Côtes de Provence is the local brew in the western end of the Riviera, with accent on rosé.

RESTAURANTS
Fréjus: good food at *Hôtel les Résidences du Colombier* (see above). In town, *Lou Calen:* 9 rue Desaugiers (tel: 94 52 36 87) is excellent, if fairly pricy (basic lunch menu F150) and with exceedingly elaborate explanations from Madame. *Tête d'Ail:* in the market square is rougher and readier under ancient vaulted ceiling. Hosts of good restaurants in St Tropez, a surprising number open all winter. *Chez Nano:* place de l'Hôtel de Ville (tel: 94 97 01 66), quite expensive with good food. *Les Mouscardins*, 16 rue Portalet (tel: 94 97 01 53), top quality, top prices, not many young people. Cheaper and fun: *Le Canastel:* rue de la Citadelle (tel: 94 97 26 60); *Bistrot de Pierre:* place de la Garonne (tel: 94 97 22 49), good for lunch outside.

GUIDEBOOKS
Michelin green guide, French Riviera/Côte d'Azur (£5.25); *The Companion Guide to the South of France*, by Archibald Lyall (Collins, £8.95); *The South of France*, American Express Pocket Guide by John Ardagh (Mitchell Beazley, £4.95).

Island of Texel

*Roger
Williams*

. . . .

THERE are three lively bars in Den Burg. One is at the De Smulpot Hotel, one is the Inden Grooten Slock (heavy-metal music, army helmet lamps) and the third is the Taveern de Tawaalf Blacken — which is where I was on a winter's Friday evening.

It was a surprise that the main town on the small island of Texel (pronounced Tessel) had any life at all. This is the first, and largest, of the Frisian islands, part of the province of Friesland, the only Dutch province which has its own language and way of life.

The islands make a dotted line from the top of Holland, along the north German coast and up to Jutland in Denmark. They are islands of shifting sands, of seals, of millions of migrating birds, of rugged Frisians ("more Dutch than the Dutch", "the Scots of Holland") and of an annual influx of Germans who like nothing better than a sandpapering wind to chasten their frolicking bodies.

I was there for an out-of-season weekend, in search of some peace, some good walks and to find out a little about the Frisians, of whom I had been profoundly ignorant.

But this was no rustic backwater. Half the island's 15,000-strong population live in Den Burg, and they seemed lively, young and prosperous as they ducked into the bar where I was sitting — breaking off from their evening's progress round the concentric circles of traffic-free shopping streets. The Frisian language is said to be much like English and the greetings ("Hi!", "Hello!") ping-ponged back and forth.

"The shops stay open until 9pm on Friday," explained a woman called Karla who was sitting up at the bar. Around six feet tall, Nordically fair and with metallic blue eyes, she wore heavy gold earrings and many diamond-studded silver bands on both hands. A typical Frisian, if ever I saw one.

"Yes," she said. "I am Frisian. We have a holiday bungalow on Texel, but I live in a small village near Leeuwarden in Friesland, on the mainland. They are not Frisians here, you know. Texel is the only one of the islands that belongs to the province of North Holland."

This came as a shock. I had come to find out about the Frisians and I was on the wrong island. Karla bought me a drink.

The Frisians were, she agreed, the Scots of Holland: intelligent, attractive, hardy, adventurous. Peter Stuyvesant was one, so was Saskia, Rembrandt's model wife. Karla and her husband, though Frisian, speak Dutch at home and their nine-year-old son is taught Fries at school. She could not recall a famous Frisian writer but said the Dutch author Jan Wolkars had recently set up home on Texel with his fourth wife. His best-known book, *Turkish Delight* had been a successful film and he had just published a book of erotic folk tales illustrated with his own, rather childish, drawings.

The best restaurant on the island, said Karla, was the Klif 23 in the old village of Den Hoorn, but the owner-chef only cooked when he felt like it. So we ate at the Smulpot Hotel, where I had booked in for a couple of nights. It was run by two energetic, lookalike brothers, Piet and Cees, and cost the equivalent of £10 a night — including a breakfast you could turn into a picnic lunch — plus a guilder (30p) for the shower.

We ate *cabeljauw* (whole cod half a metre long) with great fingers of roe, plus the usual pile of salad and vegetables. They like you to eat well in Holland: the vegetables and fruit — carrots, beans, cauliflower in omelette slices, leeks, even cooked pears — are piled wonderfully high. With a bottle of white bordeaux, the meal came to £30. We went Dutch.

Afterwards, I went to the hotel bar where Piet — or was it Cees? — shook my hand and gave me a beer on the house. The local crowd was still singing along to the best of British pop songs at 2.30am when I slipped off to bed.

Texel is a good place to walk anything off. Thirteen miles long and six miles across, it is flat as a pancake and protected by a high dyke down the Wadden Sea side and dunes on the North Sea side, which keep it safe from the tides. People drift about on sit-up-and-beg bikes, hired for about £2 at 't Horntjie where you get off the ferry, or at Zegel & Zn, near the VVV tourist office (good maps, open all year) in Den Burg.

The fifteen-mile sandy beach on the North Sea side is too long to conquer in winter daylight. Even in high summer, when the island's population increases to more than 150,000, you can, I was told, still escape the crowds. Off season, the people of Texel enjoy weekend walks and horses gallop flat out on the firm sand. It is a bracing place. Striding across wide, summer-nudist beaches wrapped up in the best that Millets has to offer — stout walking boots, thermal socks, Korean jacket, ear-flapped cap from Macau — brings a perverse kind of pleasure.

There are other benefits to gain from going out of season. Churches and small museums — local history in Den Burg, agriculture in De Waal, marine interests in the Mannonite church in Den Hoorn and, by the windmill in Oudeschild, a beachcomber's museum — are closed for the season. So there are no distractions from the hard walking to be done.

One museum that stays open, however, is the Nature Research Centre, set among the dunes just south of the resort of De Koog (open nine to five every day except Sunday, entrance 90p). This is where you learn about the island's history and its flora and fauna. The island is a stopping-off point for millions of migrating birds and about eighty species breed here each spring, the rarest of them the spoonbill and the short-eared owl.

The main reason the nature centre stays open is to look after its principal guests, a couple of dozen delightful grey seals kept in tanks. They are curious, friendly creatures, quite happy for you to go up to them, even to give them a pat. About ten cubs are bred each year to re-stock the local herds, reduced to about 350 animals. These wild seals are monitored, as are the birds, for signs of skin cancers and other diseases they pick up from industrial and other pollutants in the North and Wadden seas. Everyone on the island has a shaming knowledge of both English and industrial waste.

Texel is very fertile: known for its bulbs, particularly narcissus; for its root crops and cattle, which produce a cheese that looks like Edam but has a better taste; and

for its sheep, whose wool hangs in great coloured coils in a shop in Den Burg.

"We are not exactly self-sufficient," said the eel farmer I met that night, "but we do very well." And he explained that the sheep, unique to the island, had short back legs, which was, he said, why the lean, sliced slab I had just eaten tasted so good.

The Rotisserie 't Kerckeplein is in Oosterend, a mile from the island's fishing port of Oudeschild on the Wadden Sea. None of the villages in Texel is spectacularly beautiful and most run to little more than a main street. Oosterend is the prettiest but, being on the Wadden Sea side and away from the sandy beaches, people don't come here much, not even in high summer. There is no hotel, just one bar and the Rotisserie, a great Dutch barn of a place built, surprisingly, only eight years ago.

There was nobody else there at 8pm (kitchens are usually closed by 9.30pm) and this only seemed to add to its cosiness. A fishbowl of a glass full of small brownish shrimps fresh that morning off the

boats, was followed by the lamb with a tarragon sauce and the usual Dutch feast of salad and vegetables.

After the meal I sat in front of the fire, where I was joined by the restaurant's late arrivals. There was a young banker and a family who ran the Texval eel farm, and who had spent a year in Stirling learning production techniques.

On Sunday morning I went on the walk I had been saving up, recommended by a garage mechanic in Den Burg. Turning left just before the only petrol station on the road to Cocksdorp, I parked the car next to the dunes, then walked for half an hour over these rolling grasslands, built up by reed mats and marram grass. Small indistinct birds flitted through the bushes singing unfamiliar songs.

I had already seen a number of new birds. The island is fat with them and entire farms have been bought by the local authority to allow them to graze. There were fields full of curlews and tufty-topped lapwings, all pecking at the damp land.

Reaching the beach I turned right, and for forty-five minutes walked along the sands where, no doubt, Cor Ellen, the beachcomber who has built up the Wrecker's Museum in Oudeschild, frequently comes for a scavenge.

After a while the dunes disappeared and the beach opened up on to De Slufter creek, the island's great breeding ground. Gulls, terns, and perhaps oyster catchers and avocets lined the water's edge, so black and so white under the winter sun. Sometimes in bad weather the whole of these wetlands are flooded, but now they were crisscrossed with streams; though I managed in shoes, wellingtons would have allowed me to stride through them, rather than seeking ways around. There must have been a dozen or so people out for a Sunday walk, a few with serious, big-barrelled binoculars, most with cheery greetings just taking the fresh air. The birds were beautiful, but they were also a bonus: this was just a very pleasant, very different, wide open, faraway place to be.

At 2pm I took the twenty-minute ferry ride from the island to the naval base at Den Helder at the top of Holland. From there it was four effortless hours to Ostend, and at 2am on Monday morning I was back in London climbing in to bed — tired, relaxed and forgetting I had failed in my quest to find the Frisians.

HOTELS:
De Smulpot: Binnenburg 5-7, Den Burg (tel: 010 31 2220 2756). Around £10 a night, for a single room with breakfast.
De Lindeboom: largest in the town, overlooking the square. Groeneplaats 14, 1791 CC Den Burg (tel: 2220 2041). Around £15 a night for a single.
Also attractive: *Loodsmanswelvaren:* Herenstraat 12, Den Hoorn (tel: 2226 228). Around £15 a night for a single.

FERRY:
The ferry leaves Den Helder for Texel at 35 minutes past the hour and returns at 5 minutes past the hour from 8.05am to 9.35pm, from 7.35am on Sundays and from 6.35am on summer weekdays; £12 return for car and 1 passenger.

FURTHER INFORMATION:
VVV Tourist Information Centre Groeneplaats 9, 1791 CC Den Burg, Texel (tel: 2220 4741).

GETTING THERE:
Ferry Dover-Ostend or Zeebrugge (4-4½ hours), then 4-hour drive to Den Helder. P&O 5-day return £36 for the car, and £19 per passenger, plus berth. . Harwich-The Hook (6hr 45min day crossing, 8hr at night), then 1hr 45min drive. Sealink 5-day excursion for car and up to 5 passengers — from £130, plus berths. For connecting trains, contact Netherlands Railways, 25 Buckingham Gate, London SW1 (tel: 01-630 1735).

Verona

Richard Girling

. . . .

IF one is taking notes, one's pages quickly succumb to a flood of purple ink. Try as one might to block up their escape-holes, words like *exquisite* and *romantic* slink out on to the paper.

Everything in Verona demands some kind of superlative: oldest, finest, grandest, largest. Or at the very least *second*-largest, as in the case of the spellbinding Roman amphitheatre, beaten for size and importance only by the Colosseum itself. Two thousand years ago it was the Wembley stadium of the gladiatorial world, and no victim emerging from its subterranean tunnels as a human speck into the vast sunlit arena could have been left with much confidence in his own earthly significance. It now contains the world's largest theatrical stage, and is the setting for spectacular operatic productions of unparalleled opulence and scale. Returning to see one of these was instantly added to my list of life-time imperatives.

With the exception of one tiny fragment, the amphitheatre's flank wall has entirely disappeared, thereby exposing what was never meant to be seen — a double tier of rose-coloured stone arches supporting the inner terraces. It is the happiest of happy accidents, supplying the stylistic reference for most of Verona's bullishly confident renaissance architecture, and setting the tone for its style of life.

And what a style it is. The heart of the city is the huge Piazza Brà, the elegance of which extends even to its underground public lavatory (admission 300L — approximately 13p), where the incidental attractions include a busy postcard stall and a linnet in a cage. One side of the square is completely filled by the amphitheatre, and two other sides by monumental neo-classical palaces. The fourth, no less appropriately, is given over to a seamless parade of bars and restaurants, fronting an extra-wide pavement, the Listone, along which the Veronese habitually take their evening stroll. (No, this is not a guidebook hyperbole; they really do.)

The entire square pulsates with civilised life: family groups and peer groups, from very young to very old, all determinedly but harmoniously dedicated to the pursuit of pleasure. Day-long drinking, but not a hooligan in sight. Even a first division football match, Verona versus Inter Milan, produced nothing more threatening than an unusually large number of men and boys, all walking peacefully in the same direction.

Comparisons with England are hard to resist. One looks at the Italian people — at what they wear, what they eat and drink, their capacity for enjoyment, the way they cherish their cities — and it is hard to deny a nasty pang of envy.

"They have better weather than us," was my companion's best attempt to excuse the contrast. And it is true that, bathed in warm October sunshine, the pretence that we were sampling a "winter break" was not easy to sustain.

Highlights of the weekend?

● The fierce, medieval melodrama of the church interiors (rely on the guide-book to tell you which ones to see, but if you've got time for only one, make it San Zeno Maggiore) with their fabulous sequences of ferociously vivid hellfire frescoes and paintings. At the Duomo, remember to take some small change with you: all the best artworks are kept in darkness, and you have to put coins in a slot-meter if you want to see them.

● Juliet's House, with Shakespeare's famous balcony, if only for the entrance smothered in amatory, hearts-and-flowers graffiti. The only other graffito we noticed in Verona was painted in large orange letters on a doorway near the river: WELCOME HOME MARTINA.

● Two wonderful, traffic-free historic bridges across the River Adige: the Ponte Scaligero, en-closed between massive swallowtail battlements and entered from the castle; and the Roman Ponte Pietra. Both were destroyed by the retreating German army in 1945; both have been painstakingly and precisely restored, and offer unforgettable vistas of the city.

● Piazza Erbe, formerly the Roman forum and connected to Piazza Brà by the kind of shopping mall that tears holes in your pockets. Piazza Erbe is walled in with eight centuries' worth of architectural marvels — balconied houses, frescoed and balustraded palaces, belltowers and gateways — which alone would make it essential to any visitor's itinerary. But this is no museum-piece. The centre of the square, hidden beneath dozens of huge umbrellas that overlap like the scales of a giant reptile, is a market of sumptuous variety and ceaseless energy. Chickens turn slowly on spits, printing the air with rosemary. There are flowers, cage-birds, bric-à-brac, silk scarves, pottery, meat, and what looks like the entire Italian fruit mountain. At a pavement restaurant, even a bland lunch of luke warm veal (lubricated, crucially with ice-cold local Soave) counted as one of the travel experiences of a lifetime.

● Piazza dei Signori, just through an archway from Piazza Erbe but so far away from it that it might be in a different city altogether. Here, in enclosed tranquillity are camera-hogging specimens of romanesque and Venetian architecture, and a quiet restaurant, the outdoor tables of which are overlooked, not altogether approvingly, by a larger-than-lifesize statue of Dante.

● Giardino Giusti, a late-renaissance garden which we visited more out of duty than conviction but which provided the undisputed climax of the entire trip. It is in two parts: a lower, formal section, with specimen trees, classical statues and fountains within a sixteenth-century grid of low box hedges; and a less formal upper level, shaded by cypresses and with a zig-zag path and viewing tower offering an unhindered view across the jumbled red rooftops and towers of the ancient city. For an hour on Sunday morning, with the church bells ringing all around us and the mist slowly clearing to suck the blended earth colours of the city walls into the backdrop of their mother hills, we had the place entirely to our-

selves. Whatever else we may forget about Verona, it will never be this.

Dante, Goethe, Dickens, Catullus, Shakespeare ... the list of quotable writers on Verona is long and daunting in its eminence. For an encapsulation of its impact, however, one can offer little better than a bald English Midlander at the threshold of Piazza Erbe. Quite unselfconciously, surrounded by amused Italian shoppers he stood and *cheered* as if Aston Villa had won the Cup.

"Bugger me," he said, when his composure returned. "Will you look at *that*!" We would, we did, and — as Goethe would have done — we knew exactly what he meant.

GETTING THERE

Magic of Italy (tel: 01-743 9555) flies direct from Gatwick to Verona, departing Thursday, returning Sunday: three nights bed and breakfast from £224. Pegasus (tel: 01-773 2323) has a similar package from £257, but flies via Trieste. Richard Girling travelled with Citalia (tel: 01-686 5533) leaving London on a Friday but travelling via Bologna with rail transfer to Verona, returning Monday, with 3 nights bed and breakfast including rail ticket, from £204. Scheduled departure from Gatwick, 09.45 on Friday; scheduled arrival on return, 14.45 on Monday for this special off-peak weekend package. In May, Citalia operates a charter direct to Verona with prices from £317 for five nights bed and breakfast.

WHAT TO SEE

A good pocket-sized English-language guide-book, specifically designed for short-term visitors, is widely available in the city, price 4,000L (about £1.72). Most of the important architectural sites charge a small admission fee (example: Arena 3,000L; Roman Theatre 3,000L). For weekend visitors, the city museum in the Castelvecchio is not really worth the time it takes to walk around it. For further information contact the Italian State Tourist Office, 1 Princes Street, London W1 (tel: 01-408 1254).

WHERE TO EAT

The *Sunday Times* magazine's recent Taste of Italy series recommended two classic Veronese restaurants — *l'Dodici Apostoli* (dinner about 60,000L), and the *Rubiani* (about 35,000L). We enjoyed a third, the *Genistra* (about 55,000L), which is particularly handy for those staying at the Hotel San Marco. Both Piazza Brà and Piazza Erbe offer a wide choice of good, busy restaurants, bars and cafés. We enjoyed the *Oliva* in Piazza Brà (about 35,000L) and, especially, the *Alla Torre* in Piazza Erbe (about 40,000L).